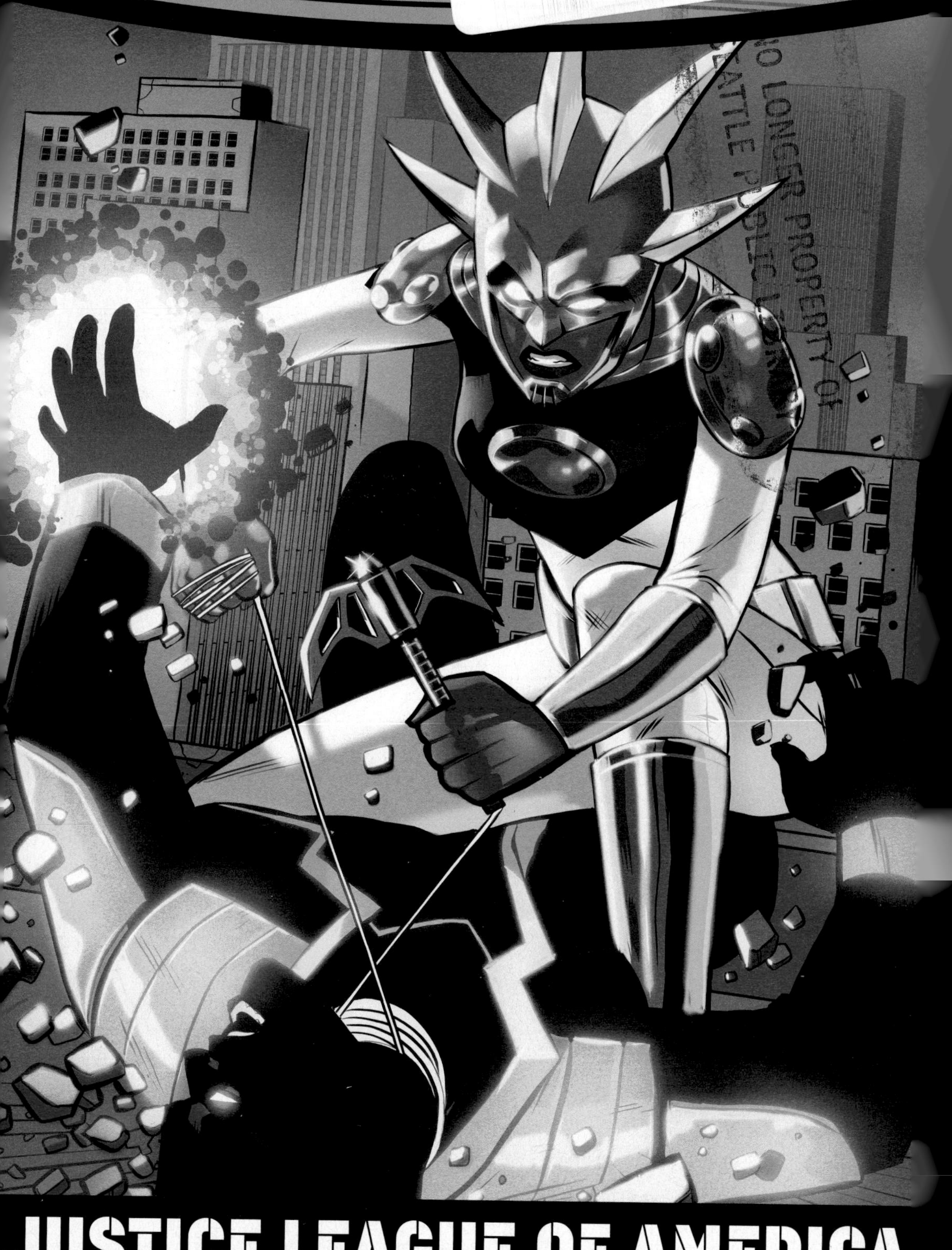

JUSTICE LEAGUE OF AMERICA

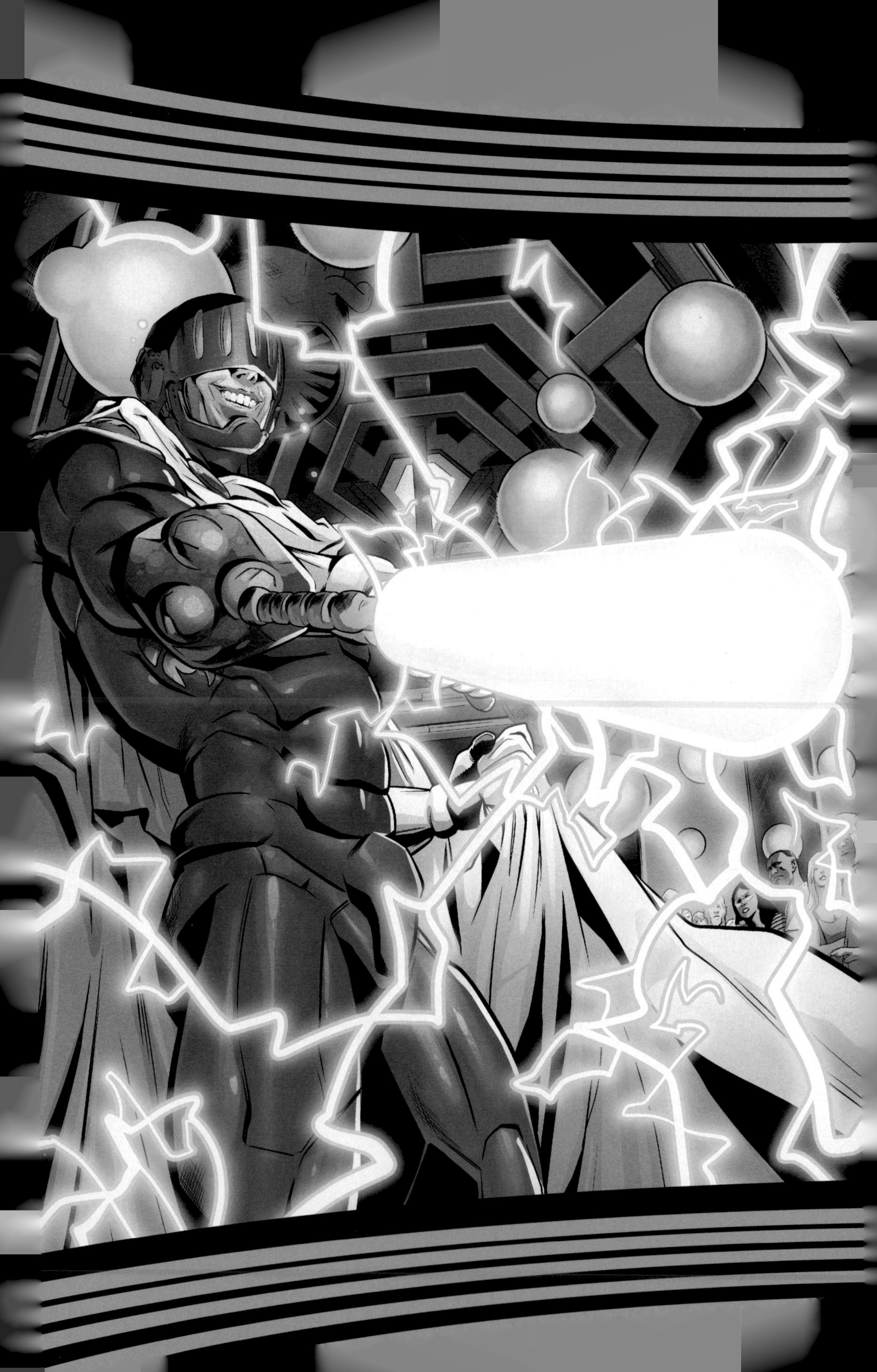

JUSTICE LEAGUE OF AMERICA
VOL.4 SURGICAL STRIKE

STEVE ORLANDO
writer

HUGO PETRUS
KELLEY JONES * **STEPHEN BYRNE**
artists

HI-FI
MICHELLE MADSEN * **STEPHEN BYRNE**
colorists

CLAYTON COWLES
JOSH REED
letterers

CARLOS D'ANDA
collection cover artist

CARLOS D'ANDA
KELLEY JONES * **STEPHEN BYRNE**
original series covers

PROMETHEUS created by **GRANT MORRISON**
VIXEN created by **GERRY CONWAY** and **BOB OKSNER**
LOBO created by **ROGER SLIFER** and **KEITH GIFFEN**

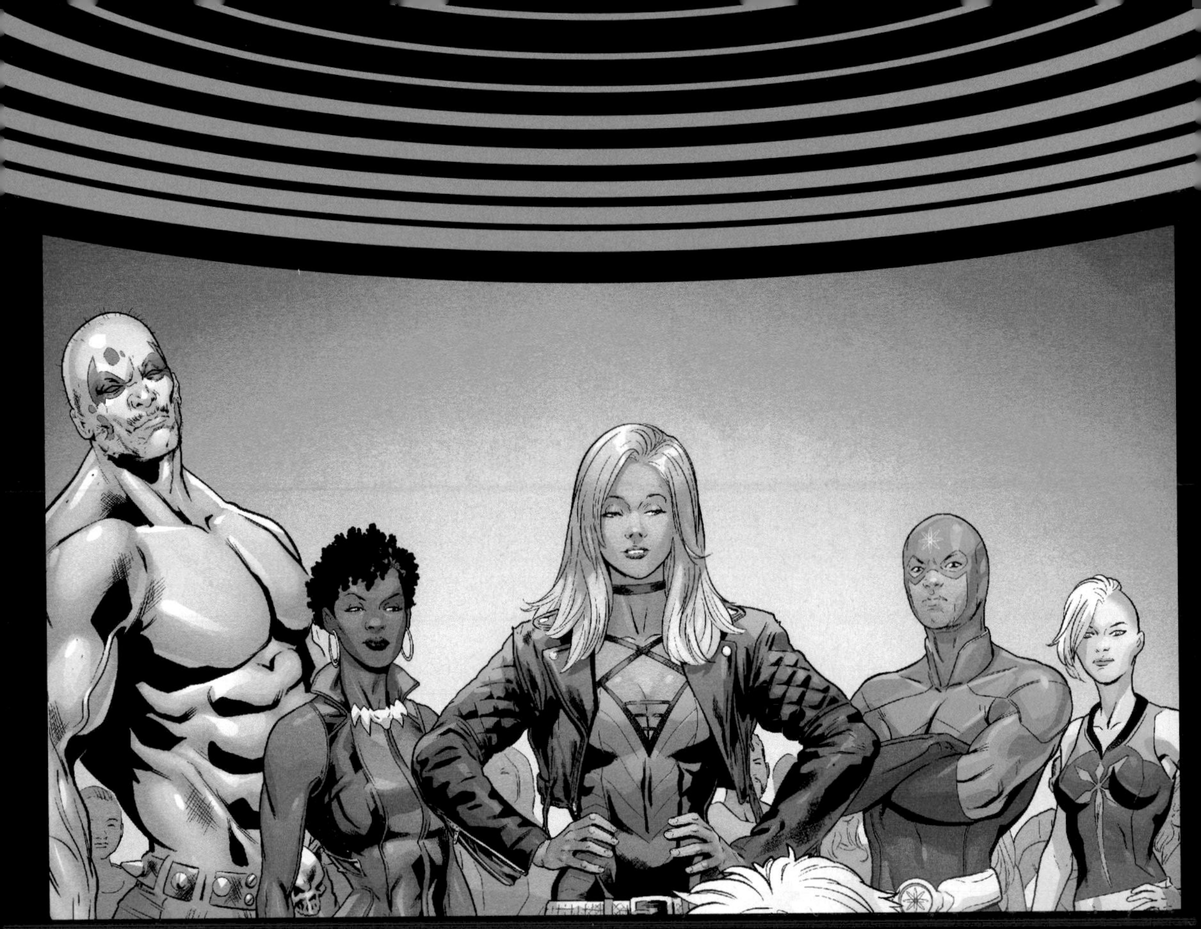

BRIAN CUNNINGHAM Editor - Original Series * **DAVE WIELGOSZ** Assistant Editor - Original Series
JEB WOODARD Group Editor - Collected Editions * **SCOTT NYBAKKEN** Editor - Collected Edition
STEVE COOK Design Director - Books * **MEGEN BELLERSEN** Publication Design

BOB HARRAS Senior VP - Editor-in-Chief, DC Comics
PAT McCALLUM Executive Editor, DC Comics

DIANE NELSON President * **DAN DiDIO** Publisher * **JIM LEE** Publisher * **GEOFF JOHNS** President & Chief Creative Officer
AMIT DESAI Executive VP - Business & Marketing Strategy, Direct to Consumer & Global Franchise Management
SAM ADES Senior VP & General Manager, Digital Services * **BOBBIE CHASE** VP & Executive Editor, Young Reader & Talent Development
MARK CHIARELLO Senior VP - Art, Design & Collected Editions * **JOHN CUNNINGHAM** Senior VP - Sales & Trade Marketing
ANNE DePIES Senior VP - Business Strategy, Finance & Administration * **DON FALLETTI** VP - Manufacturing Operations
LAWRENCE GANEM VP - Editorial Administration & Talent Relations * **ALISON GILL** Senior VP - Manufacturing & Operations
HANK KANALZ Senior VP - Editorial Strategy & Administration * **JAY KOGAN** VP - Legal Affairs * **JACK MAHAN** VP - Business Affairs
NICK J. NAPOLITANO VP - Manufacturing Administration * **EDDIE SCANNELL** VP - Consumer Marketing
COURTNEY SIMMONS Senior VP - Publicity & Communications * **JIM (SKI) SOKOLOWSKI** VP - Comic Book Specialty Sales & Trade Marketing
NANCY SPEARS VP - Mass, Book, Digital Sales & Trade Marketing * **MICHELE R. WELLS** VP - Content Strategy

JUSTICE LEAGUE OF AMERICA VOL. 4: SURGICAL STRIKE

DC Comics, 2900 West Alameda Ave., Burbank, CA 91505
Printed by LSC Communications, Kendallville, IN, USA. 6/1/18. First Printing.
ISBN: 978-1-4012-8058-1

Library of Congress Cataloging-in-Publication Data is available.

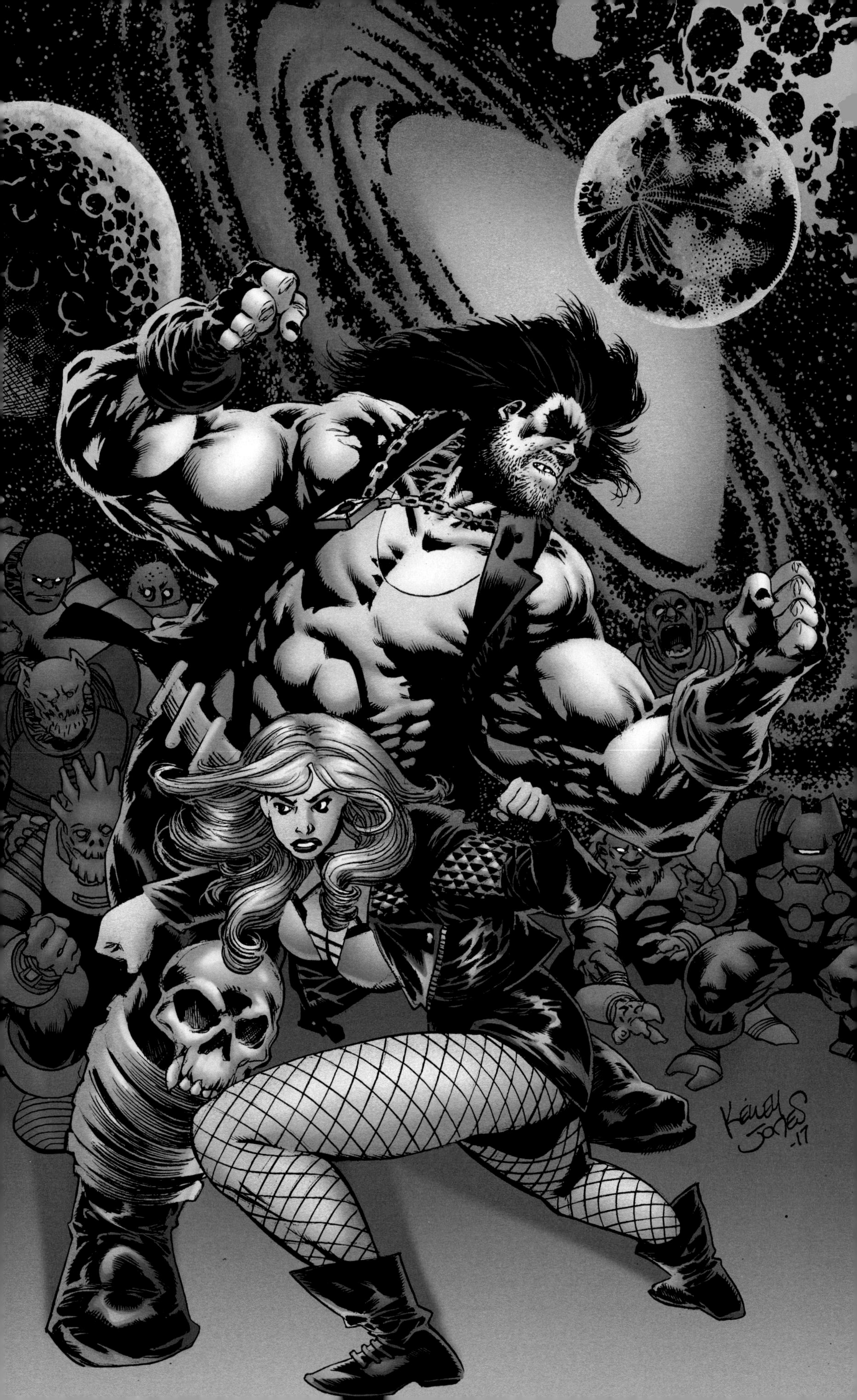
Kelley Jones -17

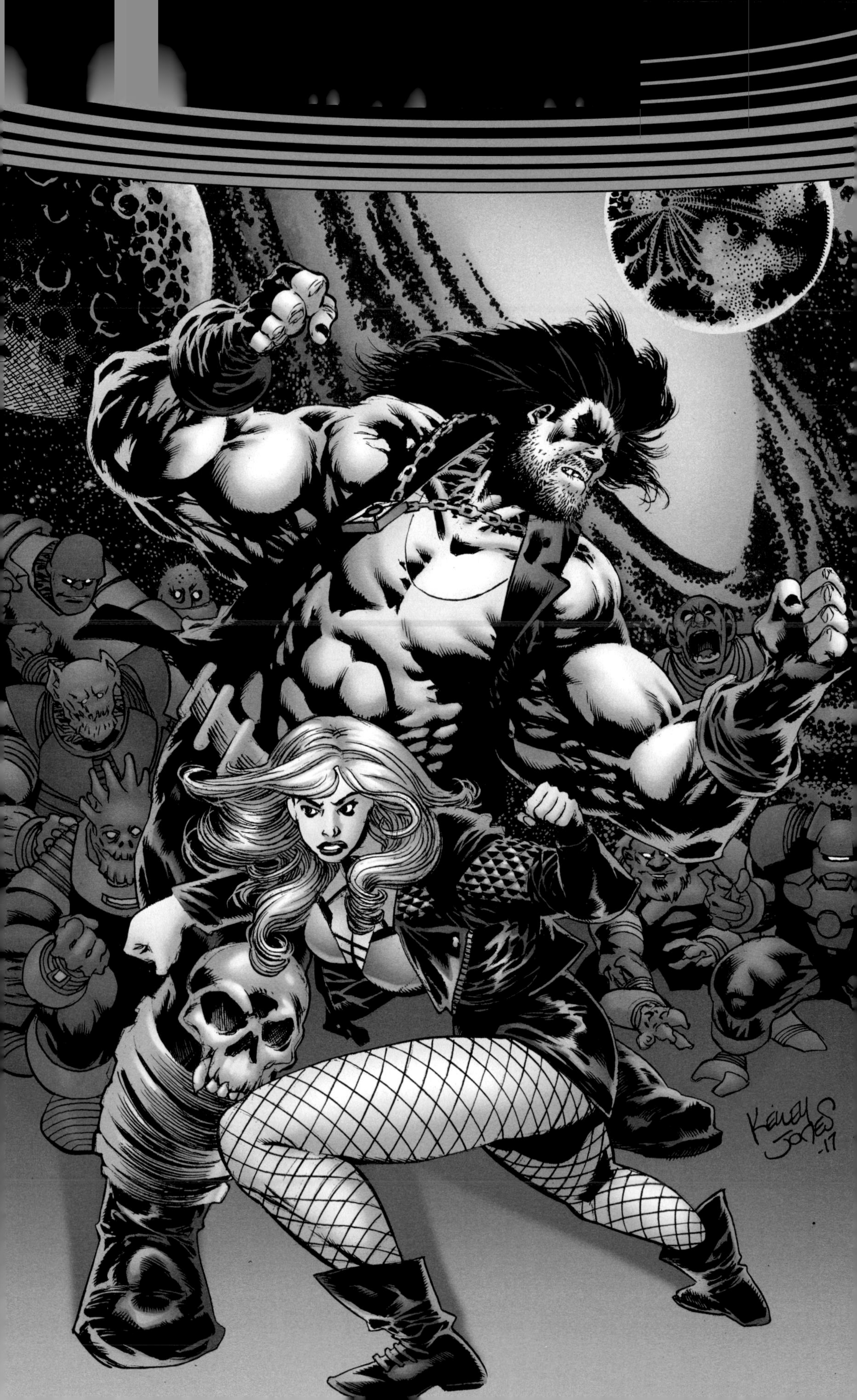
KELLEY JONES
-17

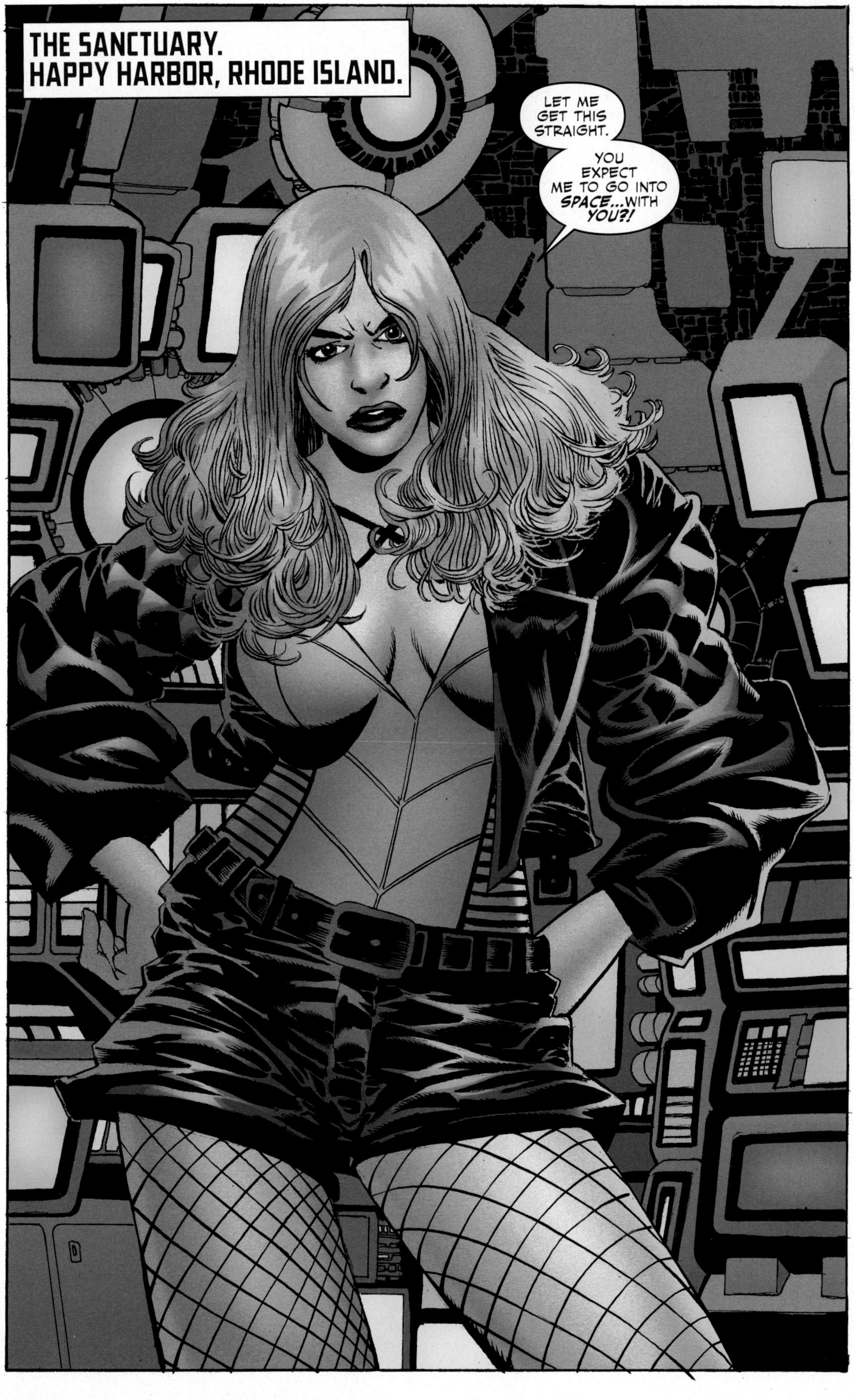
THE SANCTUARY.
HAPPY HARBOR, RHODE ISLAND.
LET ME GET THIS STRAIGHT.
YOU EXPECT ME TO GO INTO SPACE...WITH YOU?!

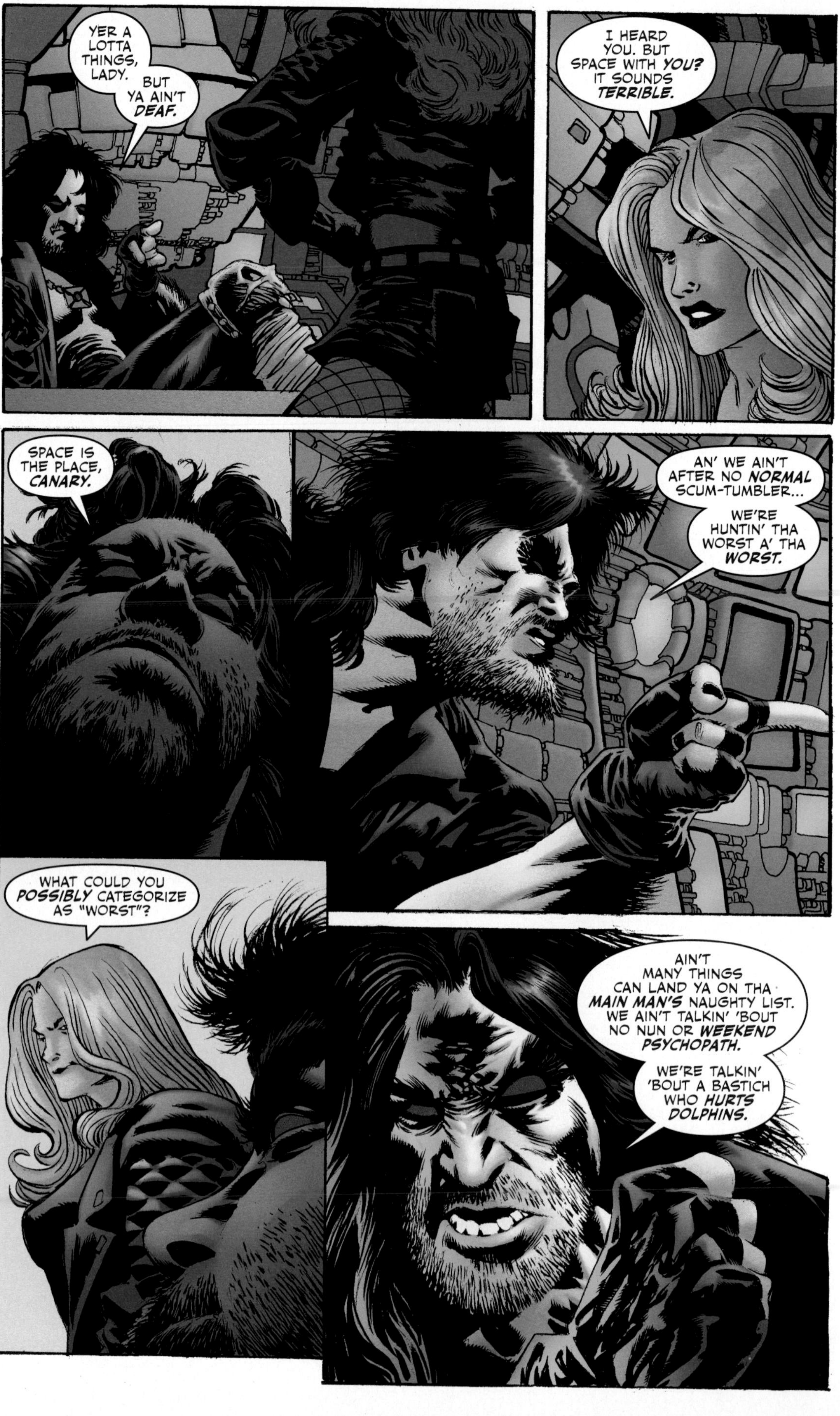
YER A LOTTA THINGS, LADY.
BUT YA AIN'T DEAF.
I HEARD YOU. BUT SPACE WITH YOU? IT SOUNDS TERRIBLE.
SPACE IS THE PLACE, CANARY.
AN' WE AIN'T AFTER NO NORMAL SCUM-TUMBLER...
WE'RE HUNTIN' THA WORST A' THA WORST.
WHAT COULD YOU POSSIBLY CATEGORIZE AS "WORST"?
AIN'T MANY THINGS CAN LAND YA ON THA MAIN MAN'S NAUGHTY LIST. WE AIN'T TALKIN' 'BOUT NO NUN OR WEEKEND PSYCHOPATH.
WE'RE TALKIN' 'BOUT A BASTICH WHO HURTS DOLPHINS.

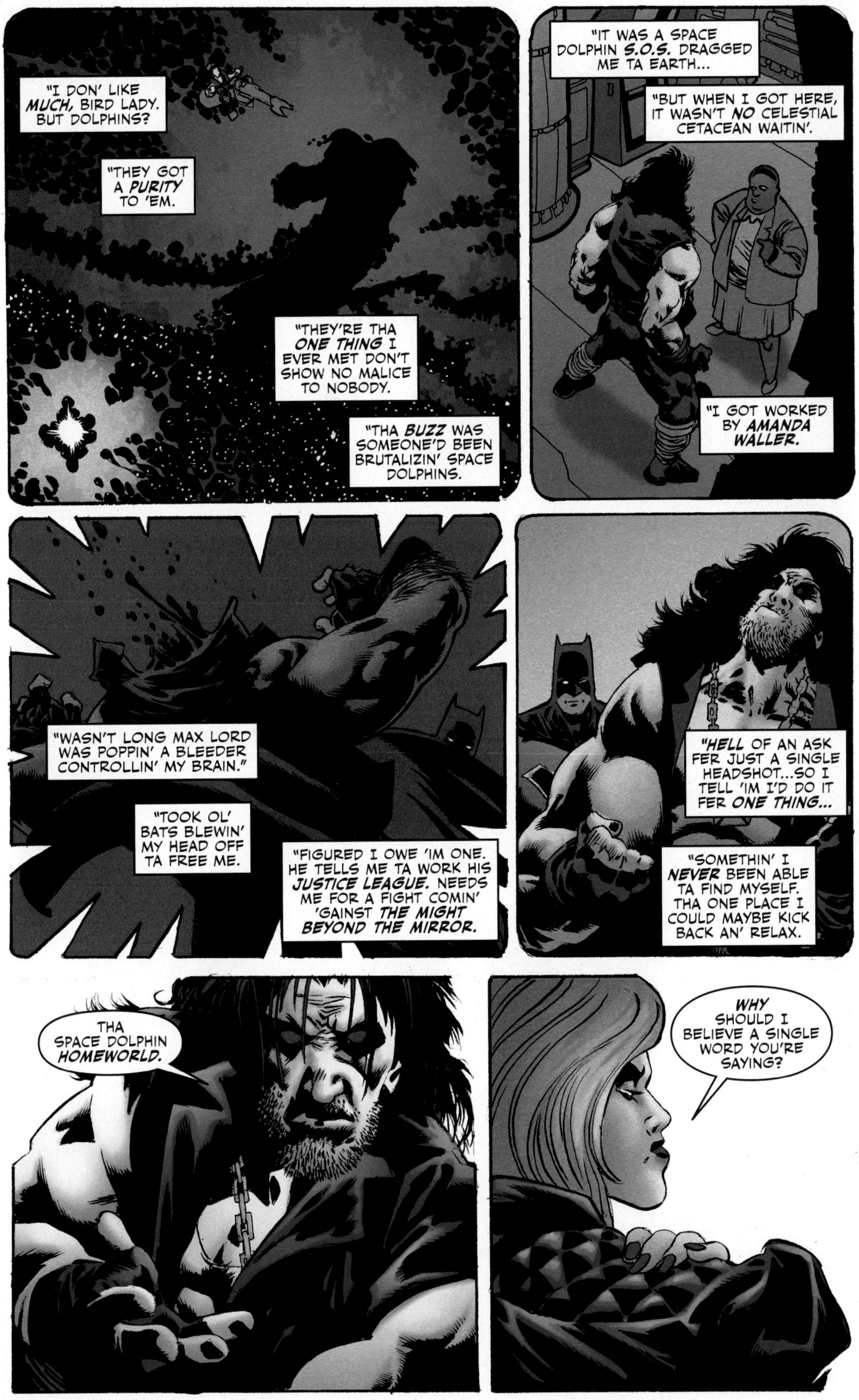
"I DON' LIKE MUCH, BIRD LADY. BUT DOLPHINS?
"THEY GOT A PURITY TO 'EM.
"THEY'RE THA ONE THING I EVER MET DON'T SHOW NO MALICE TO NOBODY.
"THA BUZZ WAS SOMEONE'D BEEN BRUTALIZIN' SPACE DOLPHINS.
"IT WAS A SPACE DOLPHIN S.O.S. DRAGGED ME TA EARTH...
"BUT WHEN I GOT HERE, IT WASN'T NO CELESTIAL CETACEAN WAITIN'.
"I GOT WORKED BY AMANDA WALLER.
"WASN'T LONG MAX LORD WAS POPPIN' A BLEEDER CONTROLLIN' MY BRAIN."
"TOOK OL' BATS BLEWIN' MY HEAD OFF TA FREE ME.
"FIGURED I OWE 'IM ONE. HE TELLS ME TA WORK HIS JUSTICE LEAGUE. NEEDS ME FOR A FIGHT COMIN' 'GAINST THE MIGHT BEYOND THE MIRROR.
"HELL OF AN ASK FER JUST A SINGLE HEADSHOT...SO I TELL 'IM I'D DO IT FER ONE THING...
"SOMETHIN' I NEVER BEEN ABLE TA FIND MYSELF. THA ONE PLACE I COULD MAYBE KICK BACK AN' RELAX.
THA SPACE DOLPHIN HOMEWORLD.
WHY SHOULD I BELIEVE A SINGLE WORD YOU'RE SAYING?

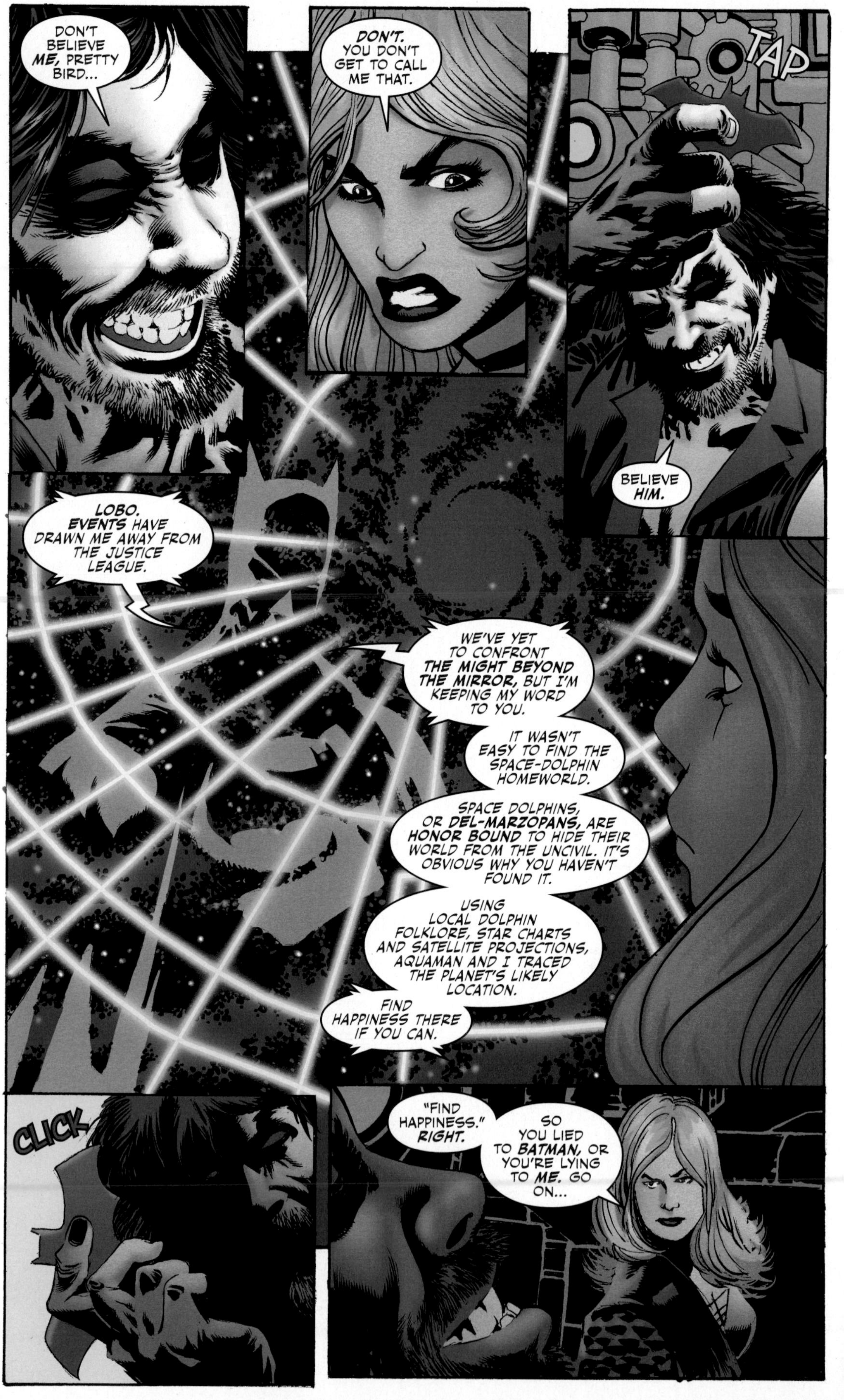
DON'T BELIEVE ME, PRETTY BIRD...
DON'T. YOU DON'T GET TO CALL ME THAT.
TAP
BELIEVE HIM.
LOBO. EVENTS HAVE DRAWN ME AWAY FROM THE JUSTICE LEAGUE.
WE'VE YET TO CONFRONT THE MIGHT BEYOND THE MIRROR, BUT I'M KEEPING MY WORD TO YOU.
IT WASN'T EASY TO FIND THE SPACE-DOLPHIN HOMEWORLD.
SPACE DOLPHINS, OR DEL-MARZOPANS, ARE HONOR BOUND TO HIDE THEIR WORLD FROM THE UNCIVIL. IT'S OBVIOUS WHY YOU HAVEN'T FOUND IT.
USING LOCAL DOLPHIN FOLKLORE, STAR CHARTS AND SATELLITE PROJECTIONS, AQUAMAN AND I TRACED THE PLANET'S LIKELY LOCATION.
FIND HAPPINESS THERE IF YOU CAN.
CLICK
"FIND HAPPINESS." RIGHT.
SO YOU LIED TO BATMAN, OR YOU'RE LYING TO ME. GO ON...

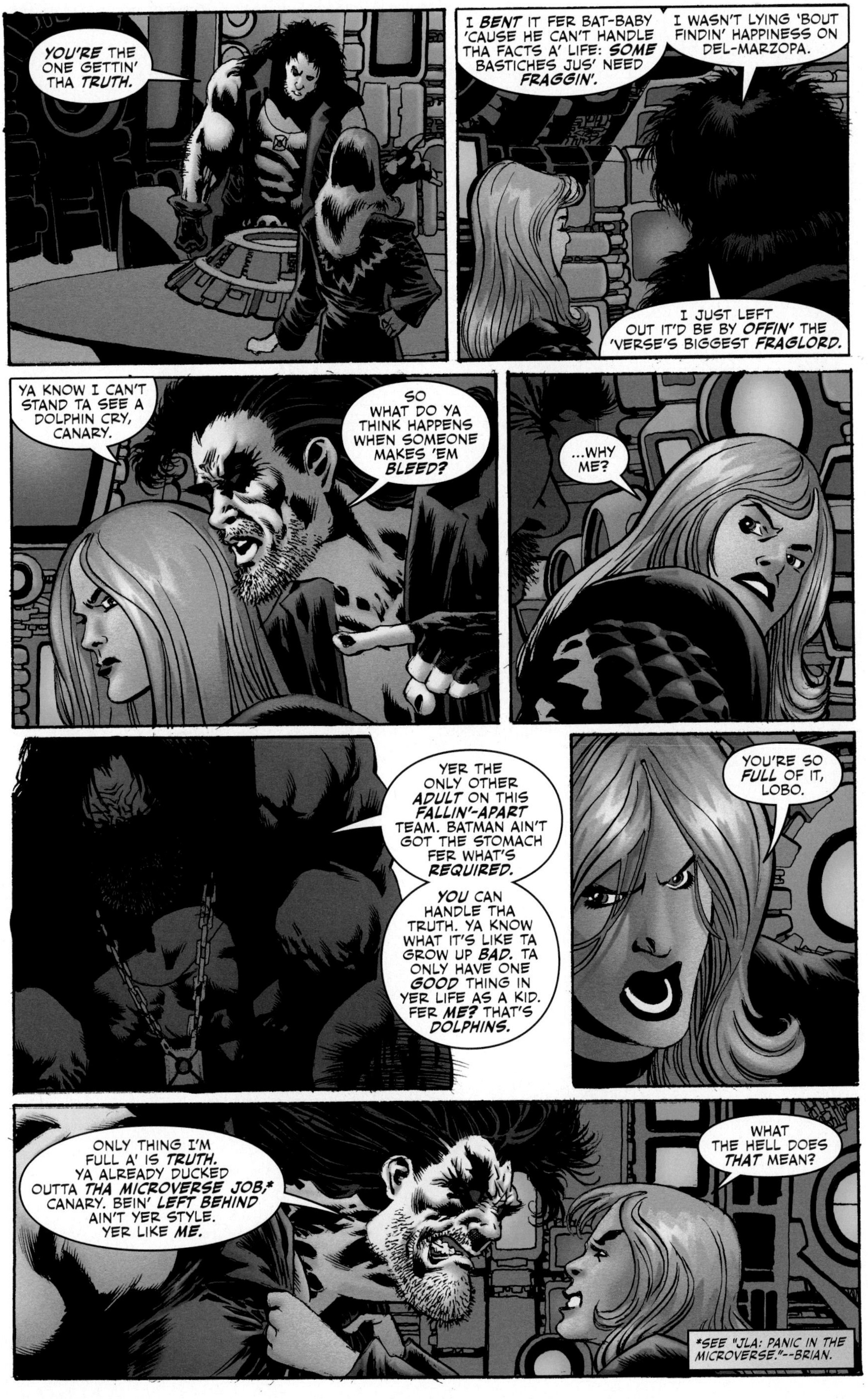
YOU'RE THE ONE GETTIN' THA TRUTH.
I BENT IT FER BAT-BABY 'CAUSE HE CAN'T HANDLE THA FACTS A' LIFE: SOME BASTICHES JUS' NEED FRAGGIN'.
I WASN'T LYING 'BOUT FINDIN' HAPPINESS ON DEL-MARZOPA.
I JUST LEFT OUT IT'D BE BY OFFIN' THE 'VERSE'S BIGGEST FRAGLORD.
YA KNOW I CAN'T STAND TA SEE A DOLPHIN CRY, CANARY.
SO WHAT DO YA THINK HAPPENS WHEN SOMEONE MAKES 'EM BLEED?
...WHY ME?
YER THE ONLY OTHER ADULT ON THIS FALLIN'-APART TEAM. BATMAN AIN'T GOT THE STOMACH FER WHAT'S REQUIRED.
YOU CAN HANDLE THA TRUTH. YA KNOW WHAT IT'S LIKE TA GROW UP BAD. TA ONLY HAVE ONE GOOD THING IN YER LIFE AS A KID. FER ME? THAT'S DOLPHINS.
YOU'RE SO FULL OF IT, LOBO.
ONLY THING I'M FULL A' IS TRUTH. YA ALREADY DUCKED OUTTA THA MICROVERSE JOB,* CANARY. BEIN' LEFT BEHIND AIN'T YER STYLE. YER LIKE ME.
WHAT THE HELL DOES THAT MEAN?
*SEE "JLA: PANIC IN THE MICROVERSE."--BRIAN.

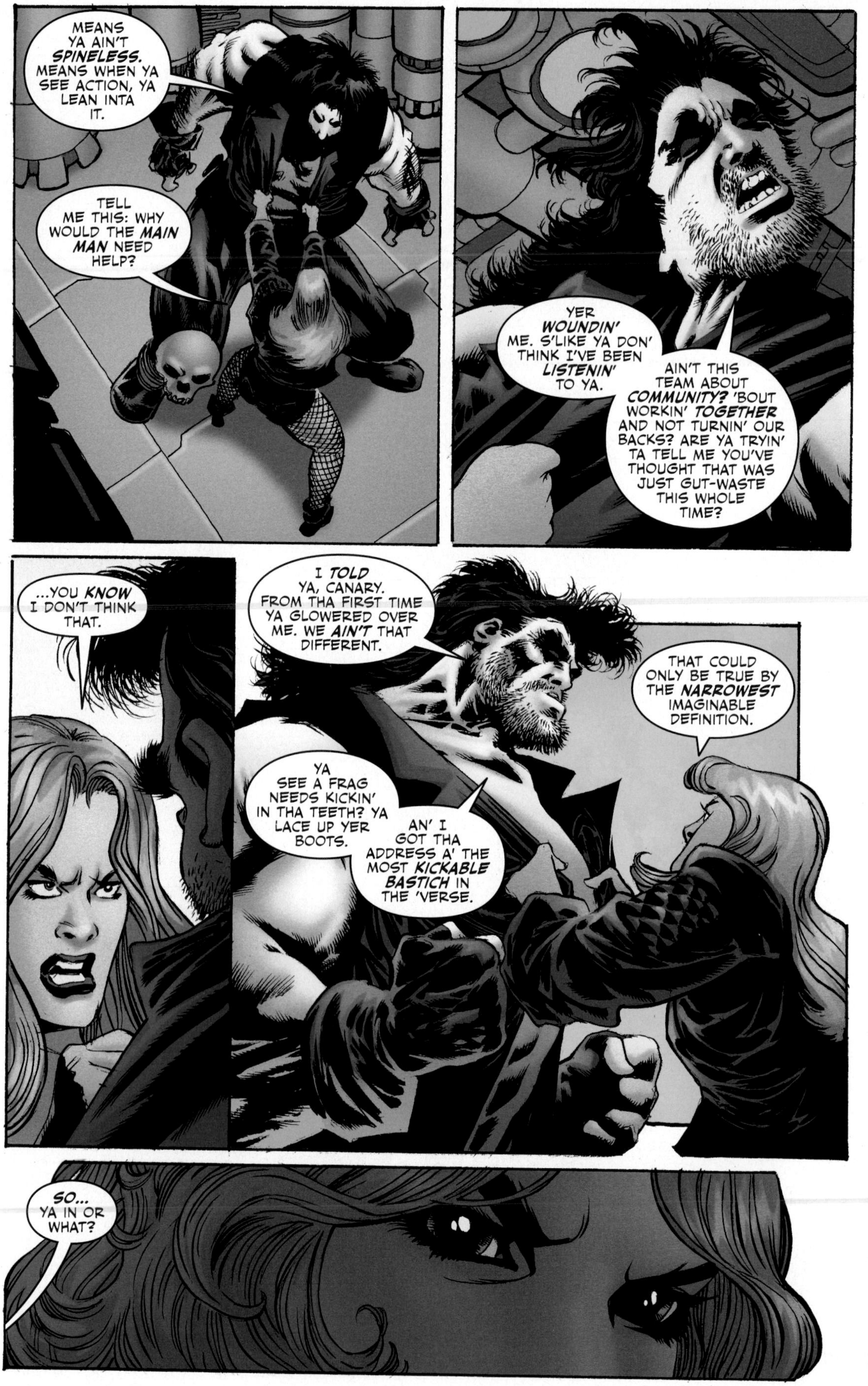
MEANS YA AIN'T SPINELESS. MEANS WHEN YA SEE ACTION, YA LEAN INTA IT.
TELL ME THIS: WHY WOULD THE MAIN MAN NEED HELP?
YER WOUNDIN' ME. S'LIKE YA DON' THINK I'VE BEEN LISTENIN' TO YA.
AIN'T THIS TEAM ABOUT COMMUNITY? 'BOUT WORKIN' TOGETHER AND NOT TURNIN' OUR BACKS? ARE YA TRYIN' TA TELL ME YOU'VE THOUGHT THAT WAS JUST GUT-WASTE THIS WHOLE TIME?
...YOU KNOW I DON'T THINK THAT.
I TOLD YA, CANARY. FROM THA FIRST TIME YA GLOWERED OVER ME. WE AIN'T THAT DIFFERENT.
THAT COULD ONLY BE TRUE BY THE NARROWEST IMAGINABLE DEFINITION.
YA SEE A FRAG NEEDS KICKIN' IN THA TEETH? YA LACE UP YER BOOTS.
AN' I GOT THA ADDRESS A' THE MOST KICKABLE BASTICH IN THE 'VERSE.
SO... YA IN OR WHAT?

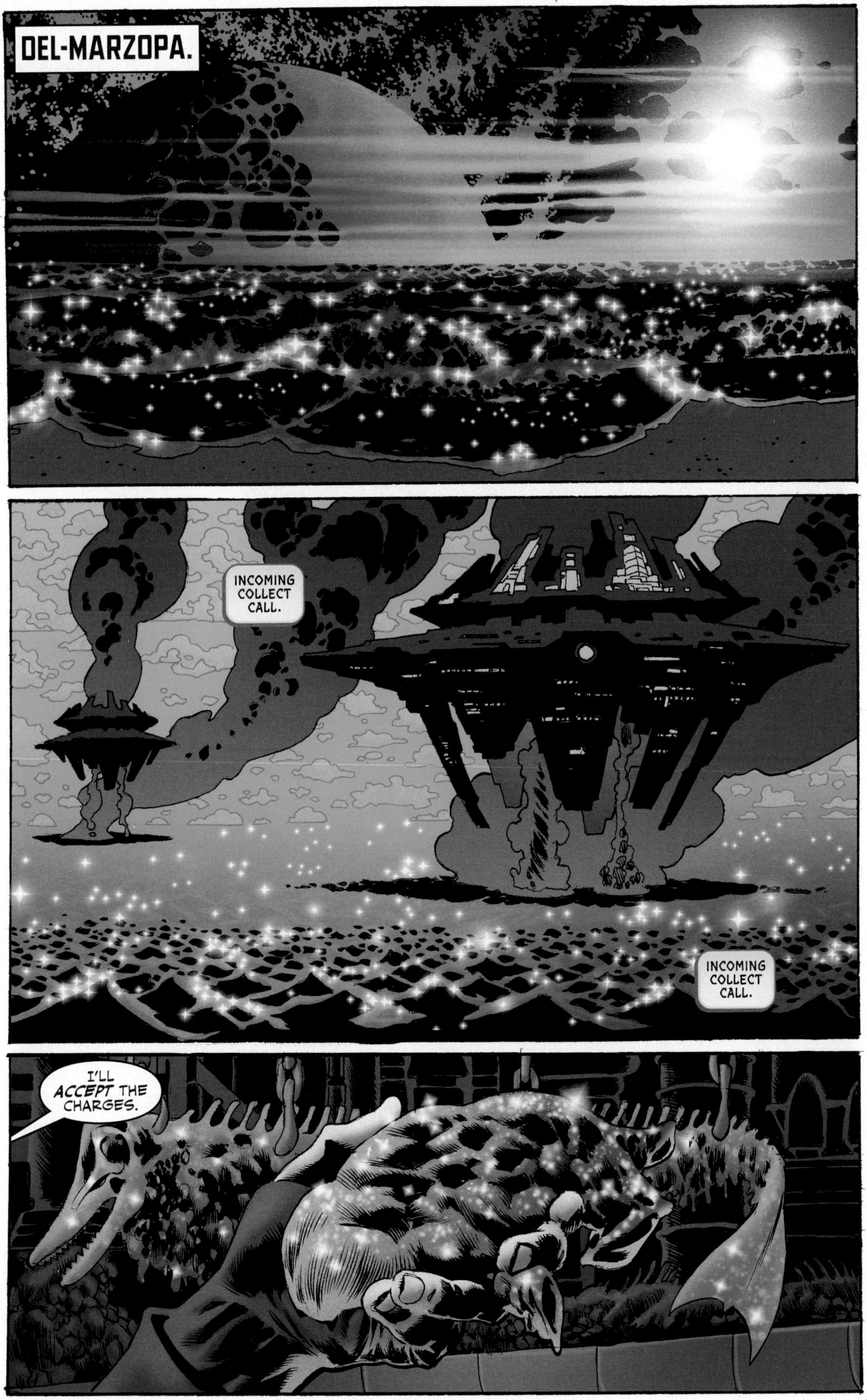
DEL-MARZOPA.
INCOMING COLLECT CALL.
INCOMING COLLECT CALL.
I'LL *ACCEPT* THE CHARGES.

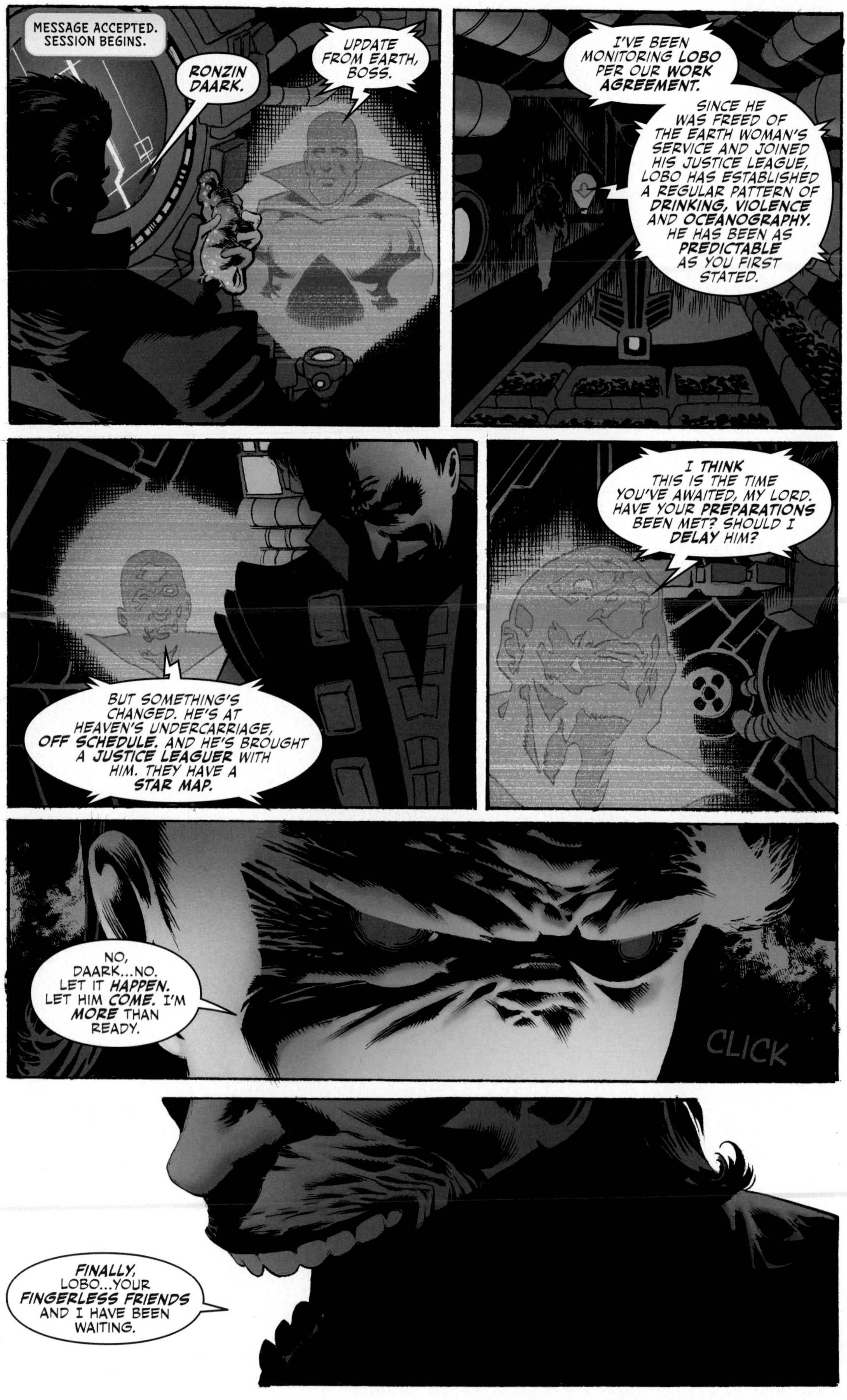
MESSAGE ACCEPTED. SESSION BEGINS.
RONZIN DAARK.
UPDATE FROM EARTH, BOSS.
I'VE BEEN MONITORING LOBO PER OUR WORK AGREEMENT.
SINCE HE WAS FREED OF THE EARTH WOMAN'S SERVICE AND JOINED HIS JUSTICE LEAGUE, LOBO HAS ESTABLISHED A REGULAR PATTERN OF DRINKING, VIOLENCE AND OCEANOGRAPHY. HE HAS BEEN AS PREDICTABLE AS YOU FIRST STATED.
BUT SOMETHING'S CHANGED. HE'S AT HEAVEN'S UNDERCARRIAGE, OFF SCHEDULE. AND HE'S BROUGHT A JUSTICE LEAGUER WITH HIM. THEY HAVE A STAR MAP.
I THINK THIS IS THE TIME YOU'VE AWAITED, MY LORD. HAVE YOUR PREPARATIONS BEEN MET? SHOULD I DELAY HIM?
NO, DAARK...NO. LET IT HAPPEN. LET HIM COME. I'M MORE THAN READY.
CLICK
FINALLY, LOBO...YOUR FINGERLESS FRIENDS AND I HAVE BEEN WAITING.

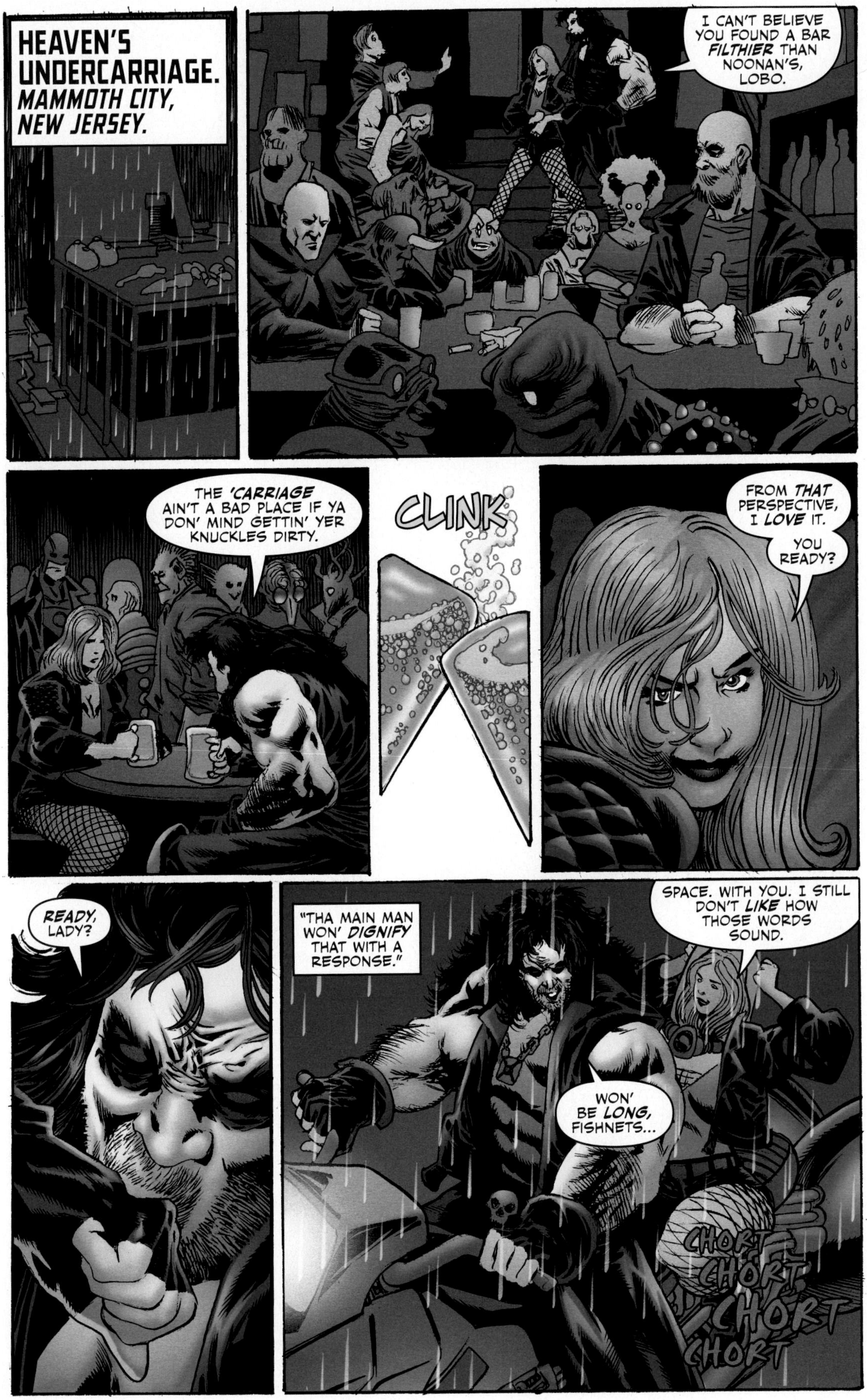
HEAVEN'S UNDERCARRIAGE. *MAMMOTH CITY, NEW JERSEY.*
I CAN'T BELIEVE YOU FOUND A BAR *FILTHIER* THAN NOONAN'S, LOBO.
THE *'CARRIAGE* AIN'T A BAD PLACE IF YA DON' MIND GETTIN' YER KNUCKLES DIRTY.
CLINK
FROM *THAT* PERSPECTIVE, I *LOVE* IT.
YOU READY?
READY, LADY?
"THA MAIN MAN WON' *DIGNIFY* THAT WITH A RESPONSE."
SPACE. WITH YOU. I STILL DON'T *LIKE* HOW THOSE WORDS SOUND.
WON' BE *LONG,* FISHNETS...
CHORT CHORT CHORT CHORT

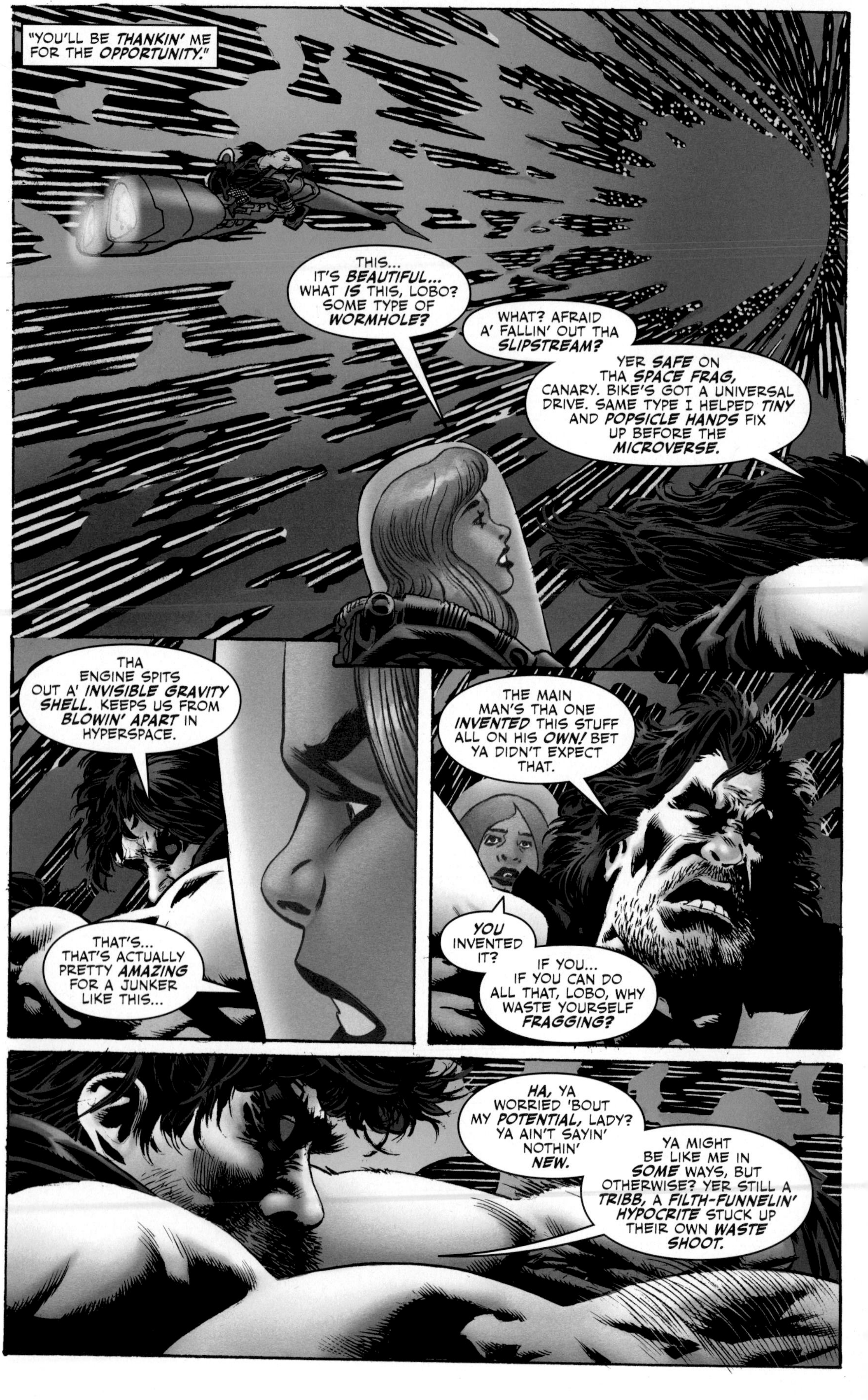
"YOU'LL BE THANKIN' ME FOR THE OPPORTUNITY."
THIS... IT'S BEAUTIFUL... WHAT IS THIS, LOBO? SOME TYPE OF WORMHOLE?
WHAT? AFRAID A' FALLIN' OUT THA SLIPSTREAM?
YER SAFE ON THA SPACE FRAG, CANARY. BIKE'S GOT A UNIVERSAL DRIVE. SAME TYPE I HELPED TINY AND POPSICLE HANDS FIX UP BEFORE THE MICROVERSE.
THA ENGINE SPITS OUT A' INVISIBLE GRAVITY SHELL. KEEPS US FROM BLOWIN' APART IN HYPERSPACE.
THAT'S... THAT'S ACTUALLY PRETTY AMAZING FOR A JUNKER LIKE THIS...
THE MAIN MAN'S THA ONE INVENTED THIS STUFF ALL ON HIS OWN! BET YA DIDN'T EXPECT THAT.
YOU INVENTED IT?
IF YOU... IF YOU CAN DO ALL THAT, LOBO, WHY WASTE YOURSELF FRAGGING?
HA, YA WORRIED 'BOUT MY POTENTIAL, LADY? YA AIN'T SAYIN' NOTHIN' NEW.
YA MIGHT BE LIKE ME IN SOME WAYS, BUT OTHERWISE? YER STILL A TRIBB, A FILTH-FUNNELIN' HYPOCRITE STUCK UP THEIR OWN WASTE SHOOT.

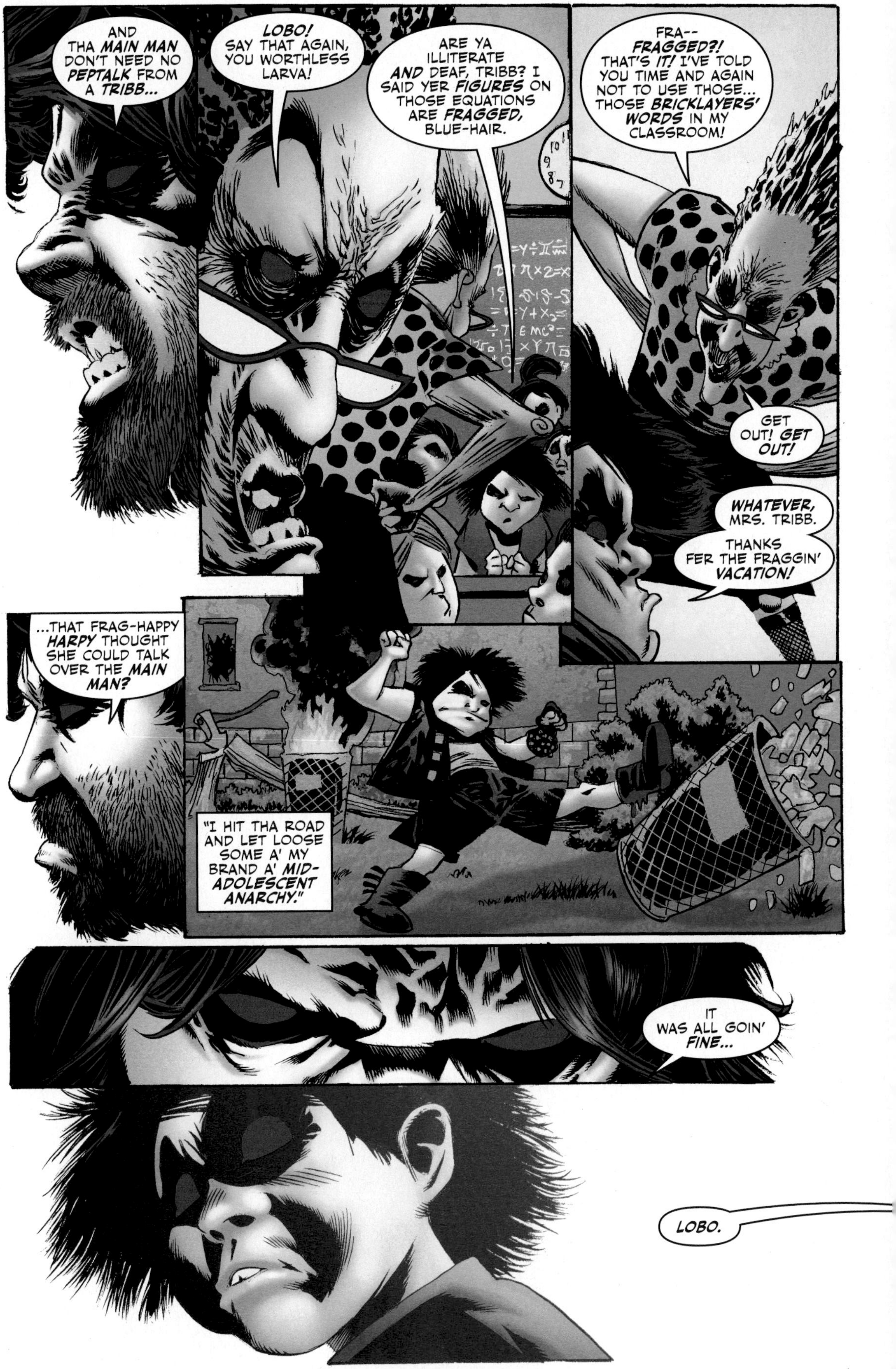
AND THA MAIN MAN DON'T NEED NO PEPTALK FROM A TRIBB...
LOBO! SAY THAT AGAIN, YOU WORTHLESS LARVA!
ARE YA ILLITERATE AND DEAF, TRIBB? I SAID YER FIGURES ON THOSE EQUATIONS ARE FRAGGED, BLUE-HAIR.
FRA-- FRAGGED?! THAT'S IT! I'VE TOLD YOU TIME AND AGAIN NOT TO USE THOSE... THOSE BRICKLAYERS' WORDS IN MY CLASSROOM!
GET OUT! GET OUT!
WHATEVER, MRS. TRIBB.
THANKS FER THE FRAGGIN' VACATION!
...THAT FRAG-HAPPY HARPY THOUGHT SHE COULD TALK OVER THE MAIN MAN?
"I HIT THA ROAD AND LET LOOSE SOME A' MY BRAND A' MID-ADOLESCENT ANARCHY."
IT WAS ALL GOIN' FINE...
LOBO.

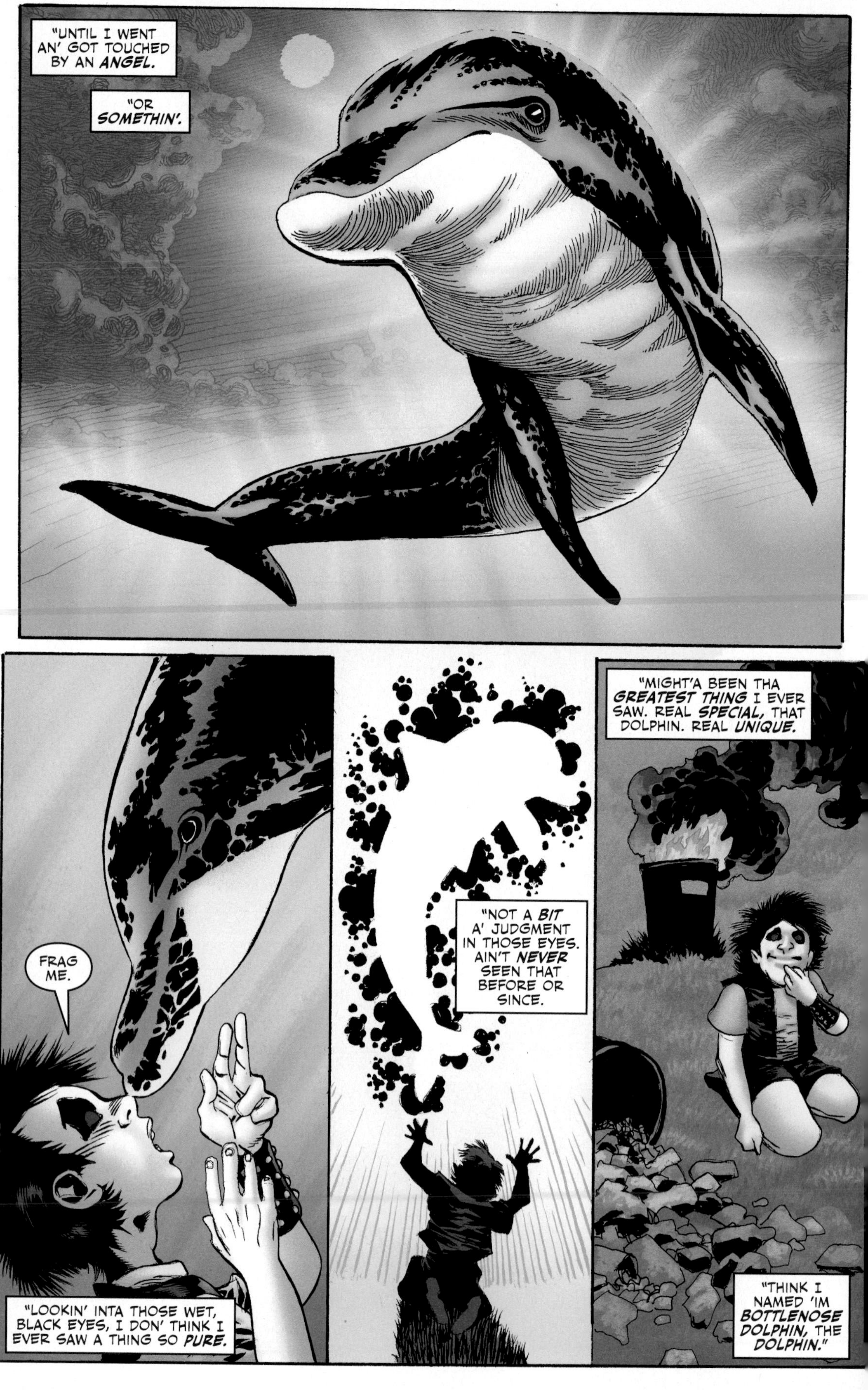
"UNTIL I WENT AN' GOT TOUCHED BY AN ANGEL.
"OR SOMETHIN'.
FRAG ME.
"LOOKIN' INTA THOSE WET, BLACK EYES, I DON' THINK I EVER SAW A THING SO PURE.
"NOT A BIT A' JUDGMENT IN THOSE EYES. AIN'T NEVER SEEN THAT BEFORE OR SINCE.
"MIGHT'A BEEN THA GREATEST THING I EVER SAW. REAL SPECIAL, THAT DOLPHIN. REAL UNIQUE.
"THINK I NAMED 'IM BOTTLENOSE DOLPHIN, THE DOLPHIN."

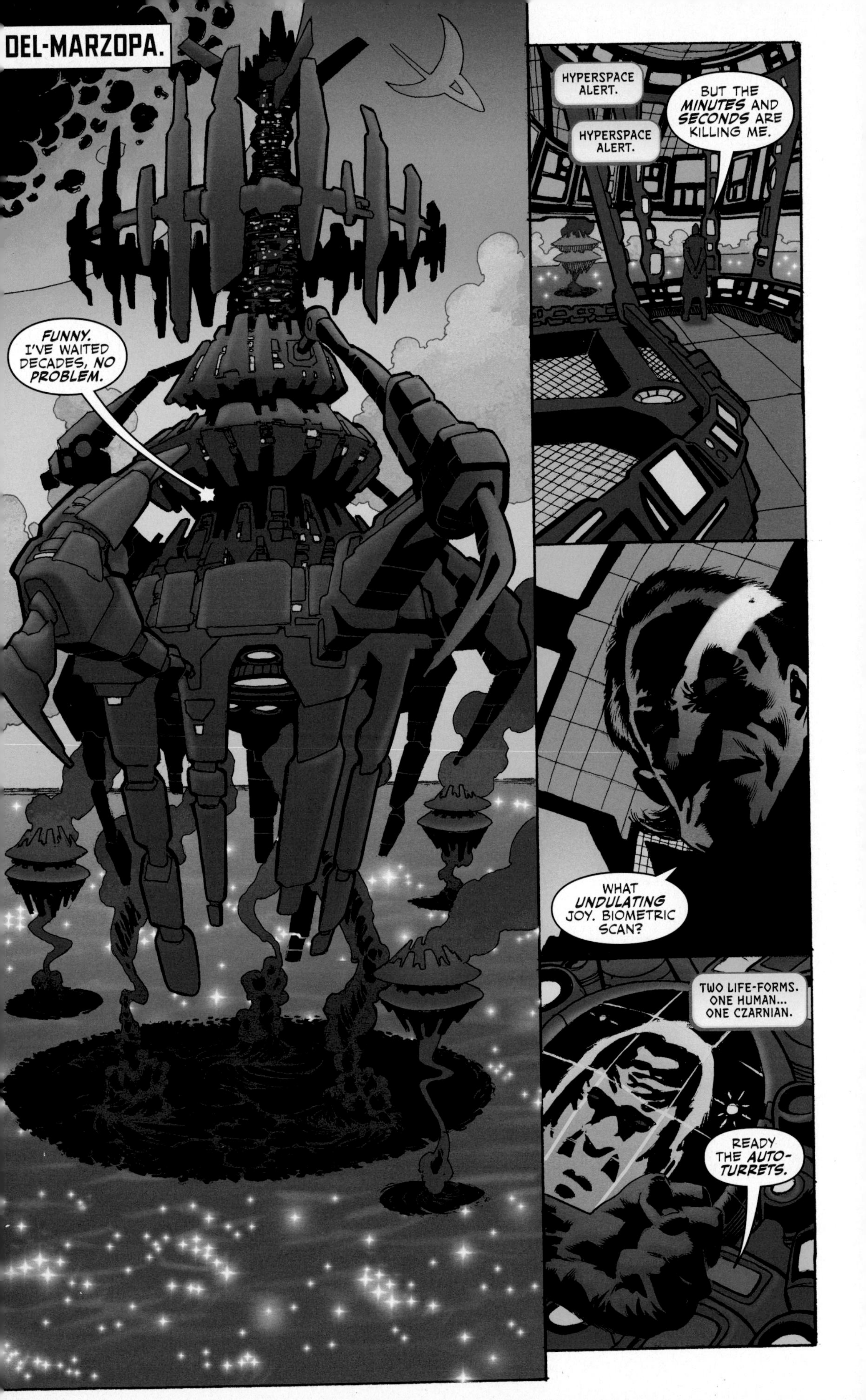
DEL-MARZOPA.
FUNNY. I'VE WAITED DECADES, NO PROBLEM.
HYPERSPACE ALERT.
HYPERSPACE ALERT.
BUT THE MINUTES AND SECONDS ARE KILLING ME.
WHAT UNDULATING JOY. BIOMETRIC SCAN?
TWO LIFE-FORMS. ONE HUMAN... ONE CZARNIAN.
READY THE AUTO-TURRETS.

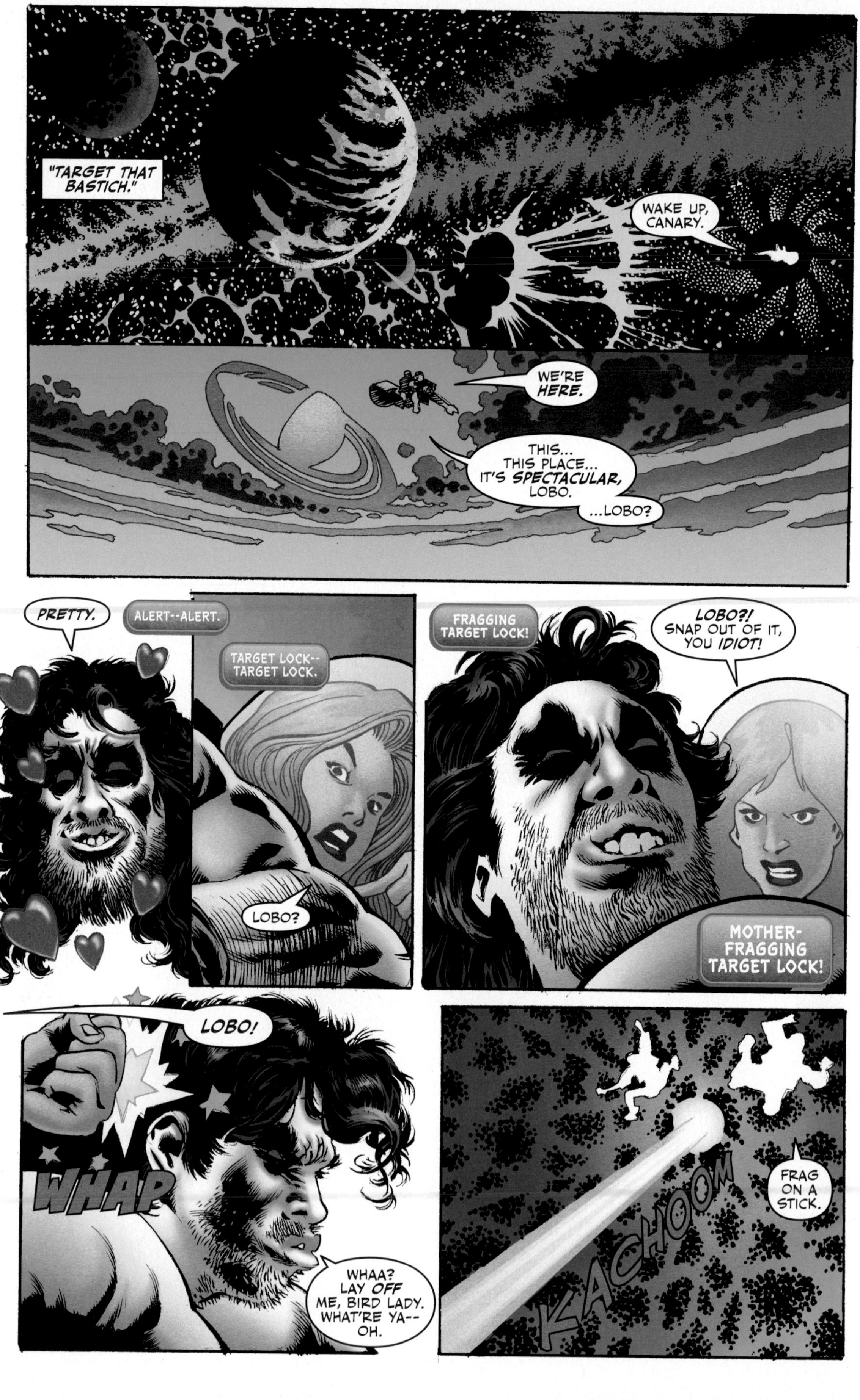
"TARGET THAT BASTICH."
WAKE UP, CANARY.
WE'RE HERE.
THIS... THIS PLACE... IT'S SPECTACULAR, LOBO.
...LOBO?
PRETTY.
ALERT--ALERT.
TARGET LOCK-- TARGET LOCK.
LOBO?
FRAGGING TARGET LOCK!
LOBO?! SNAP OUT OF IT, YOU IDIOT!
MOTHER-FRAGGING TARGET LOCK!
LOBO!
WHAP
WHAA? LAY OFF ME, BIRD LADY. WHAT'RE YA-- OH.
KACHOOM
FRAG ON A STICK.

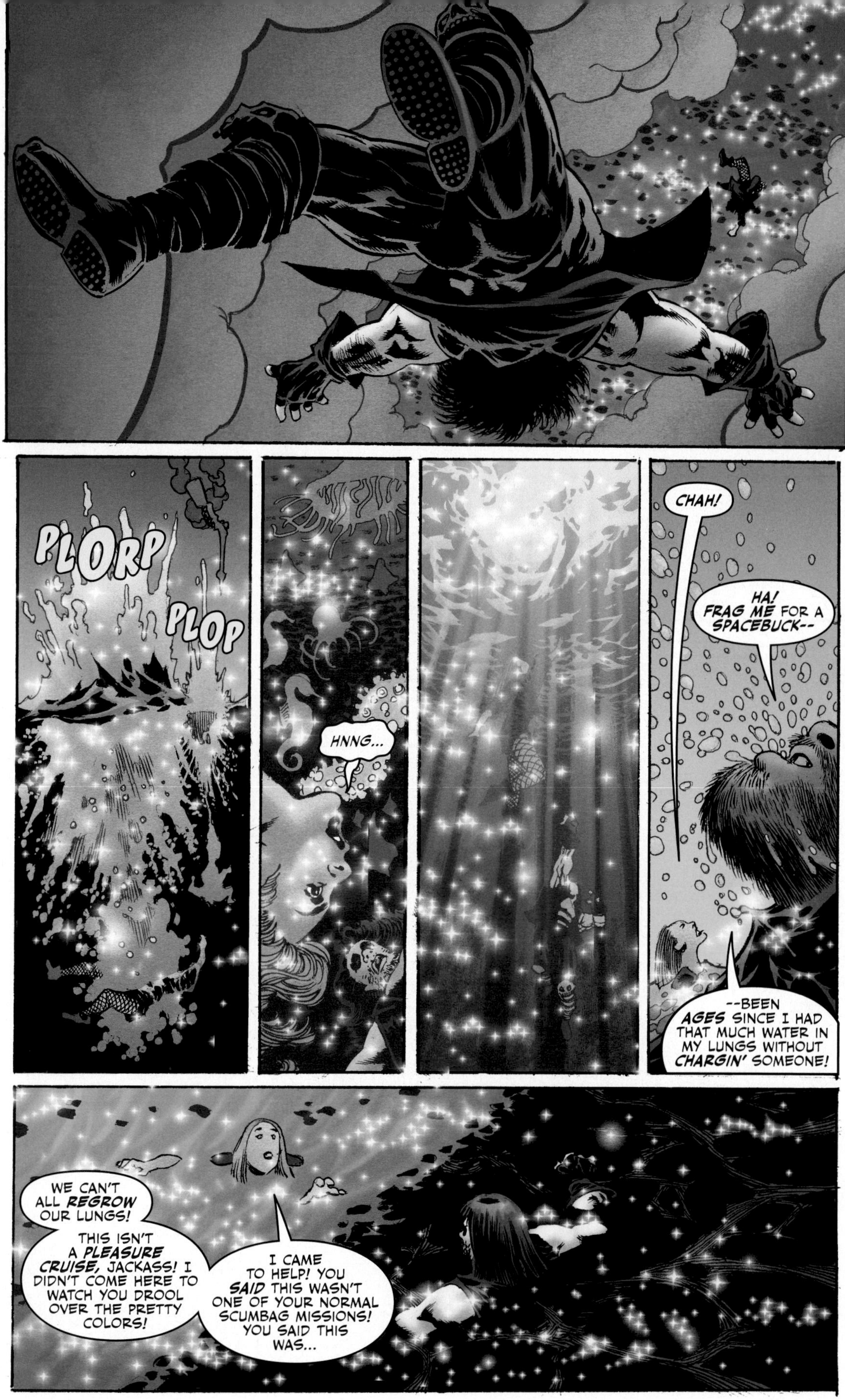
PLORP
PLOP
HNNG...
CHAH!
HA! FRAG ME FOR A SPACEBUCK--
--BEEN AGES SINCE I HAD THAT MUCH WATER IN MY LUNGS WITHOUT CHARGIN' SOMEONE!
WE CAN'T ALL REGROW OUR LUNGS!
THIS ISN'T A PLEASURE CRUISE, JACKASS! I DIDN'T COME HERE TO WATCH YOU DROOL OVER THE PRETTY COLORS!
I CAME TO HELP! YOU SAID THIS WASN'T ONE OF YOUR NORMAL SCUMBAG MISSIONS! YOU SAID THIS WAS...

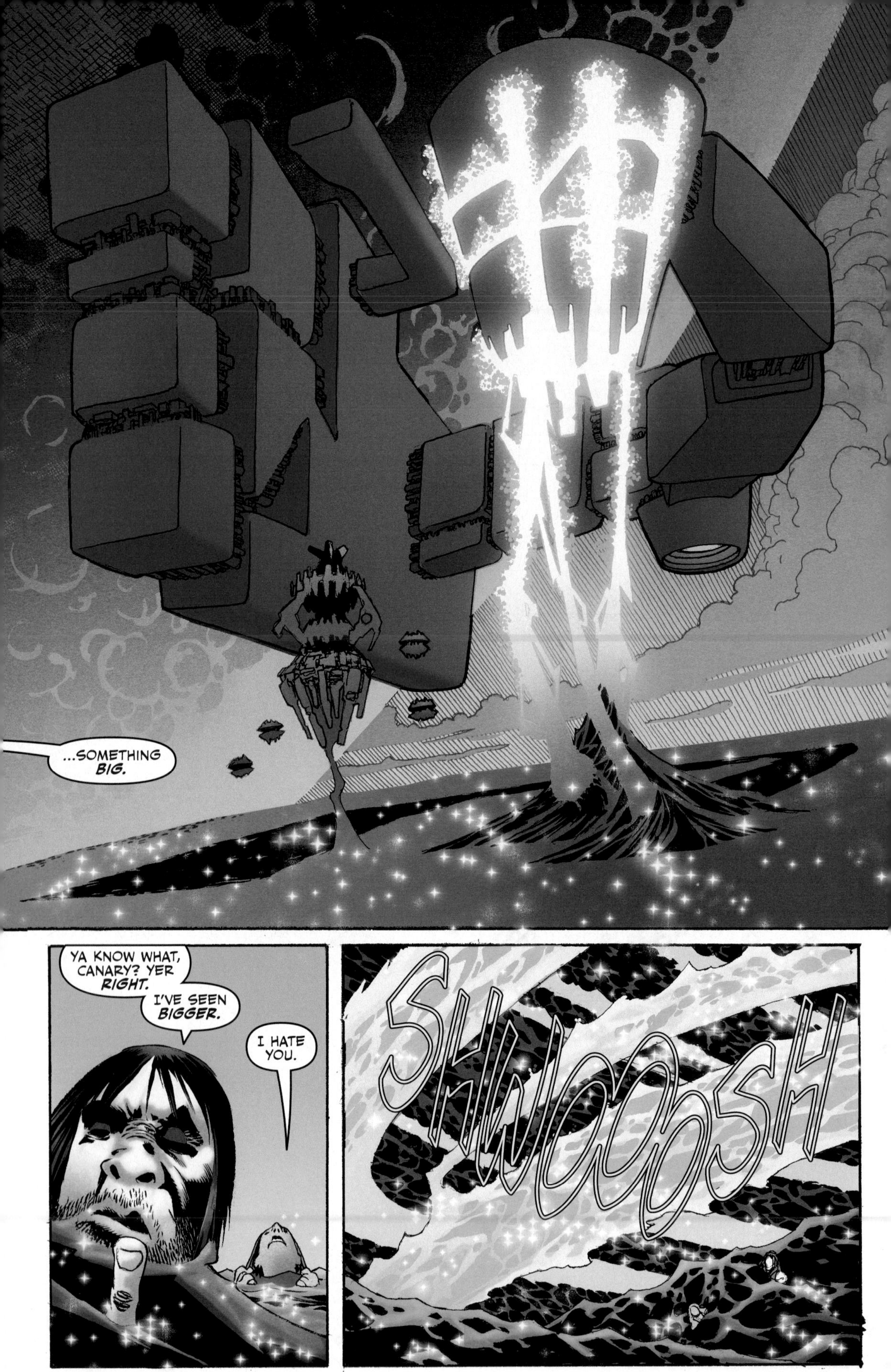
...SOMETHING BIG.
YA KNOW WHAT, CANARY? YER RIGHT.
I'VE SEEN BIGGER.
I HATE YOU.
SHWOOOSH

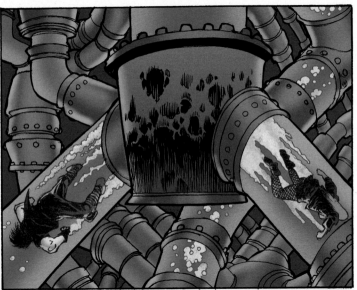

CLANG

FWAMP

HUAHGH...

LOBO.

DON'T...
DON'T FRAGGIN'
BELIEVE IT...

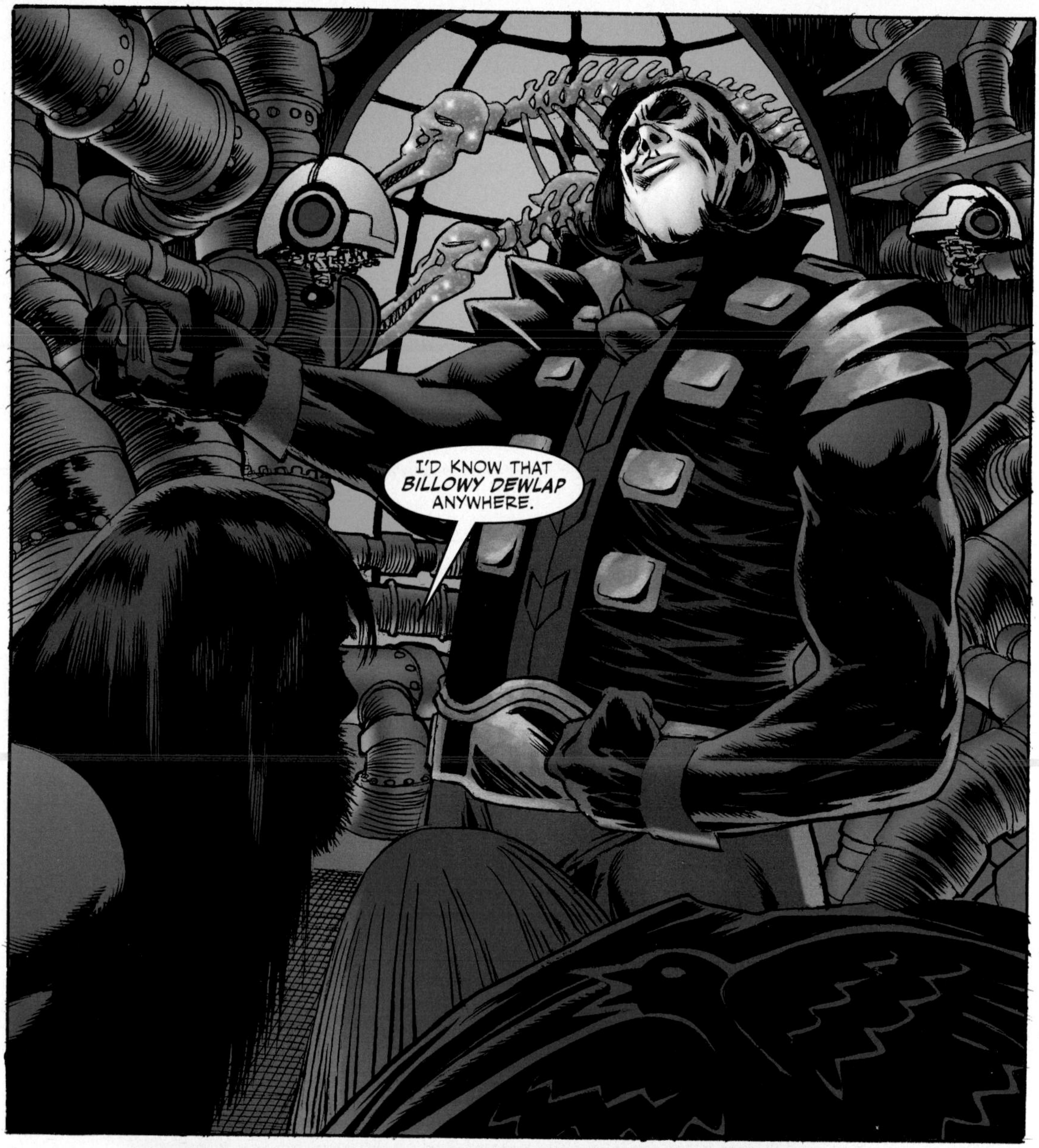
I'D KNOW THAT BILLOWY DEWLAP ANYWHERE.

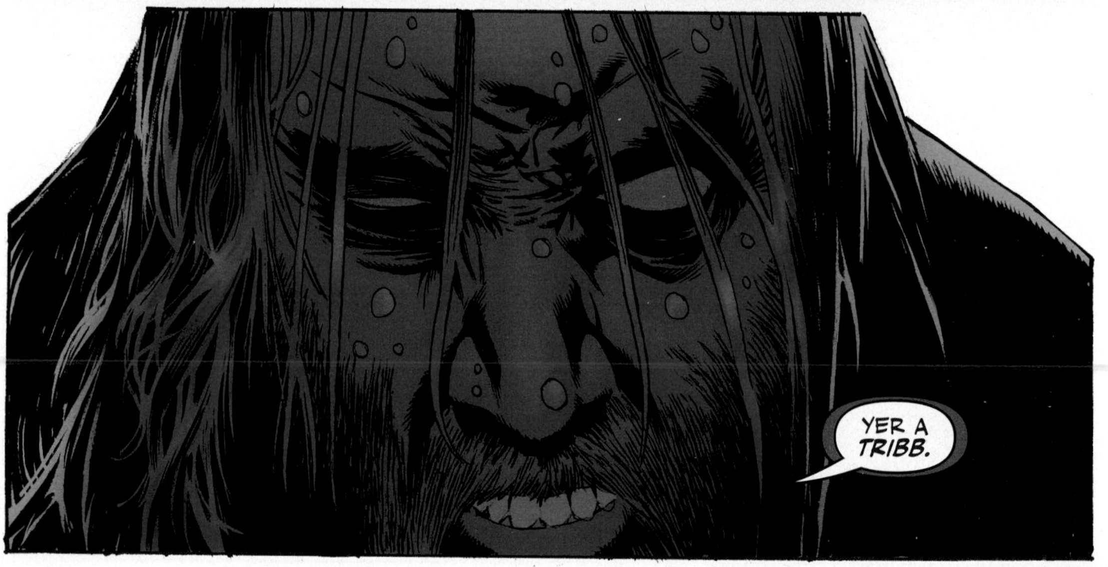
YER A TRIBB.

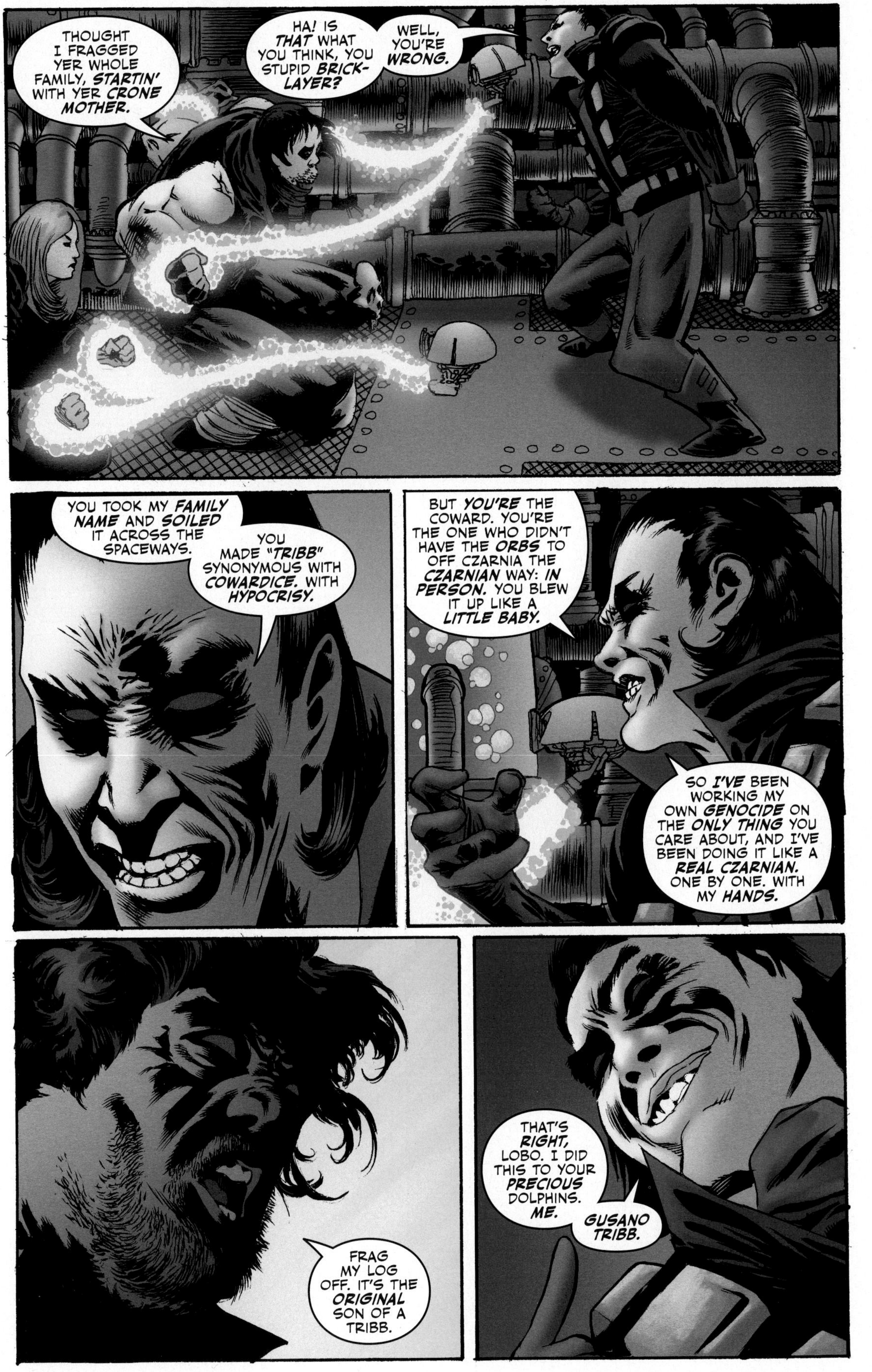
THOUGHT I FRAGGED YER WHOLE FAMILY, STARTIN' WITH YER CRONE MOTHER.
HA! IS THAT WHAT YOU THINK, YOU STUPID BRICK-LAYER?
WELL, YOU'RE WRONG.
YOU TOOK MY FAMILY NAME AND SOILED IT ACROSS THE SPACEWAYS.
YOU MADE "TRIBB" SYNONYMOUS WITH COWARDICE. WITH HYPOCRISY.
BUT YOU'RE THE COWARD. YOU'RE THE ONE WHO DIDN'T HAVE THE ORBS TO OFF CZARNIA THE CZARNIAN WAY: IN PERSON. YOU BLEW IT UP LIKE A LITTLE BABY.
SO I'VE BEEN WORKING MY OWN GENOCIDE ON THE ONLY THING YOU CARE ABOUT, AND I'VE BEEN DOING IT LIKE A REAL CZARNIAN. ONE BY ONE. WITH MY HANDS.
FRAG MY LOG OFF. IT'S THE ORIGINAL SON OF A TRIBB.
THAT'S RIGHT, LOBO. I DID THIS TO YOUR PRECIOUS DOLPHINS. ME.
GUSANO TRIBB.

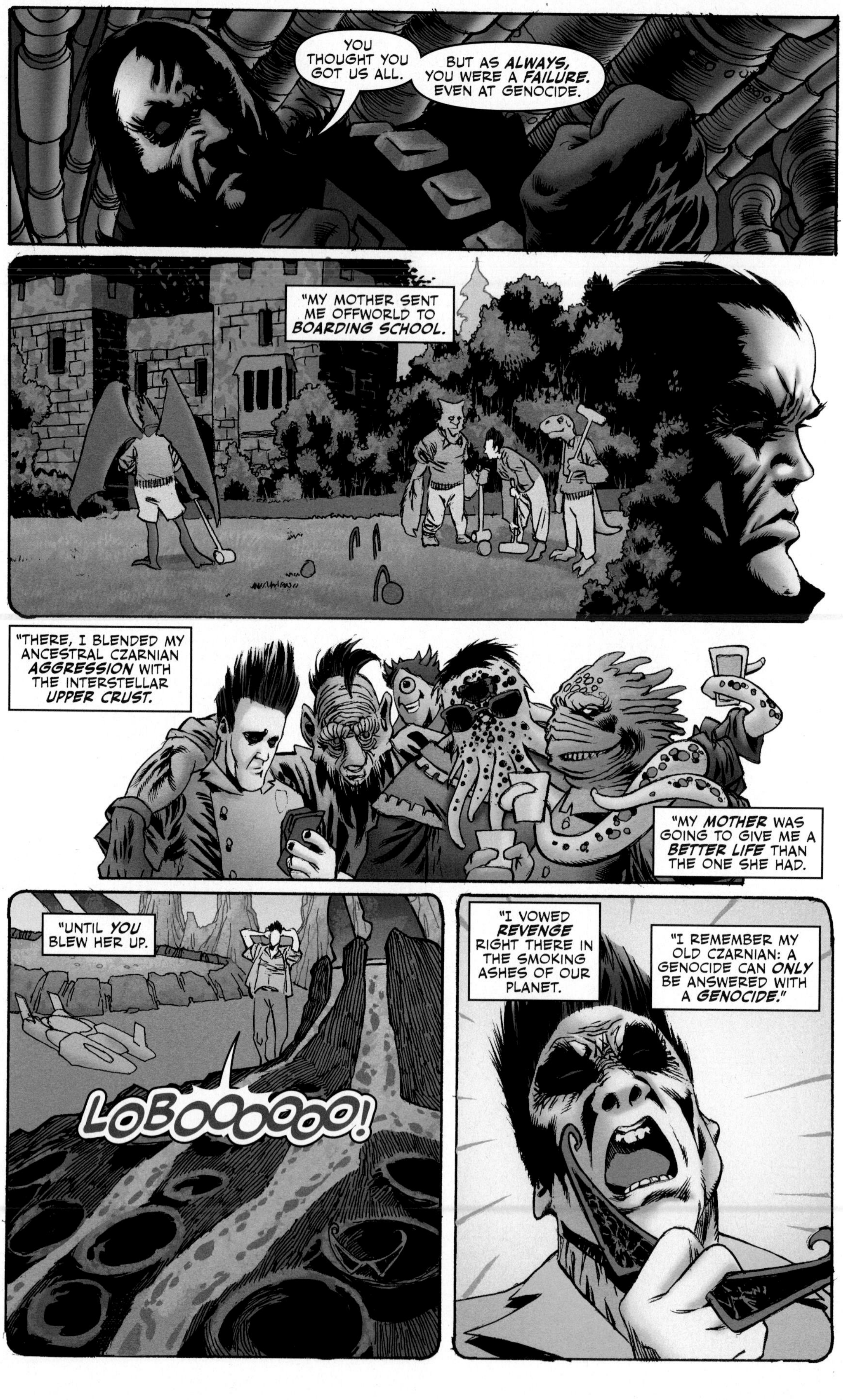
YOU THOUGHT YOU GOT US ALL.
BUT AS ALWAYS, YOU WERE A FAILURE. EVEN AT GENOCIDE.
"MY MOTHER SENT ME OFFWORLD TO BOARDING SCHOOL.
"THERE, I BLENDED MY ANCESTRAL CZARNIAN AGGRESSION WITH THE INTERSTELLAR UPPER CRUST.
"MY MOTHER WAS GOING TO GIVE ME A BETTER LIFE THAN THE ONE SHE HAD.
"UNTIL YOU BLEW HER UP.
LOBOOOOOO!
"I VOWED REVENGE RIGHT THERE IN THE SMOKING ASHES OF OUR PLANET.
"I REMEMBER MY OLD CZARNIAN: A GENOCIDE CAN ONLY BE ANSWERED WITH A GENOCIDE."

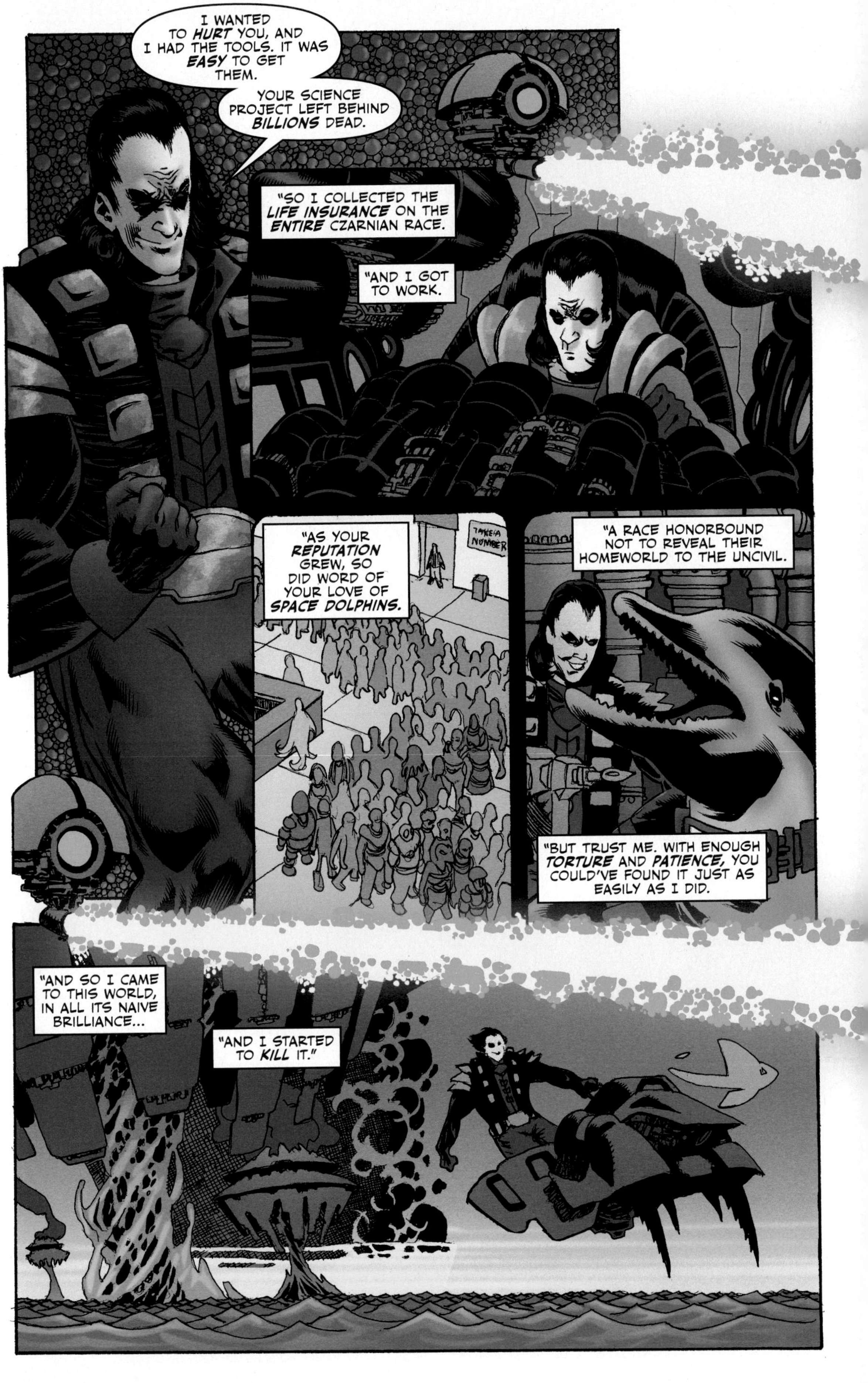

I WANTED TO HURT YOU, AND I HAD THE TOOLS. IT WAS EASY TO GET THEM.
YOUR SCIENCE PROJECT LEFT BEHIND BILLIONS DEAD.
"SO I COLLECTED THE LIFE INSURANCE ON THE ENTIRE CZARNIAN RACE.
"AND I GOT TO WORK.
"AS YOUR REPUTATION GREW, SO DID WORD OF YOUR LOVE OF SPACE DOLPHINS.
TAKE A NUMBER
"A RACE HONORBOUND NOT TO REVEAL THEIR HOMEWORLD TO THE UNCIVIL.
"BUT TRUST ME. WITH ENOUGH TORTURE AND PATIENCE, YOU COULD'VE FOUND IT JUST AS EASILY AS I DID.
"AND SO I CAME TO THIS WORLD, IN ALL ITS NAIVE BRILLIANCE...
"AND I STARTED TO KILL IT."

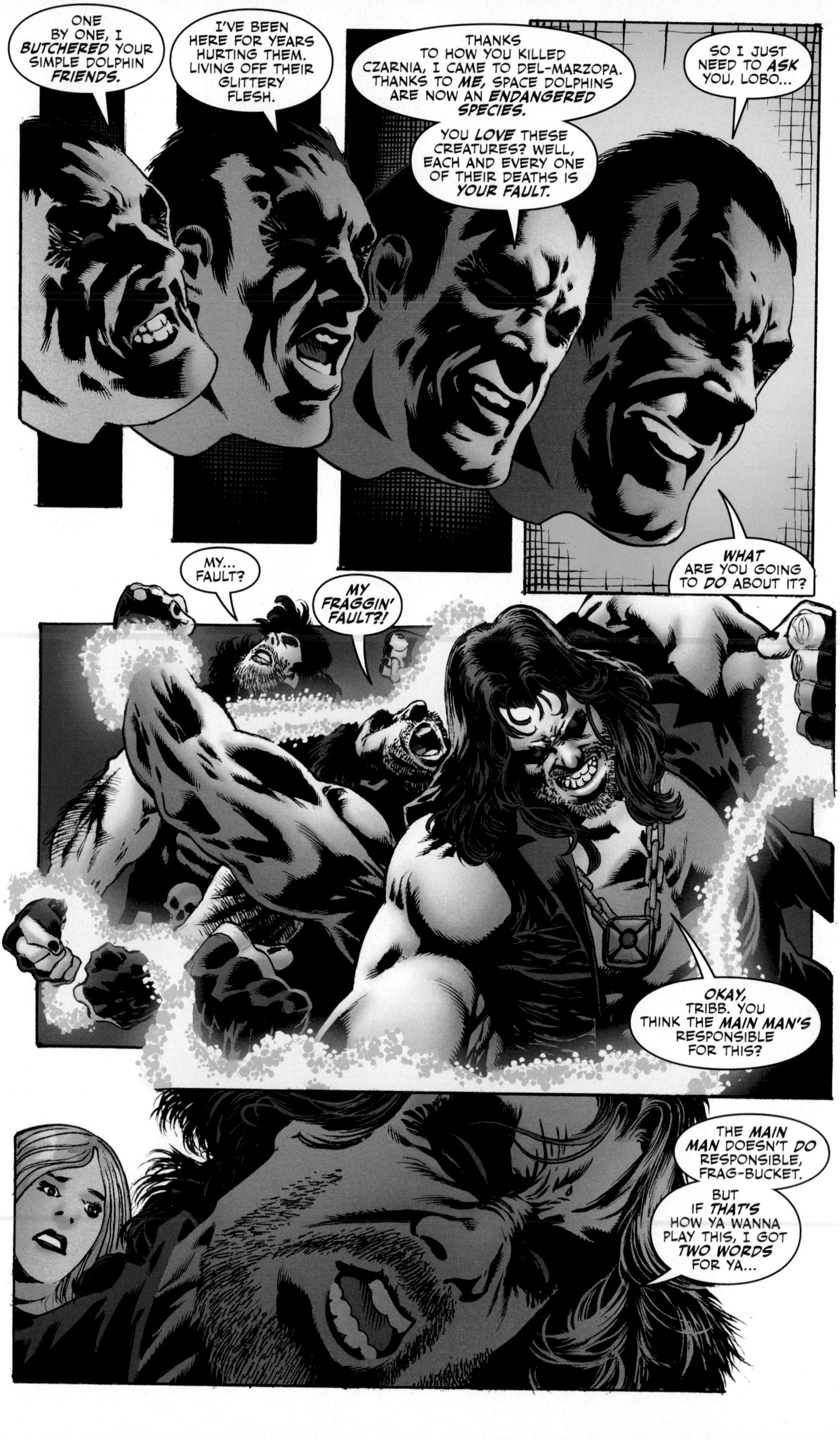
ONE BY ONE, I BUTCHERED YOUR SIMPLE DOLPHIN FRIENDS.
I'VE BEEN HERE FOR YEARS HURTING THEM. LIVING OFF THEIR GLITTERY FLESH.
THANKS TO HOW YOU KILLED CZARNIA, I CAME TO DEL-MARZOPA. THANKS TO ME, SPACE DOLPHINS ARE NOW AN ENDANGERED SPECIES.
YOU LOVE THESE CREATURES? WELL, EACH AND EVERY ONE OF THEIR DEATHS IS YOUR FAULT.
SO I JUST NEED TO ASK YOU, LOBO...
WHAT ARE YOU GOING TO DO ABOUT IT?
MY... FAULT?
MY FRAGGIN' FAULT?!
OKAY, TRIBB. YOU THINK THE MAIN MAN'S RESPONSIBLE FOR THIS?
THE MAIN MAN DOESN'T DO RESPONSIBLE, FRAG-BUCKET.
BUT IF THAT'S HOW YA WANNA PLAY THIS, I GOT TWO WORDS FOR YA...

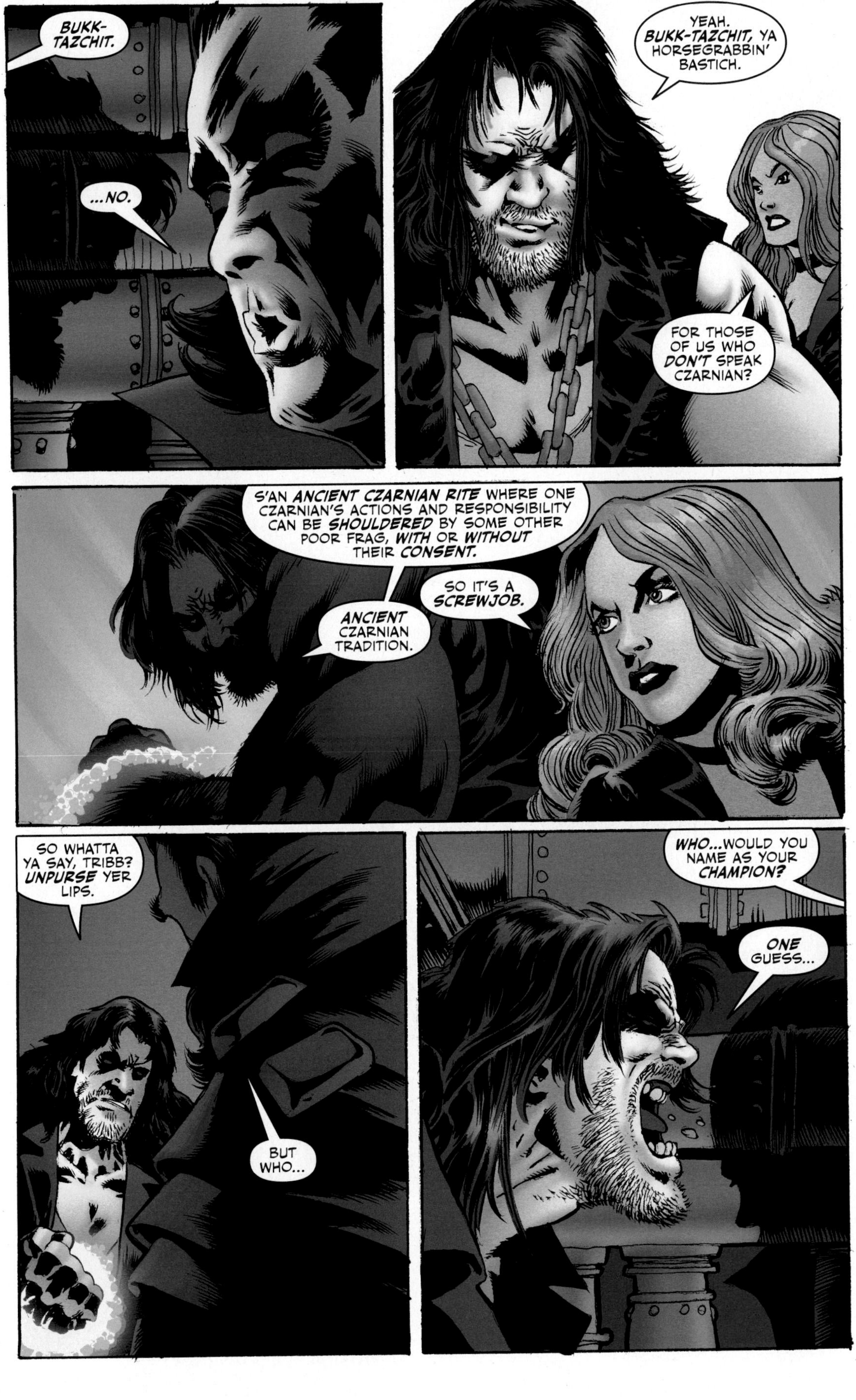
BUKK-TAZCHIT.
...NO.
YEAH. BUKK-TAZCHIT, YA HORSEGRABBIN' BASTICH.
FOR THOSE OF US WHO DON'T SPEAK CZARNIAN?
S'AN ANCIENT CZARNIAN RITE WHERE ONE CZARNIAN'S ACTIONS AND RESPONSIBILITY CAN BE SHOULDERED BY SOME OTHER POOR FRAG, WITH OR WITHOUT THEIR CONSENT.
SO IT'S A SCREWJOB.
ANCIENT CZARNIAN TRADITION.
SO WHATTA YA SAY, TRIBB? UNPURSE YER LIPS.
BUT WHO...
WHO...WOULD YOU NAME AS YOUR CHAMPION?
ONE GUESS...

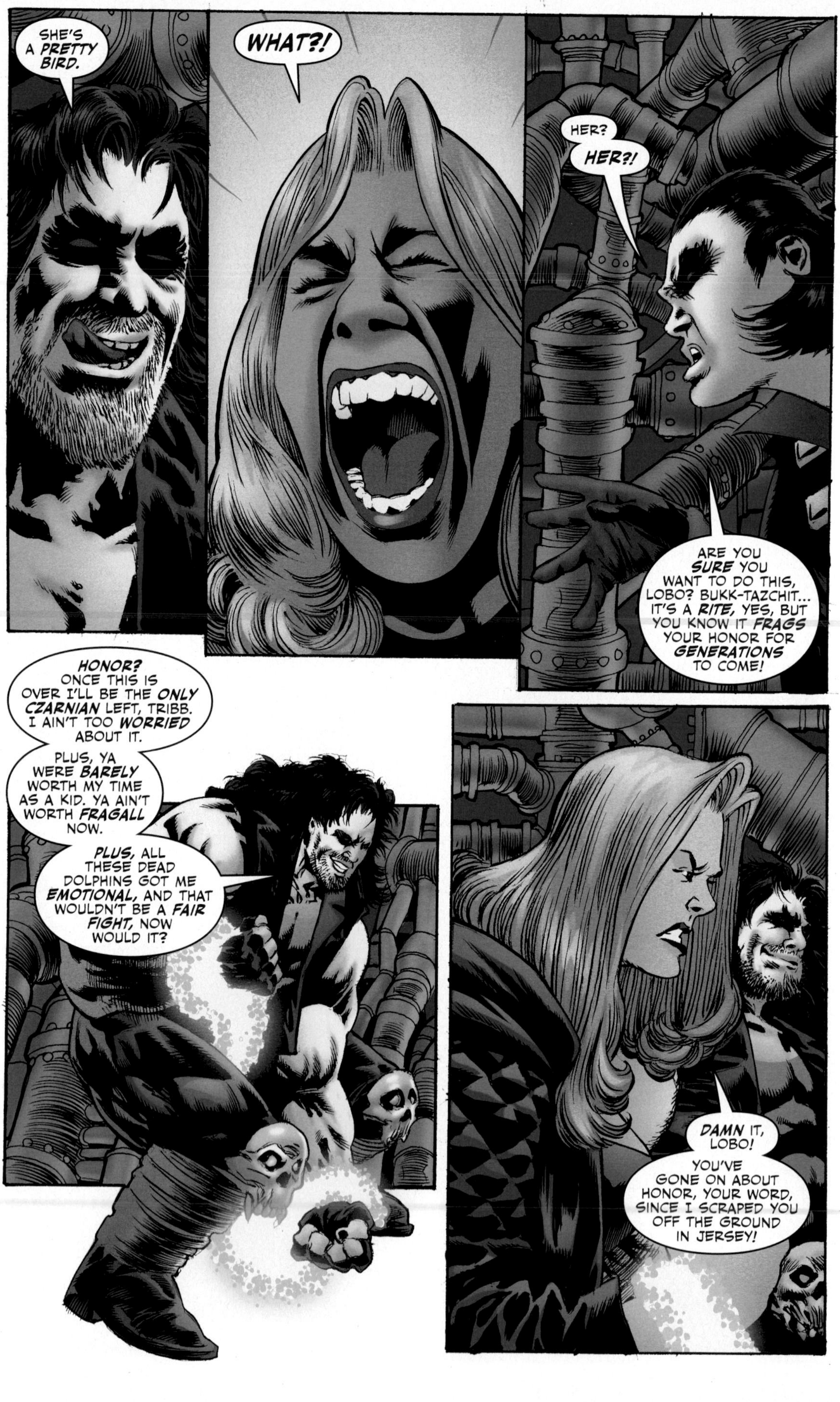
SHE'S A PRETTY BIRD.
WHAT?!
HER? HER?!
ARE YOU SURE YOU WANT TO DO THIS, LOBO? BUKK-TAZCHIT... IT'S A RITE, YES, BUT YOU KNOW IT FRAGS YOUR HONOR FOR GENERATIONS TO COME!
HONOR? ONCE THIS IS OVER I'LL BE THE ONLY CZARNIAN LEFT, TRIBB. I AIN'T TOO WORRIED ABOUT IT.
PLUS, YA WERE BARELY WORTH MY TIME AS A KID. YA AIN'T WORTH FRAGALL NOW.
PLUS, ALL THESE DEAD DOLPHINS GOT ME EMOTIONAL, AND THAT WOULDN'T BE A FAIR FIGHT, NOW WOULD IT?
DAMN IT, LOBO!
YOU'VE GONE ON ABOUT HONOR, YOUR WORD, SINCE I SCRAPED YOU OFF THE GROUND IN JERSEY!

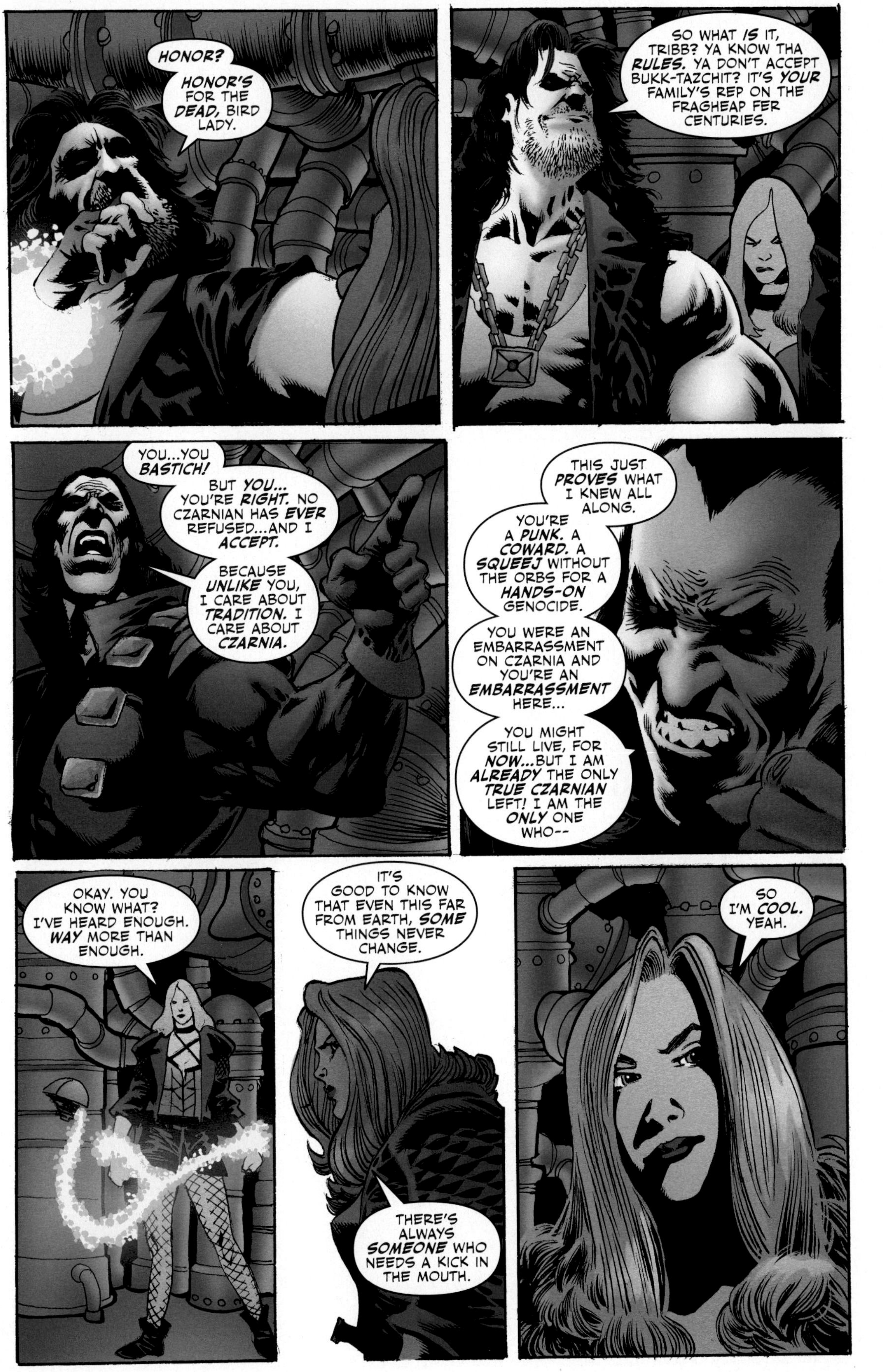
HONOR?
HONOR'S FOR THE DEAD, BIRD LADY.
SO WHAT IS IT, TRIBB? YA KNOW THA RULES. YA DON'T ACCEPT BUKK-TAZCHIT? IT'S YOUR FAMILY'S REP ON THE FRAGHEAP FER CENTURIES.
YOU...YOU BASTICH!
BUT YOU... YOU'RE RIGHT. NO CZARNIAN HAS EVER REFUSED...AND I ACCEPT.
BECAUSE UNLIKE YOU, I CARE ABOUT TRADITION. I CARE ABOUT CZARNIA.
THIS JUST PROVES WHAT I KNEW ALL ALONG.
YOU'RE A PUNK. A COWARD. A SQUEEJ WITHOUT THE ORBS FOR A HANDS-ON GENOCIDE.
YOU WERE AN EMBARRASSMENT ON CZARNIA AND YOU'RE AN EMBARRASSMENT HERE...
YOU MIGHT STILL LIVE, FOR NOW...BUT I AM ALREADY THE ONLY TRUE CZARNIAN LEFT! I AM THE ONLY ONE WHO--
OKAY. YOU KNOW WHAT? I'VE HEARD ENOUGH. WAY MORE THAN ENOUGH.
IT'S GOOD TO KNOW THAT EVEN THIS FAR FROM EARTH, SOME THINGS NEVER CHANGE.
THERE'S ALWAYS SOMEONE WHO NEEDS A KICK IN THE MOUTH.
SO I'M COOL. YEAH.

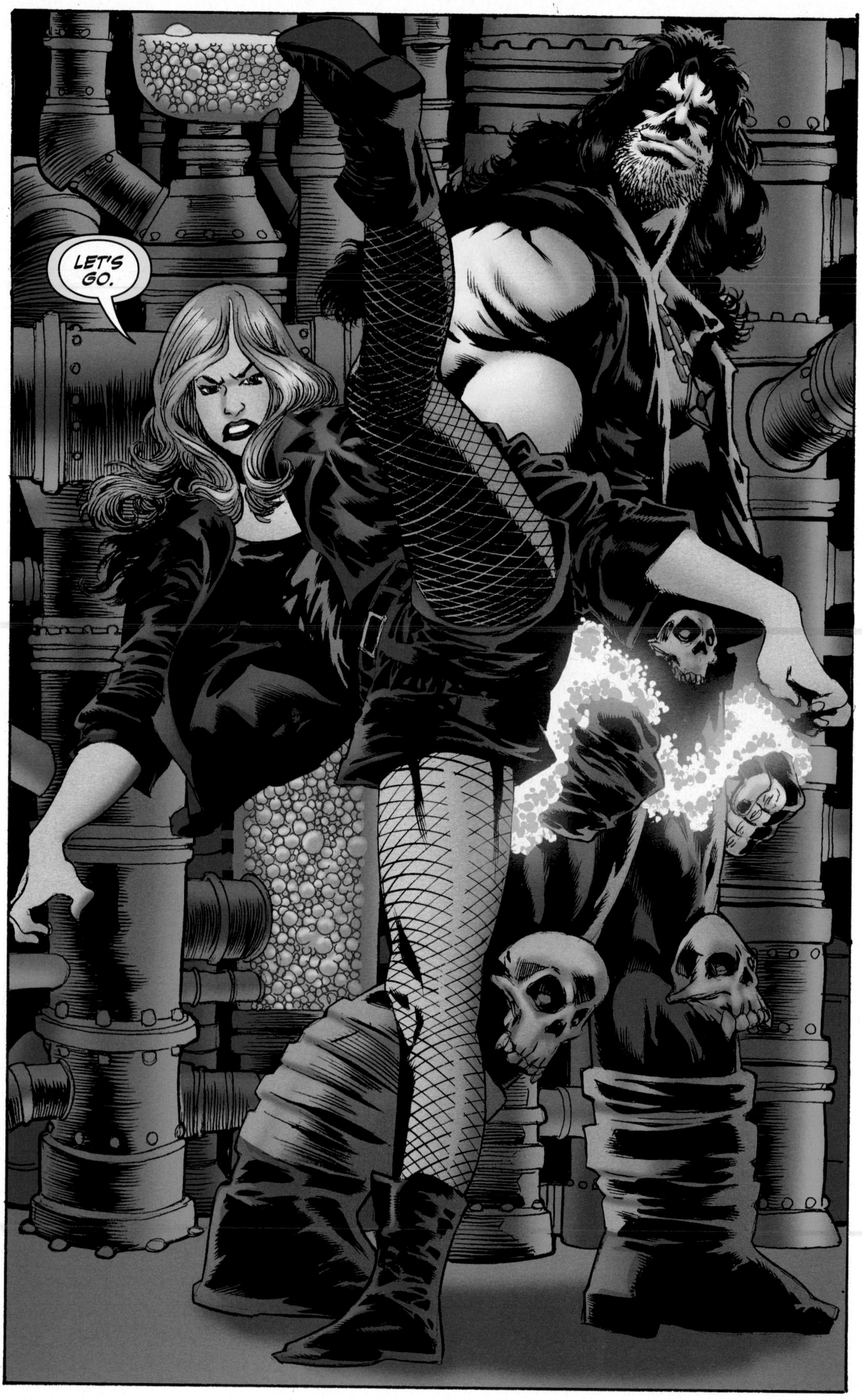
LET'S GO.

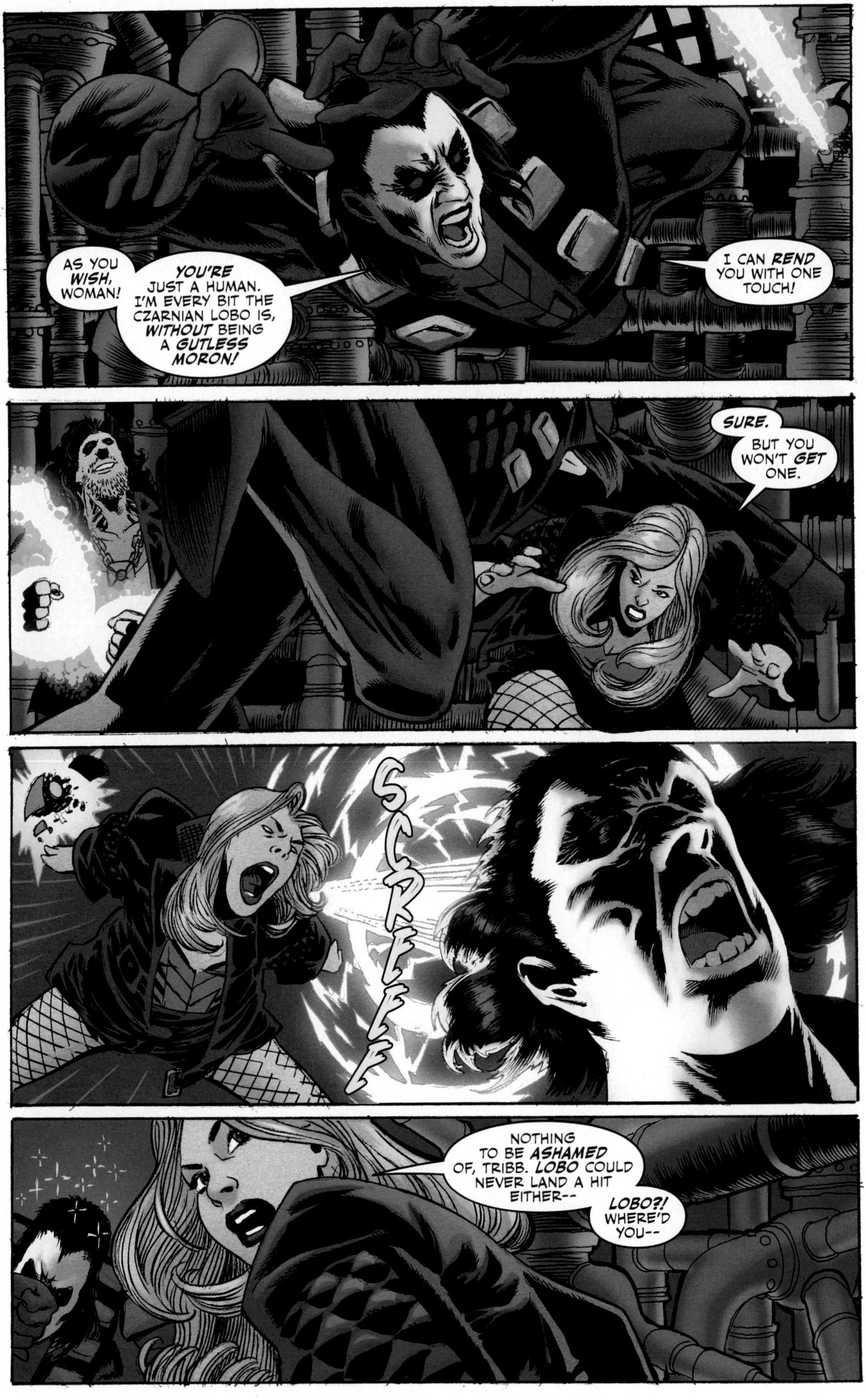
AS YOU WISH, WOMAN!
YOU'RE JUST A HUMAN. I'M EVERY BIT THE CZARNIAN LOBO IS, WITHOUT BEING A GUTLESS MORON!
I CAN REND YOU WITH ONE TOUCH!
SURE.
BUT YOU WON'T GET ONE.
SCREEEEE
NOTHING TO BE ASHAMED OF, TRIBB. LOBO COULD NEVER LAND A HIT EITHER--
LOBO?! WHERE'D YOU--

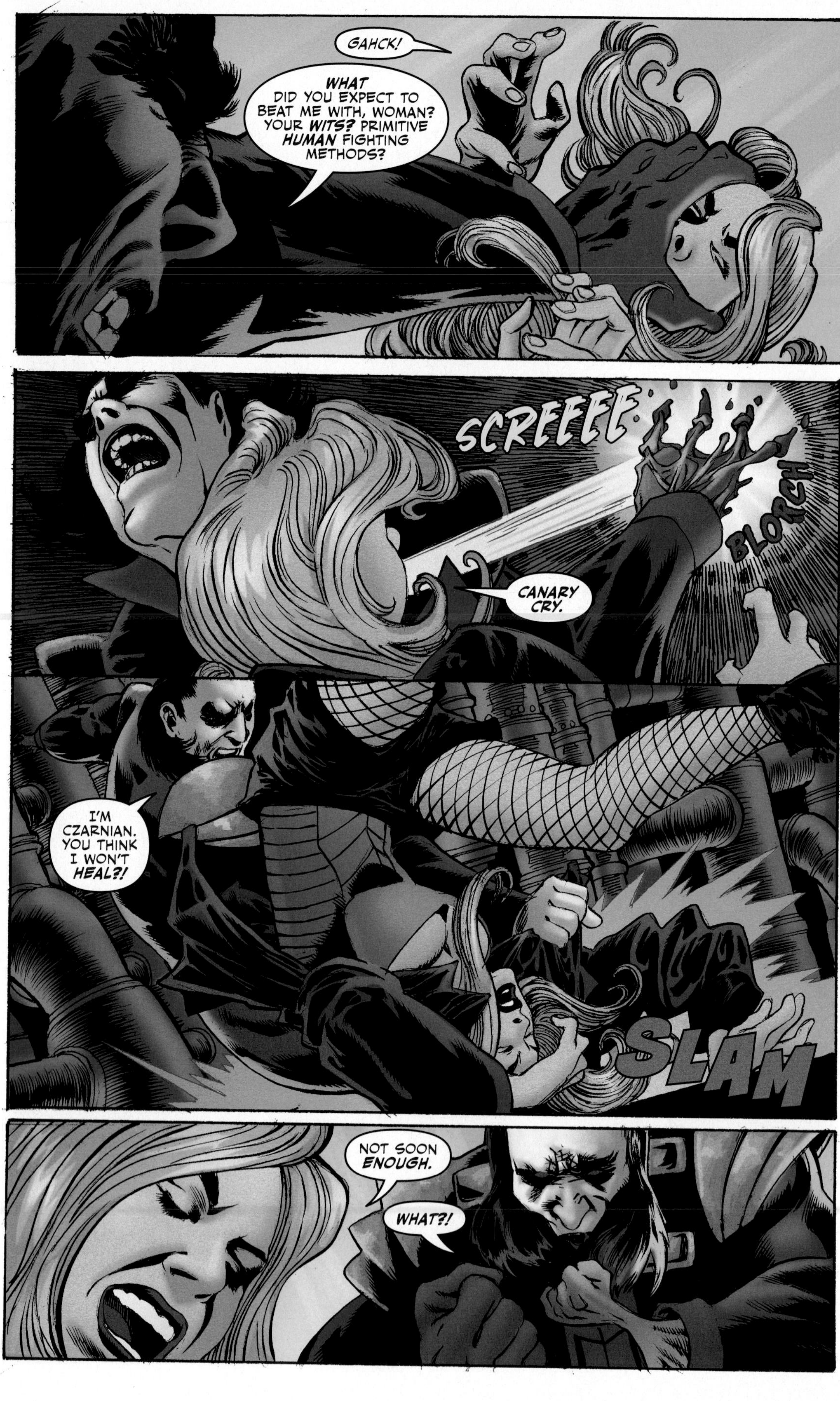
GAHCK!
WHAT DID YOU EXPECT TO BEAT ME WITH, WOMAN? YOUR WITS? PRIMITIVE HUMAN FIGHTING METHODS?
SCREEEEE
BLORCH
CANARY CRY.
I'M CZARNIAN. YOU THINK I WON'T HEAL?!
SLAM
NOT SOON ENOUGH.
WHAT?!

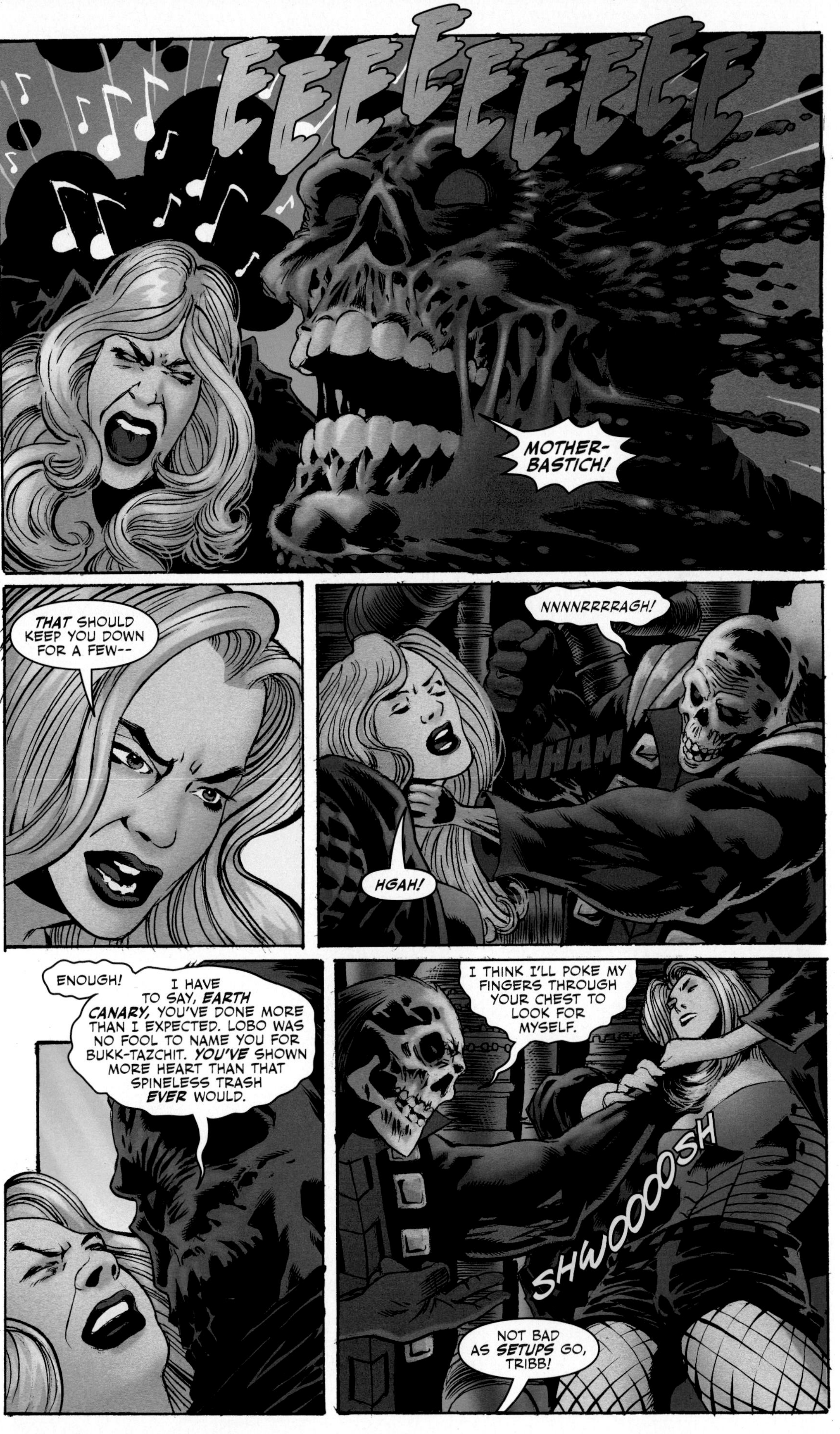
EEEEEEEEEEE
MOTHER-BASTICH!
THAT SHOULD KEEP YOU DOWN FOR A FEW--
NNNNRRRRAGH!
WHAM
HGAH!
ENOUGH!
I HAVE TO SAY, EARTH CANARY, YOU'VE DONE MORE THAN I EXPECTED. LOBO WAS NO FOOL TO NAME YOU FOR BUKK-TAZCHIT. YOU'VE SHOWN MORE HEART THAN THAT SPINELESS TRASH EVER WOULD.
I THINK I'LL POKE MY FINGERS THROUGH YOUR CHEST TO LOOK FOR MYSELF.
SHWOOOOSH
NOT BAD AS SETUPS GO, TRIBB!

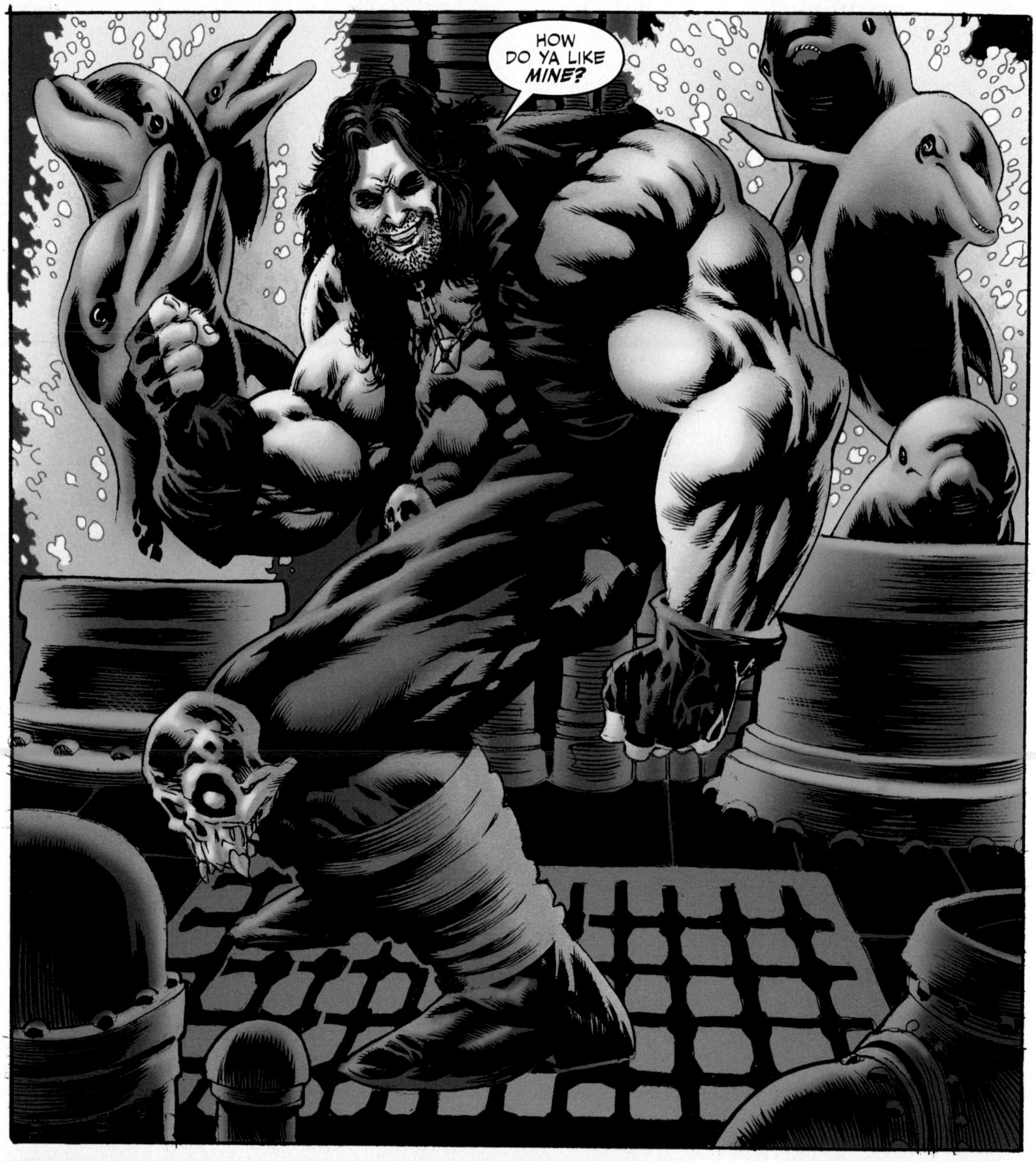
HOW DO YA LIKE MINE?

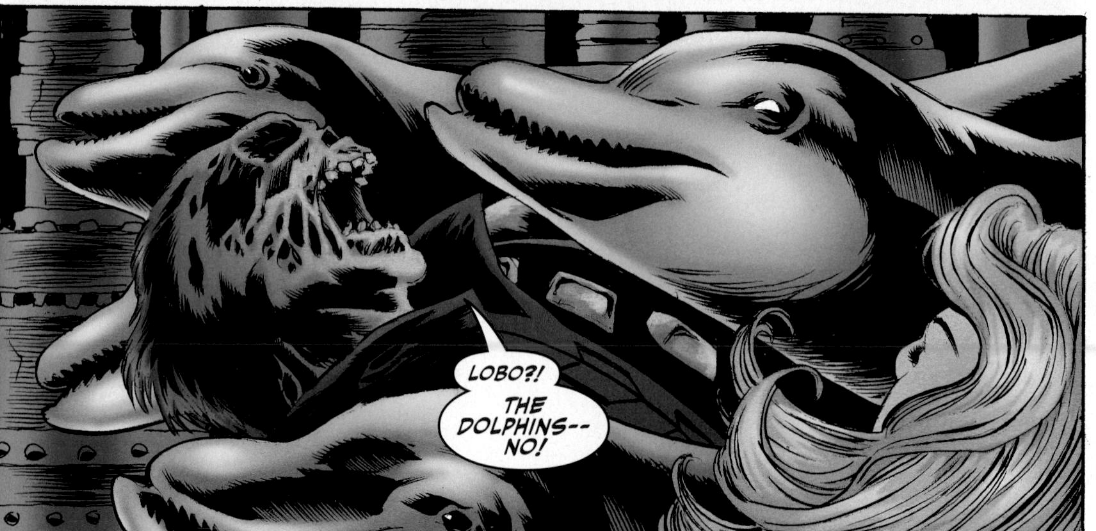
LOBO?! THE DOLPHINS-- NO!

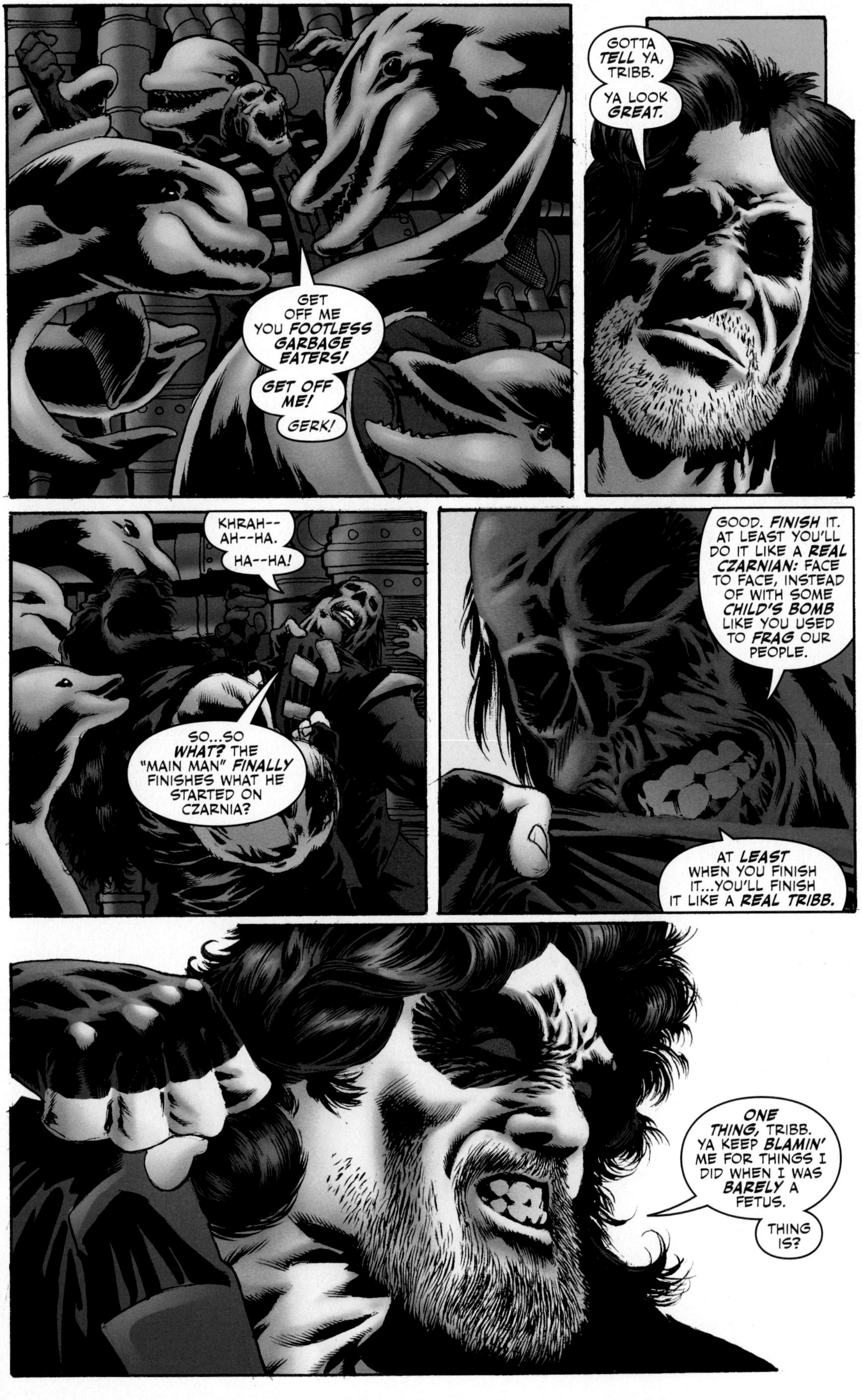
GET OFF ME YOU FOOTLESS GARBAGE EATERS!
GET OFF ME!
GERK!
GOTTA TELL YA, TRIBB.
YA LOOK GREAT.
KHRAH--AH--HA.
HA--HA!
SO...SO WHAT? THE "MAIN MAN" FINALLY FINISHES WHAT HE STARTED ON CZARNIA?
GOOD. FINISH IT. AT LEAST YOU'LL DO IT LIKE A REAL CZARNIAN: FACE TO FACE, INSTEAD OF WITH SOME CHILD'S BOMB LIKE YOU USED TO FRAG OUR PEOPLE.
AT LEAST WHEN YOU FINISH IT...YOU'LL FINISH IT LIKE A REAL TRIBB.
ONE THING, TRIBB. YA KEEP BLAMIN' ME FOR THINGS I DID WHEN I WAS BARELY A FETUS.
THING IS?

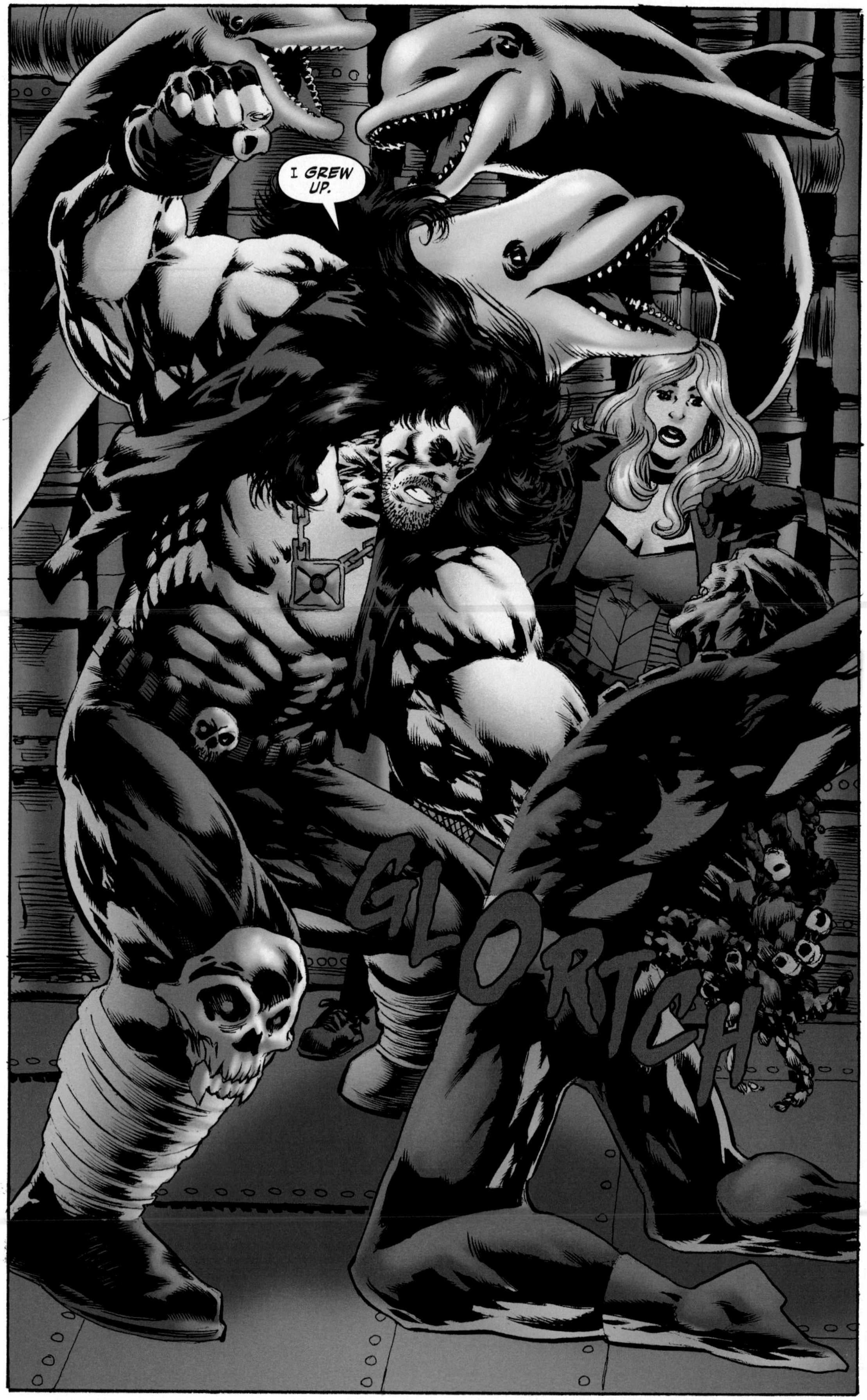
I GREW UP.
GLORTCH

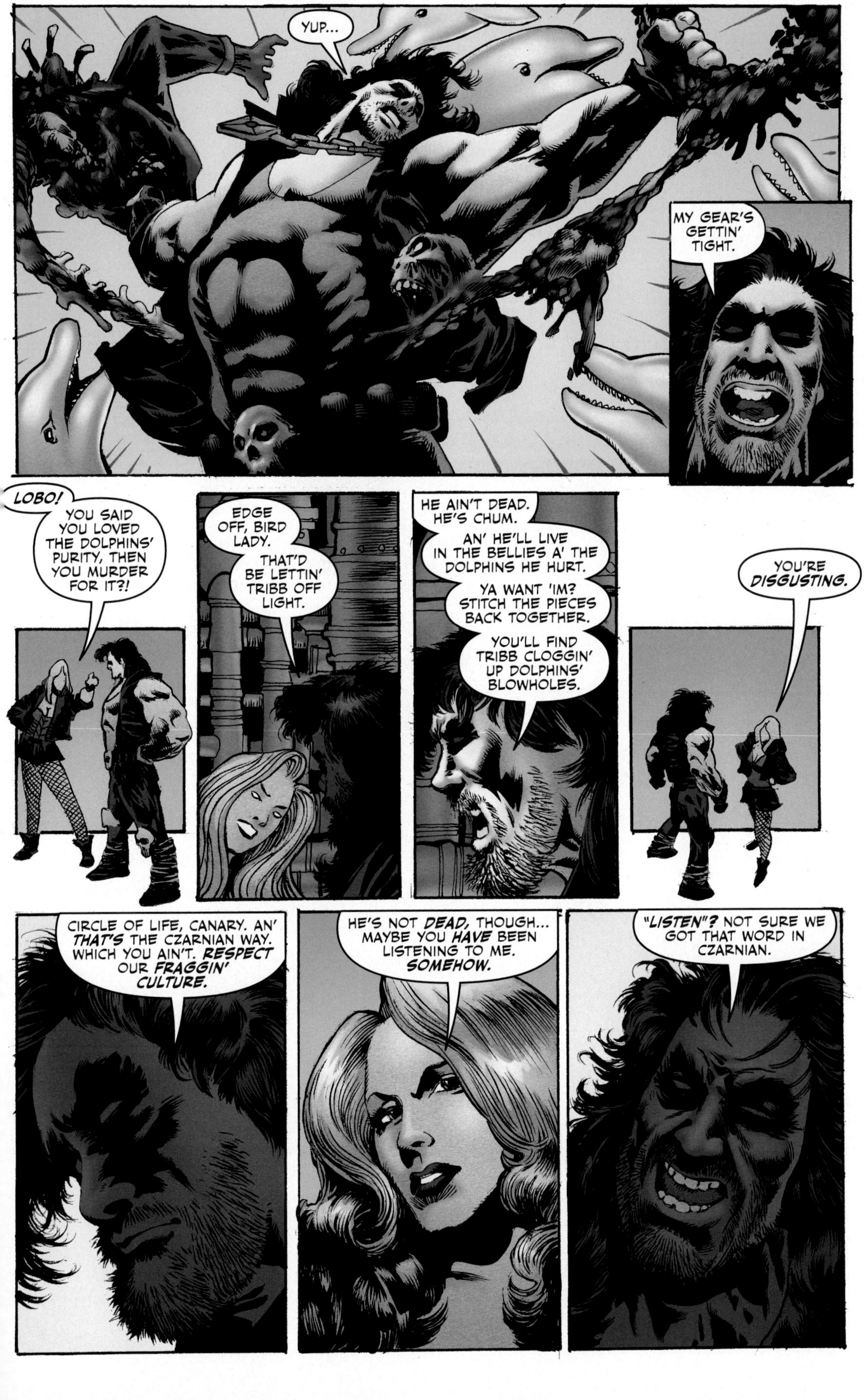
YUP...
MY GEAR'S GETTIN' TIGHT.
LOBO!
YOU SAID YOU LOVED THE DOLPHINS' PURITY, THEN YOU MURDER FOR IT?!
EDGE OFF, BIRD LADY.
THAT'D BE LETTIN' TRIBB OFF LIGHT.
HE AIN'T DEAD. HE'S CHUM.
AN' HE'LL LIVE IN THE BELLIES A' THE DOLPHINS HE HURT.
YA WANT 'IM? STITCH THE PIECES BACK TOGETHER.
YOU'LL FIND TRIBB CLOGGIN' UP DOLPHINS' BLOWHOLES.
YOU'RE DISGUSTING.
CIRCLE OF LIFE, CANARY. AN' THAT'S THE CZARNIAN WAY. WHICH YOU AIN'T. RESPECT OUR FRAGGIN' CULTURE.
HE'S NOT DEAD, THOUGH... MAYBE YOU HAVE BEEN LISTENING TO ME. SOMEHOW.
"LISTEN"? NOT SURE WE GOT THAT WORD IN CZARNIAN.

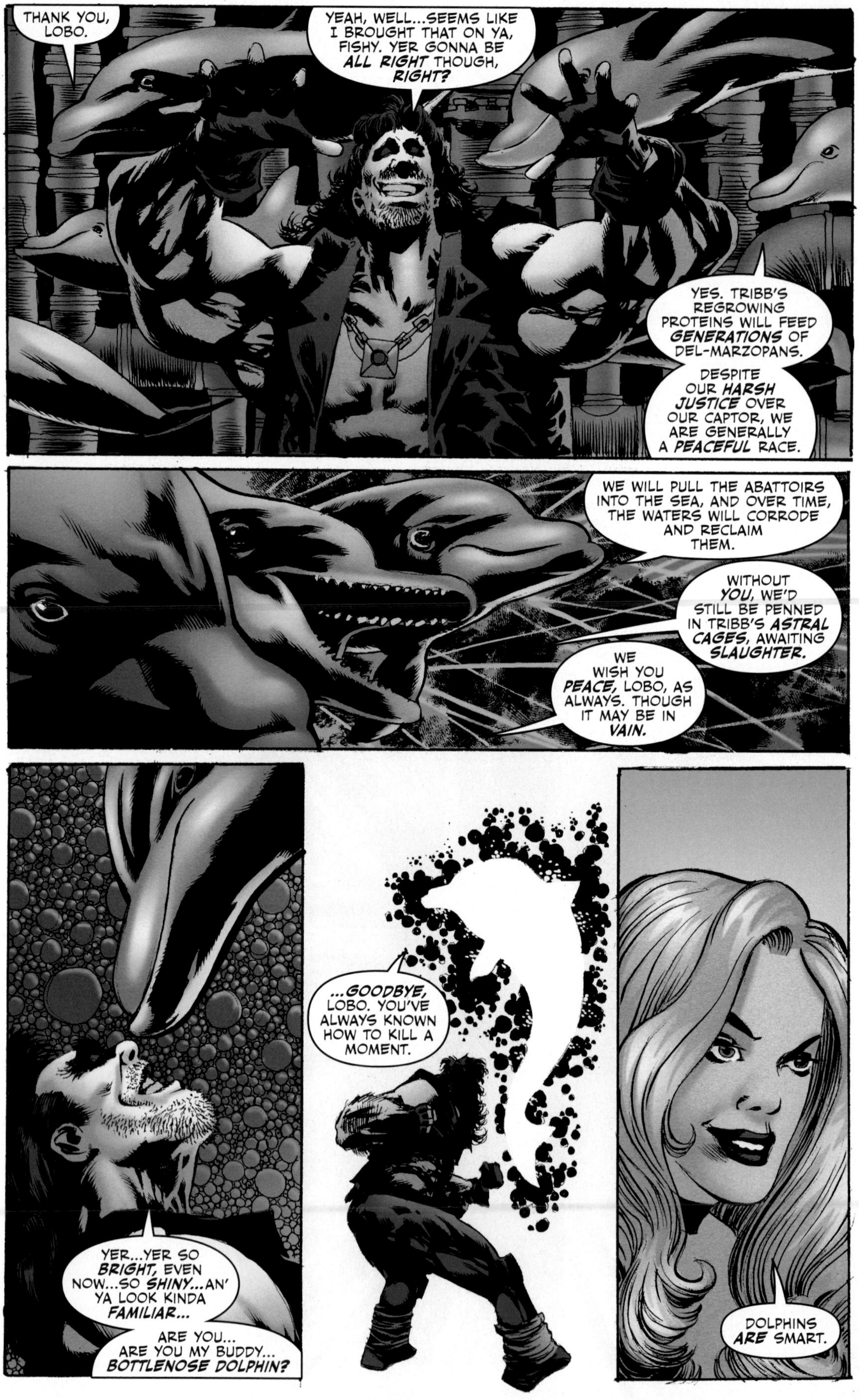
THANK YOU, LOBO.
YEAH, WELL...SEEMS LIKE I BROUGHT THAT ON YA, FISHY. YER GONNA BE ALL RIGHT THOUGH, RIGHT?
YES. TRIBB'S REGROWING PROTEINS WILL FEED GENERATIONS OF DEL-MARZOPANS.
DESPITE OUR HARSH JUSTICE OVER OUR CAPTOR, WE ARE GENERALLY A PEACEFUL RACE.
WE WILL PULL THE ABATTOIRS INTO THE SEA, AND OVER TIME, THE WATERS WILL CORRODE AND RECLAIM THEM.
WITHOUT YOU, WE'D STILL BE PENNED IN TRIBB'S ASTRAL CAGES, AWAITING SLAUGHTER.
WE WISH YOU PEACE, LOBO, AS ALWAYS. THOUGH IT MAY BE IN VAIN.
YER...YER SO BRIGHT, EVEN NOW...SO SHINY...AN' YA LOOK KINDA FAMILIAR...
ARE YOU... ARE YOU MY BUDDY... BOTTLENOSE DOLPHIN?
...GOODBYE, LOBO. YOU'VE ALWAYS KNOWN HOW TO KILL A MOMENT.
DOLPHINS ARE SMART.

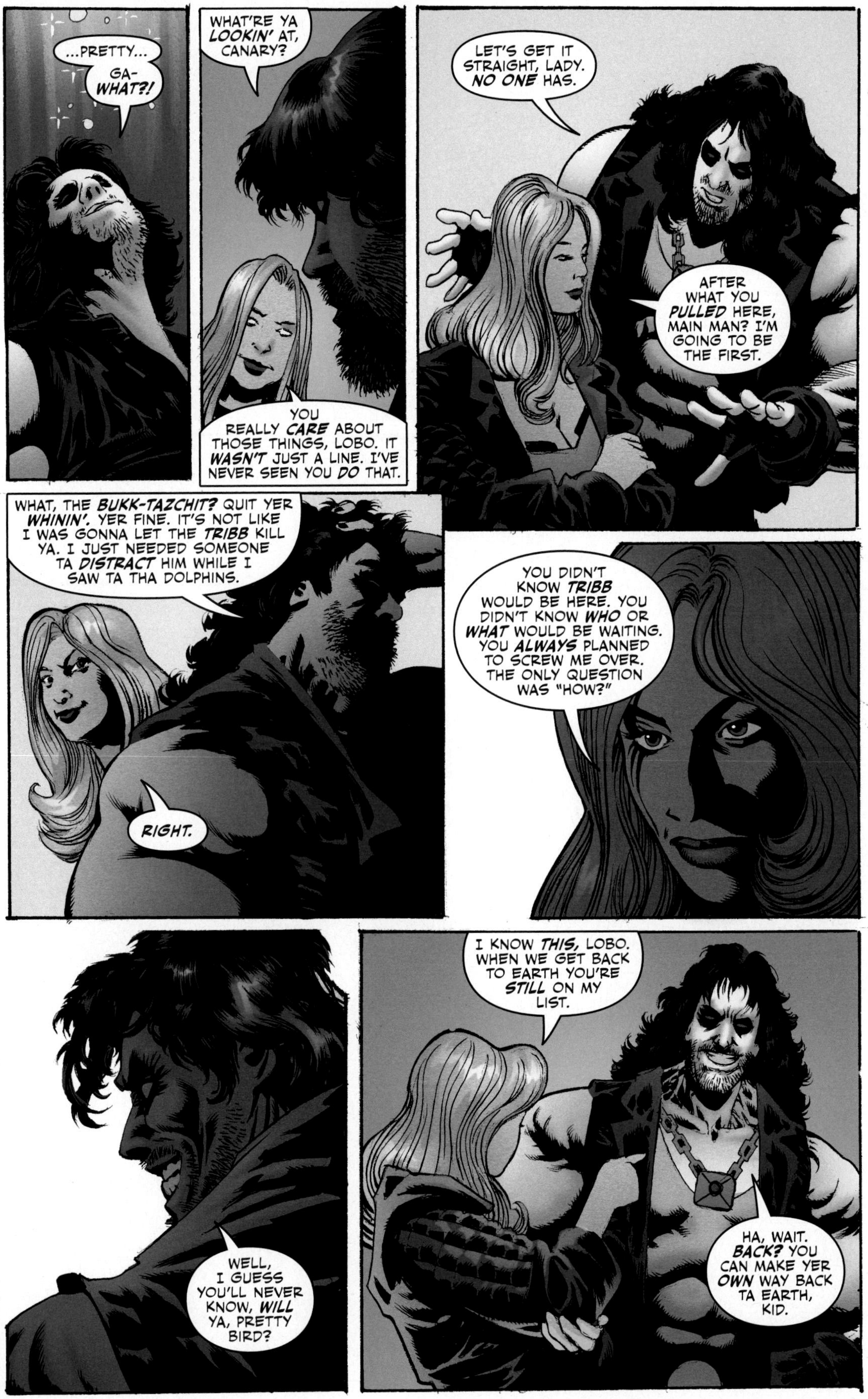
...PRETTY... GA-WHAT?!
WHAT'RE YA LOOKIN' AT, CANARY?
YOU REALLY CARE ABOUT THOSE THINGS, LOBO. IT WASN'T JUST A LINE. I'VE NEVER SEEN YOU DO THAT.
LET'S GET IT STRAIGHT, LADY. NO ONE HAS.
AFTER WHAT YOU PULLED HERE, MAIN MAN? I'M GOING TO BE THE FIRST.
WHAT, THE BUKK-TAZCHIT? QUIT YER WHININ'. YER FINE. IT'S NOT LIKE I WAS GONNA LET THE TRIBB KILL YA. I JUST NEEDED SOMEONE TA DISTRACT HIM WHILE I SAW TA THA DOLPHINS.
RIGHT.
YOU DIDN'T KNOW TRIBB WOULD BE HERE. YOU DIDN'T KNOW WHO OR WHAT WOULD BE WAITING. YOU ALWAYS PLANNED TO SCREW ME OVER. THE ONLY QUESTION WAS "HOW?"
WELL, I GUESS YOU'LL NEVER KNOW, WILL YA, PRETTY BIRD?
I KNOW THIS, LOBO. WHEN WE GET BACK TO EARTH YOU'RE STILL ON MY LIST.
HA, WAIT. BACK? YOU CAN MAKE YER OWN WAY BACK TA EARTH, KID.

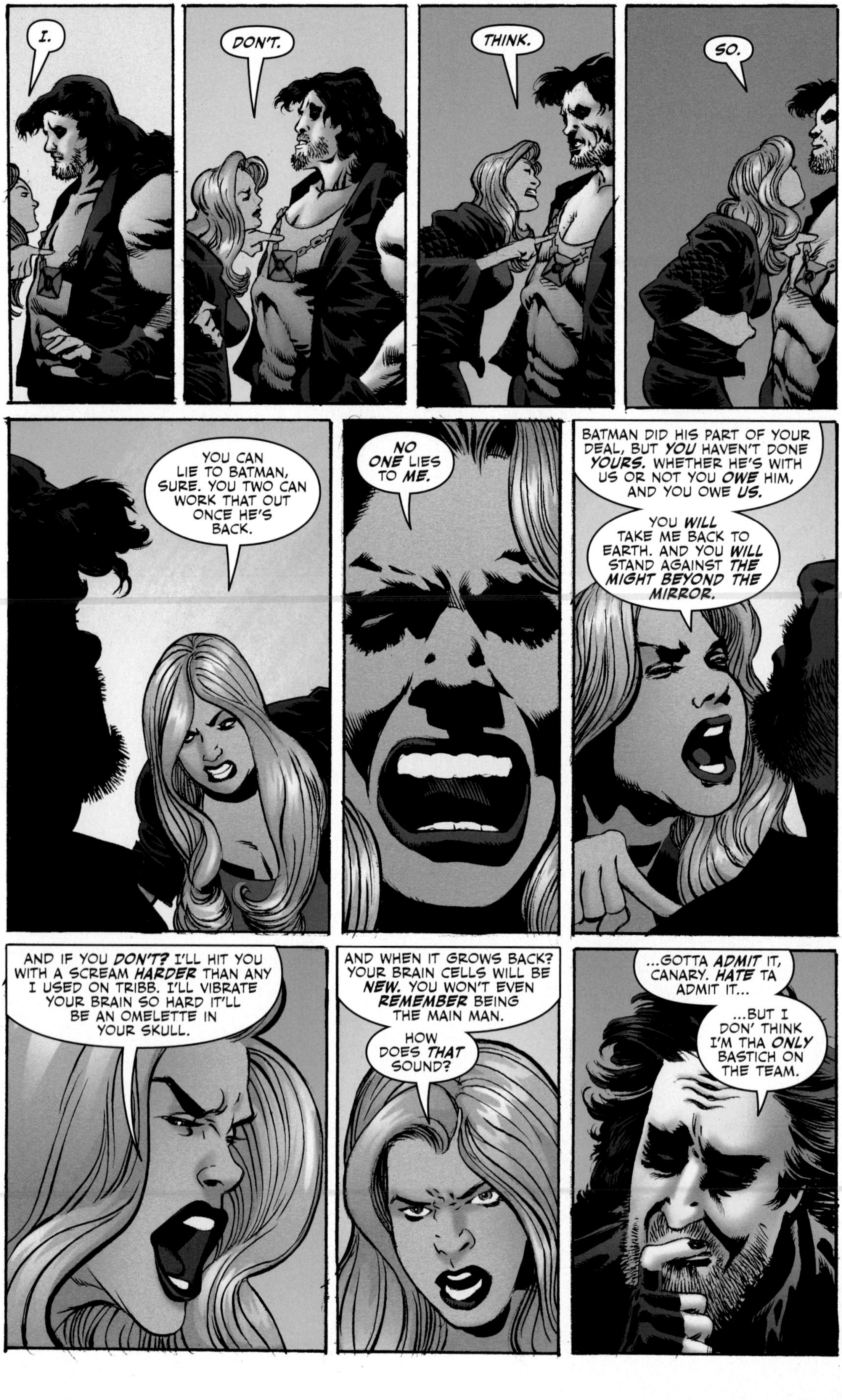
I.
DON'T.
THINK.
SO.
YOU CAN LIE TO BATMAN, SURE. YOU TWO CAN WORK THAT OUT ONCE HE'S BACK.
NO ONE LIES TO ME.
BATMAN DID HIS PART OF YOUR DEAL, BUT YOU HAVEN'T DONE YOURS. WHETHER HE'S WITH US OR NOT YOU OWE HIM, AND YOU OWE US.
YOU WILL TAKE ME BACK TO EARTH. AND YOU WILL STAND AGAINST THE MIGHT BEYOND THE MIRROR.
AND IF YOU DON'T? I'LL HIT YOU WITH A SCREAM HARDER THAN ANY I USED ON TRIBB. I'LL VIBRATE YOUR BRAIN SO HARD IT'LL BE AN OMELETTE IN YOUR SKULL.
AND WHEN IT GROWS BACK? YOUR BRAIN CELLS WILL BE NEW. YOU WON'T EVEN REMEMBER BEING THE MAIN MAN.
HOW DOES THAT SOUND?
...GOTTA ADMIT IT, CANARY. HATE TA ADMIT IT...
...BUT I DON' THINK I'M THA ONLY BASTICH ON THE TEAM.

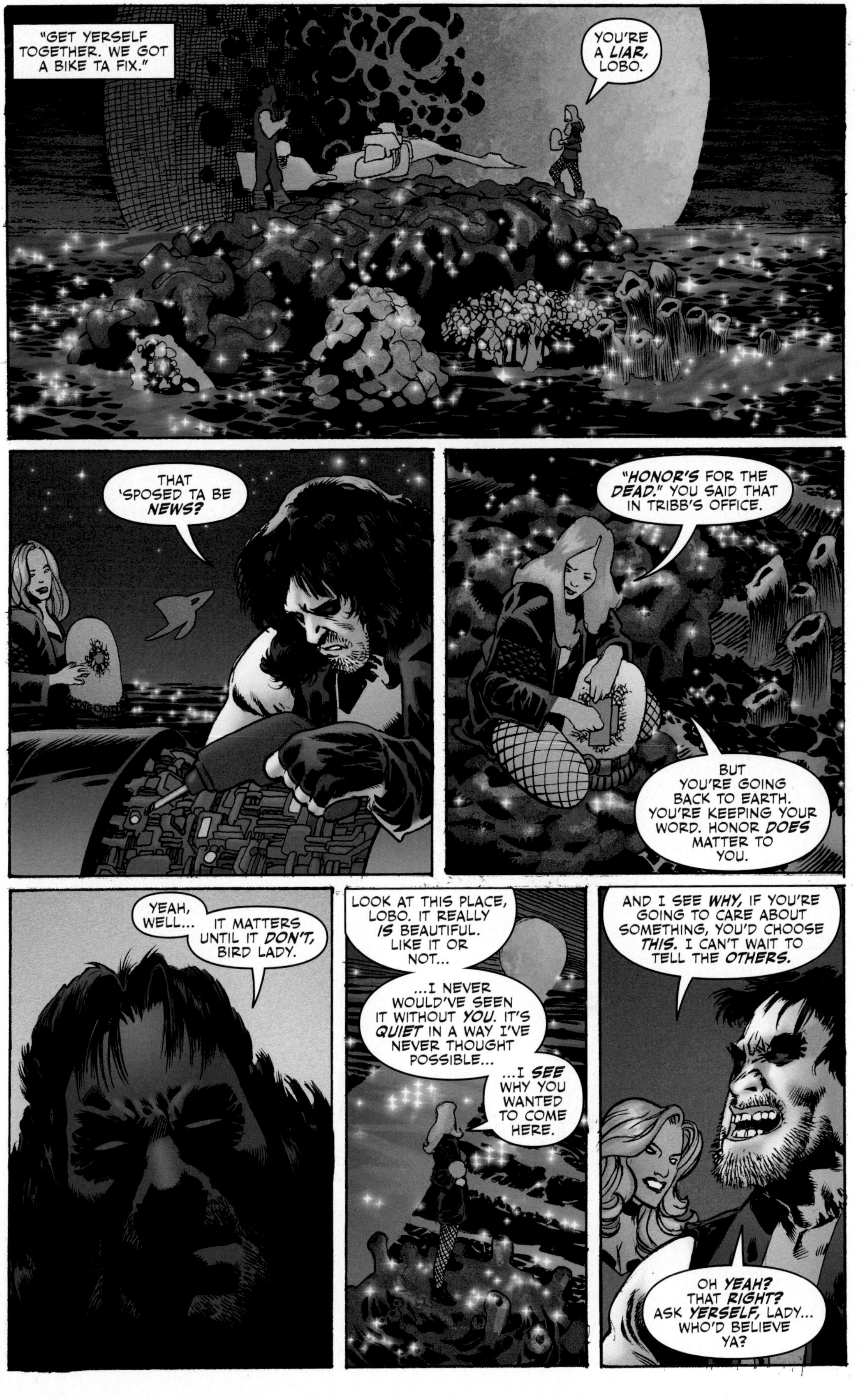
"GET YERSELF TOGETHER. WE GOT A BIKE TA FIX."
YOU'RE A LIAR, LOBO.
THAT 'SPOSED TA BE NEWS?
"HONOR'S FOR THE DEAD." YOU SAID THAT IN TRIBB'S OFFICE.
BUT YOU'RE GOING BACK TO EARTH. YOU'RE KEEPING YOUR WORD. HONOR DOES MATTER TO YOU.
YEAH, WELL...
IT MATTERS UNTIL IT DON'T, BIRD LADY.
LOOK AT THIS PLACE, LOBO. IT REALLY IS BEAUTIFUL. LIKE IT OR NOT...
...I NEVER WOULD'VE SEEN IT WITHOUT YOU. IT'S QUIET IN A WAY I'VE NEVER THOUGHT POSSIBLE...
...I SEE WHY YOU WANTED TO COME HERE.
AND I SEE WHY, IF YOU'RE GOING TO CARE ABOUT SOMETHING, YOU'D CHOOSE THIS. I CAN'T WAIT TO TELL THE OTHERS.
OH YEAH? THAT RIGHT? ASK YERSELF, LADY... WHO'D BELIEVE YA?

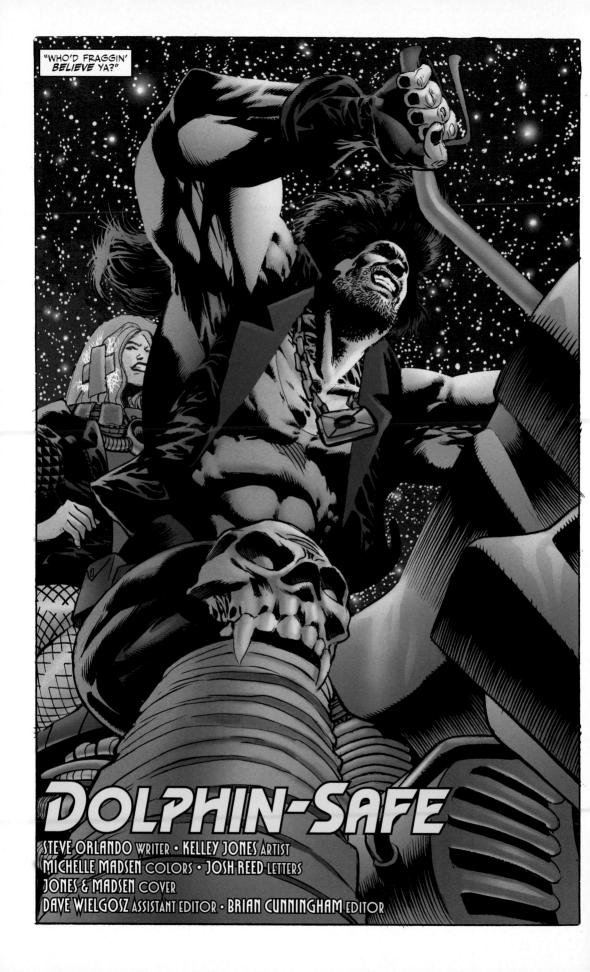

"WHO'D FRAGGIN' *BELIEVE* YA?"

DOLPHIN-SAFE

STEVE ORLANDO WRITER • KELLEY JONES ARTIST

MICHELLE MADSEN COLORS • JOSH REED LETTERS

JONES & MADSEN COVER

DAVE WIELGOSZ ASSISTANT EDITOR • BRIAN CUNNINGHAM EDITOR

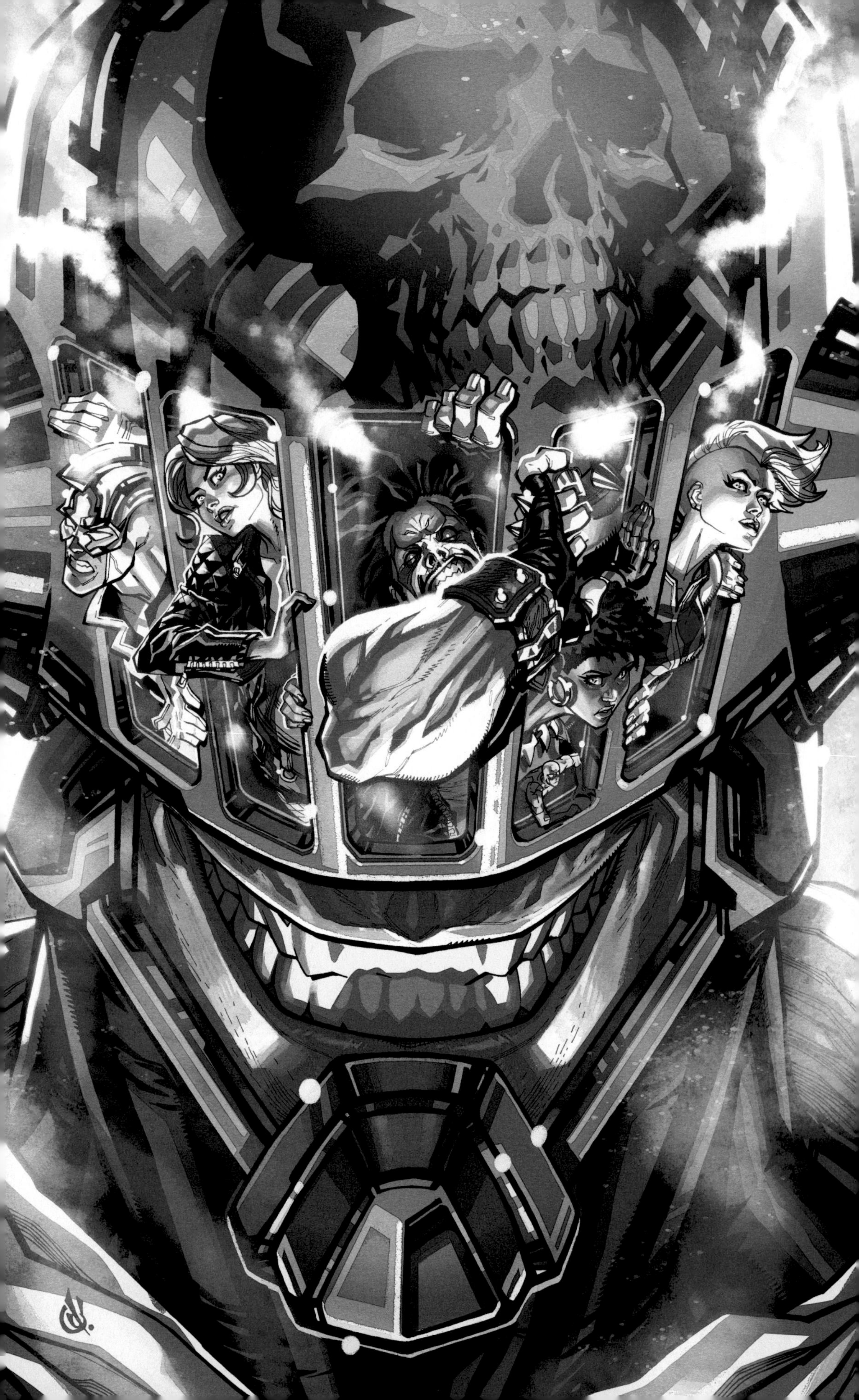

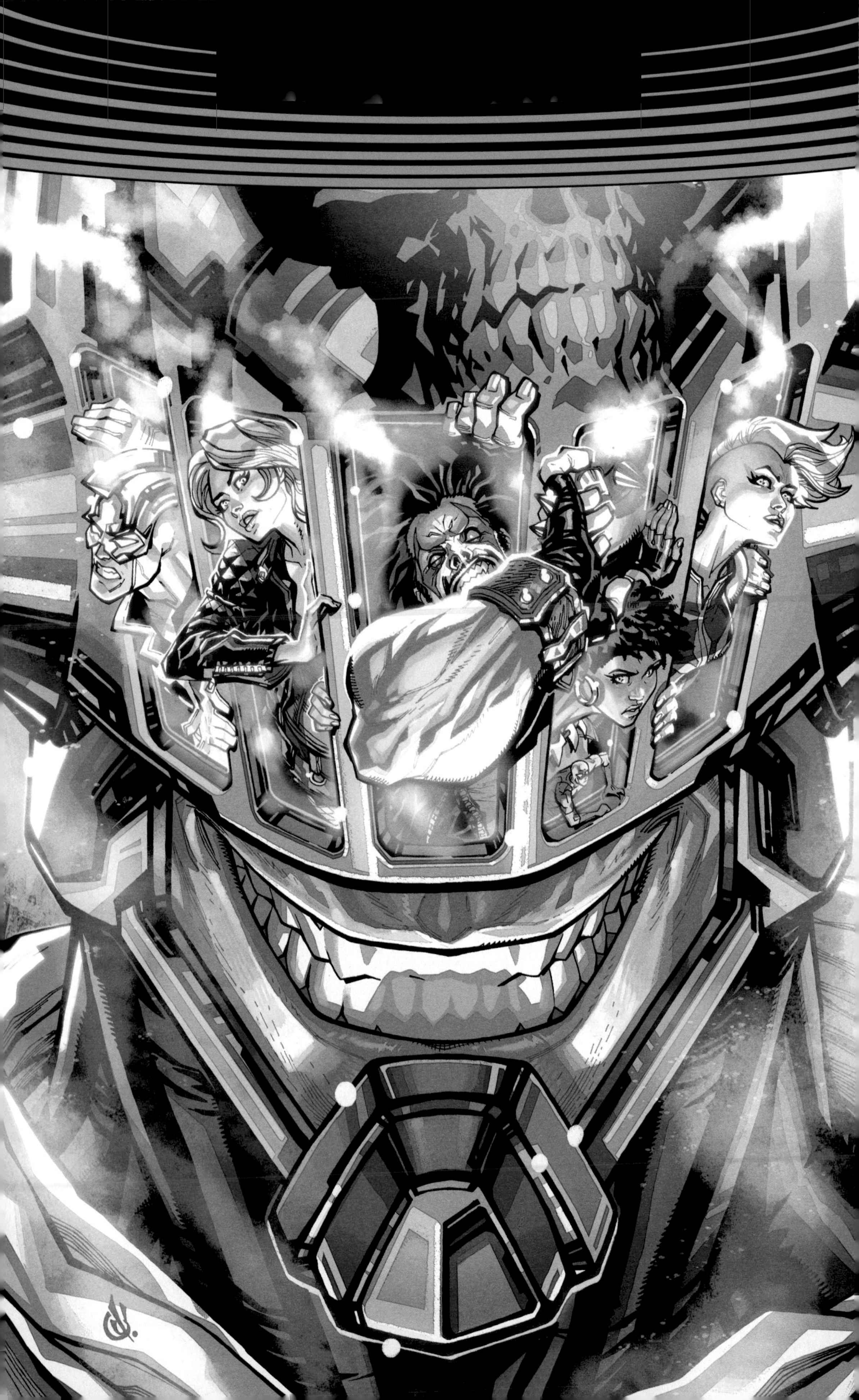

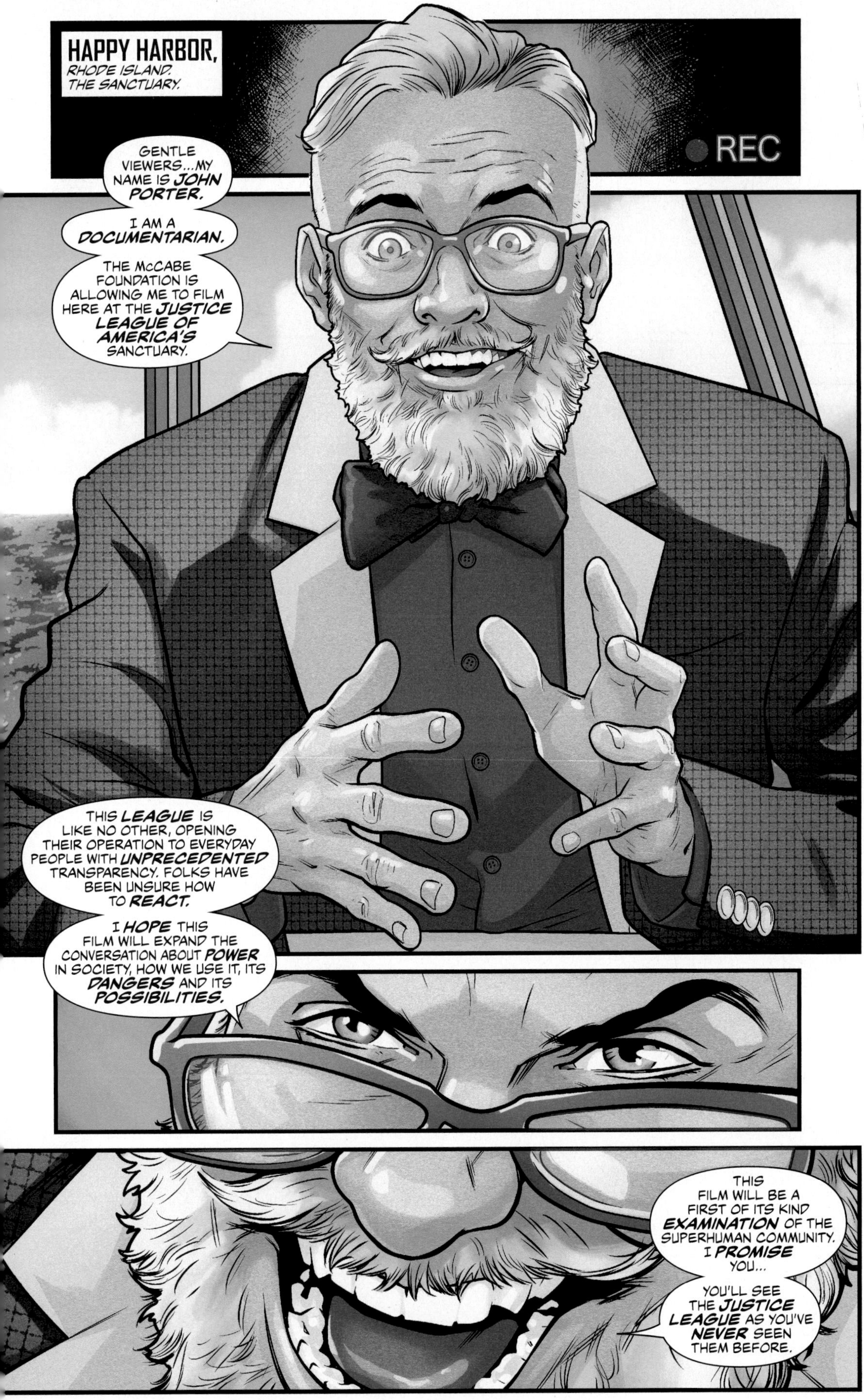
HAPPY HARBOR,
RHODE ISLAND.
THE SANCTUARY.
REC
GENTLE VIEWERS...MY NAME IS JOHN PORTER.
I AM A DOCUMENTARIAN.
THE McCABE FOUNDATION IS ALLOWING ME TO FILM HERE AT THE JUSTICE LEAGUE OF AMERICA'S SANCTUARY.
THIS LEAGUE IS LIKE NO OTHER, OPENING THEIR OPERATION TO EVERYDAY PEOPLE WITH UNPRECEDENTED TRANSPARENCY. FOLKS HAVE BEEN UNSURE HOW TO REACT.
I HOPE THIS FILM WILL EXPAND THE CONVERSATION ABOUT POWER IN SOCIETY, HOW WE USE IT, ITS DANGERS AND ITS POSSIBILITIES.
THIS FILM WILL BE A FIRST OF ITS KIND EXAMINATION OF THE SUPERHUMAN COMMUNITY. I PROMISE YOU...
YOU'LL SEE THE JUSTICE LEAGUE AS YOU'VE NEVER SEEN THEM BEFORE.

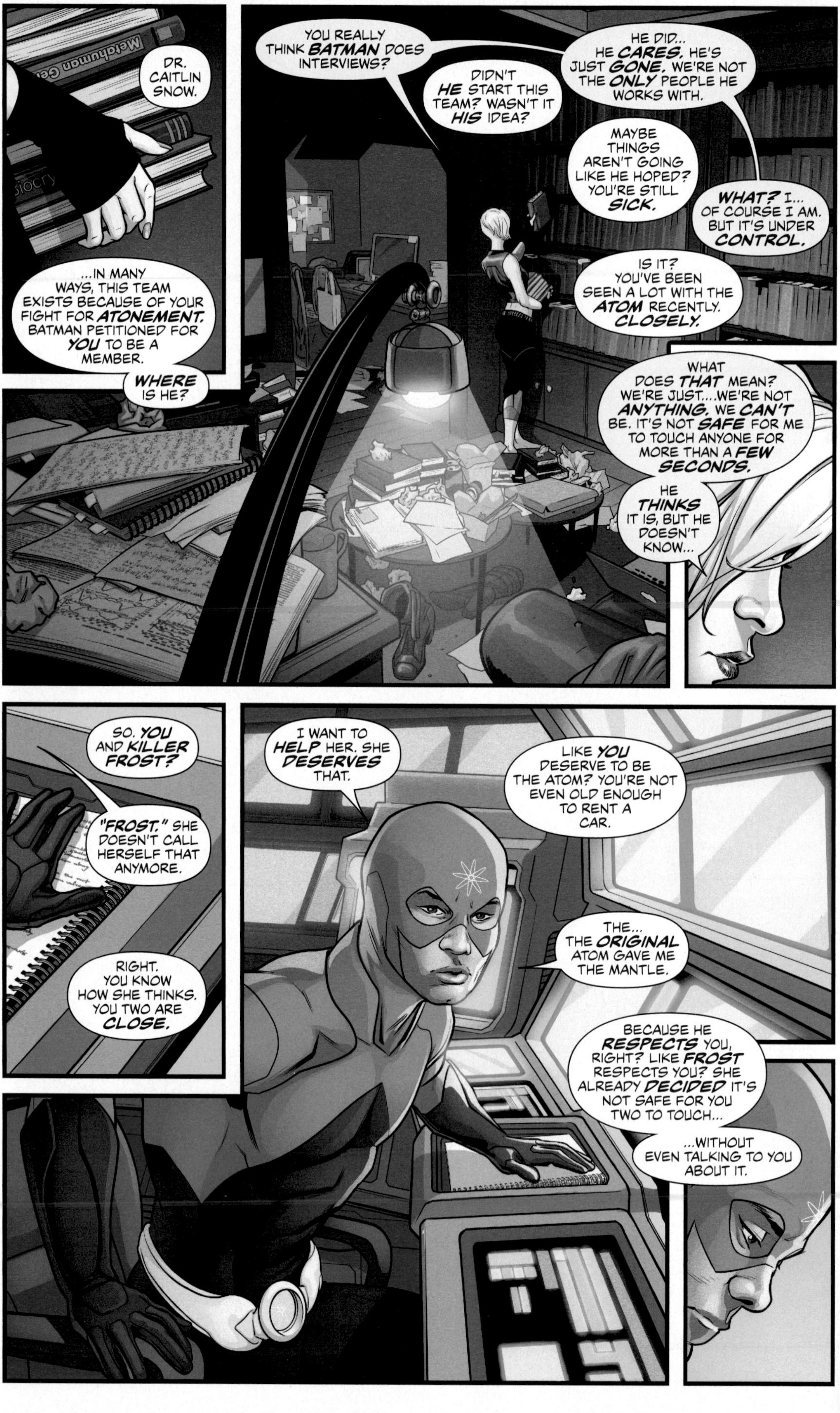
Metahuman Ge
DR. CAITLIN SNOW.
...IN MANY WAYS, THIS TEAM EXISTS BECAUSE OF YOUR FIGHT FOR ATONEMENT. BATMAN PETITIONED FOR YOU TO BE A MEMBER.
WHERE IS HE?
YOU REALLY THINK BATMAN DOES INTERVIEWS?
DIDN'T HE START THIS TEAM? WASN'T IT HIS IDEA?
HE DID... HE CARES. HE'S JUST GONE. WE'RE NOT THE ONLY PEOPLE HE WORKS WITH.
MAYBE THINGS AREN'T GOING LIKE HE HOPED? YOU'RE STILL SICK.
WHAT? I... OF COURSE I AM. BUT IT'S UNDER CONTROL.
IS IT? YOU'VE BEEN SEEN A LOT WITH THE ATOM RECENTLY. CLOSELY.
WHAT DOES THAT MEAN? WE'RE JUST....WE'RE NOT ANYTHING. WE CAN'T BE. IT'S NOT SAFE FOR ME TO TOUCH ANYONE FOR MORE THAN A FEW SECONDS.
HE THINKS IT IS, BUT HE DOESN'T KNOW...
SO. YOU AND KILLER FROST?
"FROST." SHE DOESN'T CALL HERSELF THAT ANYMORE.
RIGHT. YOU KNOW HOW SHE THINKS. YOU TWO ARE CLOSE.
I WANT TO HELP HER. SHE DESERVES THAT.
LIKE YOU DESERVE TO BE THE ATOM? YOU'RE NOT EVEN OLD ENOUGH TO RENT A CAR.
THE... THE ORIGINAL ATOM GAVE ME THE MANTLE.
BECAUSE HE RESPECTS YOU, RIGHT? LIKE FROST RESPECTS YOU? SHE ALREADY DECIDED IT'S NOT SAFE FOR YOU TWO TO TOUCH...
...WITHOUT EVEN TALKING TO YOU ABOUT IT.

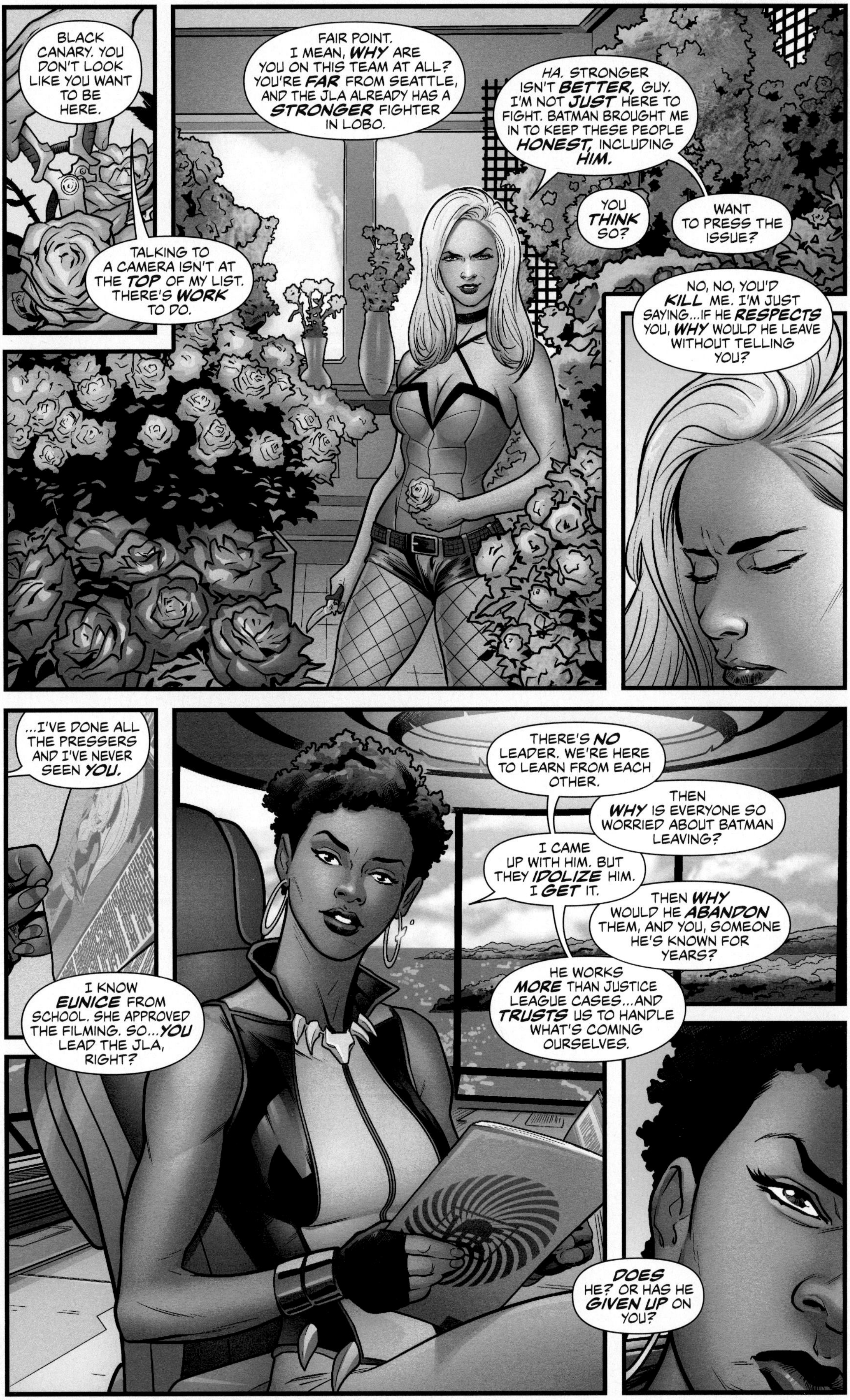
BLACK CANARY. YOU DON'T LOOK LIKE YOU WANT TO BE HERE.
TALKING TO A CAMERA ISN'T AT THE TOP OF MY LIST. THERE'S WORK TO DO.
FAIR POINT. I MEAN, WHY ARE YOU ON THIS TEAM AT ALL? YOU'RE FAR FROM SEATTLE, AND THE JLA ALREADY HAS A STRONGER FIGHTER IN LOBO.
HA. STRONGER ISN'T BETTER, GUY. I'M NOT JUST HERE TO FIGHT. BATMAN BROUGHT ME IN TO KEEP THESE PEOPLE HONEST, INCLUDING HIM.
YOU THINK SO?
WANT TO PRESS THE ISSUE?
NO, NO, YOU'D KILL ME. I'M JUST SAYING...IF HE RESPECTS YOU, WHY WOULD HE LEAVE WITHOUT TELLING YOU?
...I'VE DONE ALL THE PRESSERS AND I'VE NEVER SEEN YOU.
I KNOW EUNICE FROM SCHOOL. SHE APPROVED THE FILMING. SO...YOU LEAD THE JLA, RIGHT?
THERE'S NO LEADER. WE'RE HERE TO LEARN FROM EACH OTHER.
THEN WHY IS EVERYONE SO WORRIED ABOUT BATMAN LEAVING?
I CAME UP WITH HIM. BUT THEY IDOLIZE HIM. I GET IT.
THEN WHY WOULD HE ABANDON THEM, AND YOU, SOMEONE HE'S KNOWN FOR YEARS?
HE WORKS MORE THAN JUSTICE LEAGUE CASES...AND TRUSTS US TO HANDLE WHAT'S COMING OURSELVES.
DOES HE? OR HAS HE GIVEN UP ON YOU?

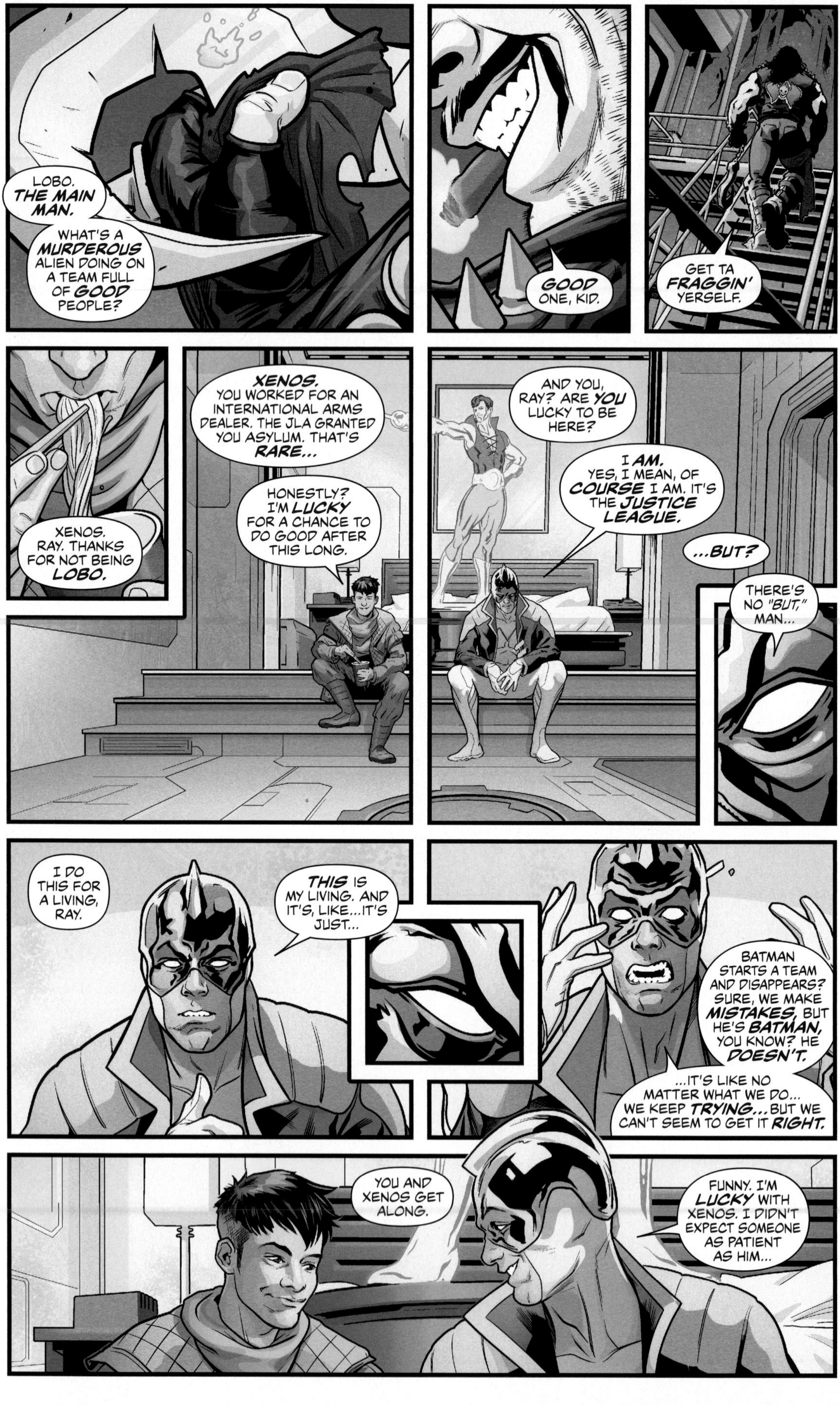
LOBO. THE MAIN MAN.
WHAT'S A MURDEROUS ALIEN DOING ON A TEAM FULL OF GOOD PEOPLE?
GOOD ONE, KID.
GET TA FRAGGIN' YERSELF.
XENOS. RAY. THANKS FOR NOT BEING LOBO.
XENOS. YOU WORKED FOR AN INTERNATIONAL ARMS DEALER. THE JLA GRANTED YOU ASYLUM. THAT'S RARE...
HONESTLY? I'M LUCKY FOR A CHANCE TO DO GOOD AFTER THIS LONG.
AND YOU, RAY? ARE YOU LUCKY TO BE HERE?
I AM. YES, I MEAN, OF COURSE I AM. IT'S THE JUSTICE LEAGUE.
...BUT?
THERE'S NO "BUT," MAN...
I DO THIS FOR A LIVING, RAY.
THIS IS MY LIVING. AND IT'S, LIKE...IT'S JUST...
BATMAN STARTS A TEAM AND DISAPPEARS? SURE, WE MAKE MISTAKES, BUT HE'S BATMAN, YOU KNOW? HE DOESN'T.
...IT'S LIKE NO MATTER WHAT WE DO... WE KEEP TRYING... BUT WE CAN'T SEEM TO GET IT RIGHT.
YOU AND XENOS GET ALONG.
FUNNY. I'M LUCKY WITH XENOS. I DIDN'T EXPECT SOMEONE AS PATIENT AS HIM...

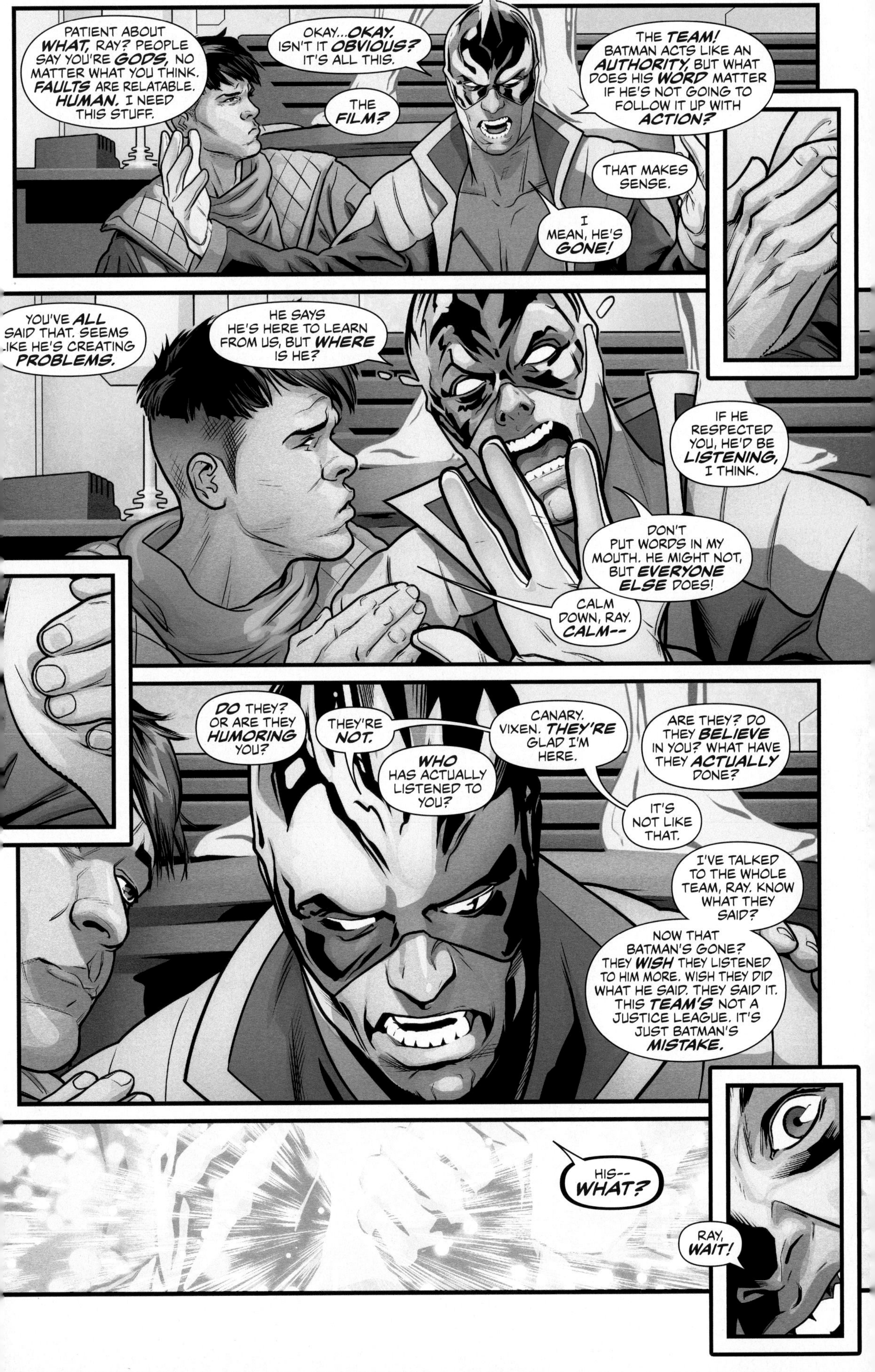
PATIENT ABOUT WHAT, RAY? PEOPLE SAY YOU'RE GODS, NO MATTER WHAT YOU THINK. FAULTS ARE RELATABLE. HUMAN. I NEED THIS STUFF.
OKAY...OKAY. ISN'T IT OBVIOUS? IT'S ALL THIS.
THE FILM?
THE TEAM! BATMAN ACTS LIKE AN AUTHORITY, BUT WHAT DOES HIS WORD MATTER IF HE'S NOT GOING TO FOLLOW IT UP WITH ACTION?
THAT MAKES SENSE.
I MEAN, HE'S GONE!
YOU'VE ALL SAID THAT. SEEMS LIKE HE'S CREATING PROBLEMS.
HE SAYS HE'S HERE TO LEARN FROM US, BUT WHERE IS HE?
IF HE RESPECTED YOU, HE'D BE LISTENING, I THINK.
DON'T PUT WORDS IN MY MOUTH. HE MIGHT NOT, BUT EVERYONE ELSE DOES!
CALM DOWN, RAY. CALM--
DO THEY? OR ARE THEY HUMORING YOU?
THEY'RE NOT.
WHO HAS ACTUALLY LISTENED TO YOU?
CANARY. VIXEN. THEY'RE GLAD I'M HERE.
ARE THEY? DO THEY BELIEVE IN YOU? WHAT HAVE THEY ACTUALLY DONE?
IT'S NOT LIKE THAT.
I'VE TALKED TO THE WHOLE TEAM, RAY. KNOW WHAT THEY SAID?
NOW THAT BATMAN'S GONE? THEY WISH THEY LISTENED TO HIM MORE. WISH THEY DID WHAT HE SAID. THEY SAID IT. THIS TEAM'S NOT A JUSTICE LEAGUE. IT'S JUST BATMAN'S MISTAKE.
HIS-- WHAT?
RAY, WAIT!

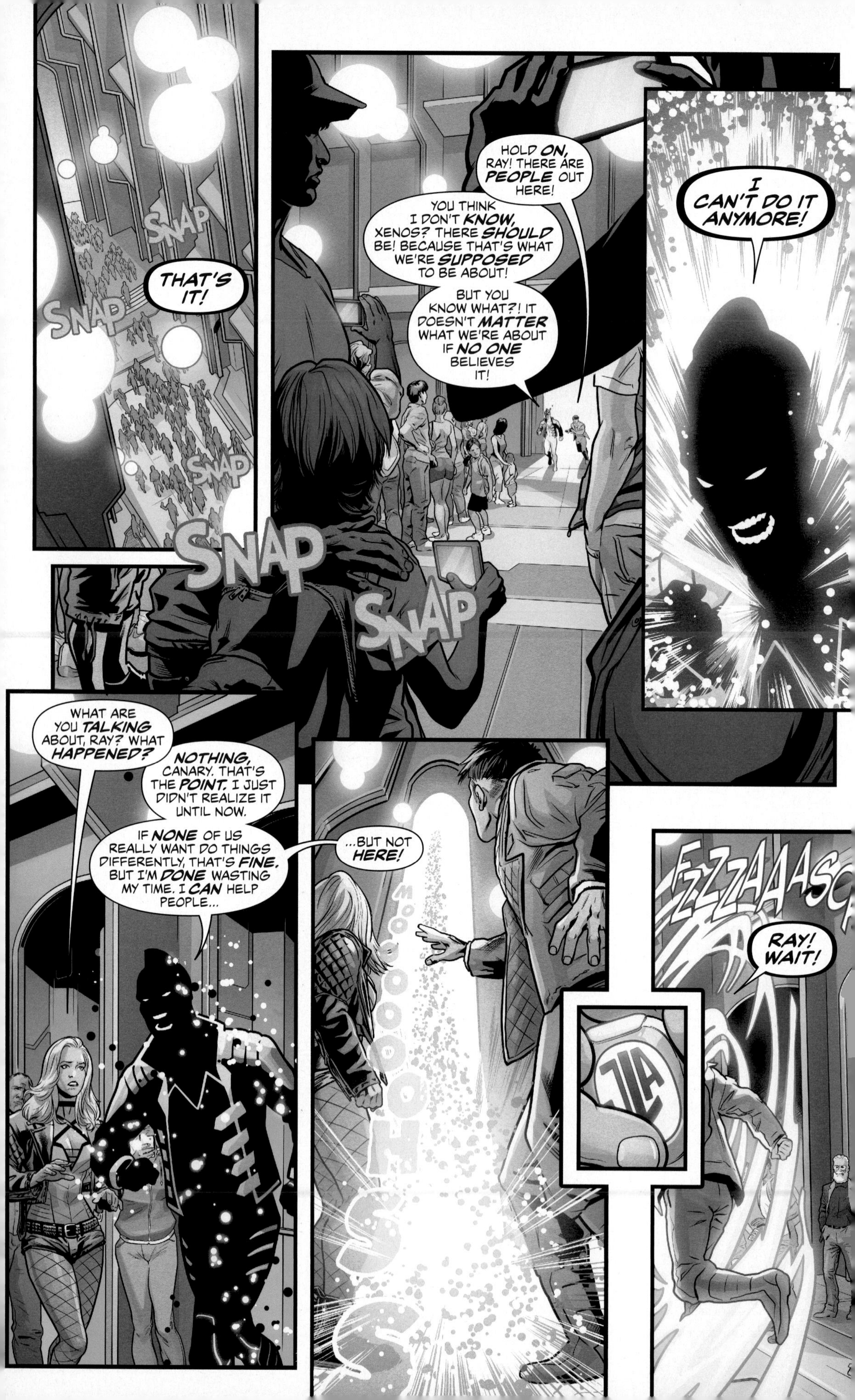
SNAP
THAT'S IT!
SNAP
SNAP
SNAP
SNAP
HOLD ON, RAY! THERE ARE PEOPLE OUT HERE!
YOU THINK I DON'T KNOW, XENOS? THERE SHOULD BE! BECAUSE THAT'S WHAT WE'RE SUPPOSED TO BE ABOUT!
BUT YOU KNOW WHAT?! IT DOESN'T MATTER WHAT WE'RE ABOUT IF NO ONE BELIEVES IT!
I CAN'T DO IT ANYMORE!
WHAT ARE YOU TALKING ABOUT, RAY? WHAT HAPPENED?
NOTHING, CANARY. THAT'S THE POINT. I JUST DIDN'T REALIZE IT UNTIL NOW.
IF NONE OF US REALLY WANT DO THINGS DIFFERENTLY, THAT'S FINE. BUT I'M DONE WASTING MY TIME. I CAN HELP PEOPLE...
...BUT NOT HERE!
FZZZAAASCH
RAY! WAIT!

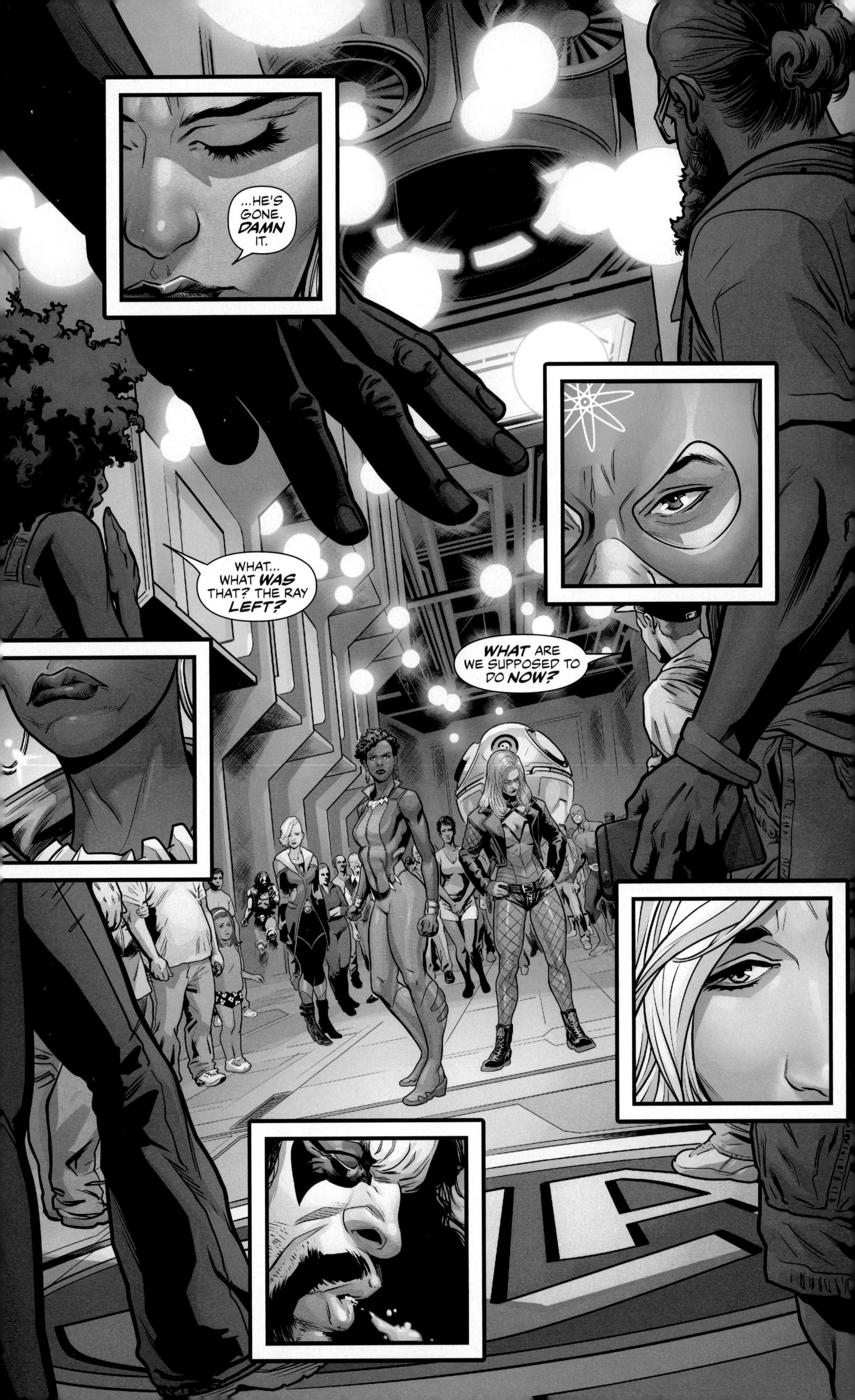
...HE'S GONE. DAMN IT.
WHAT... WHAT WAS THAT? THE RAY LEFT?
WHAT ARE WE SUPPOSED TO DO NOW?

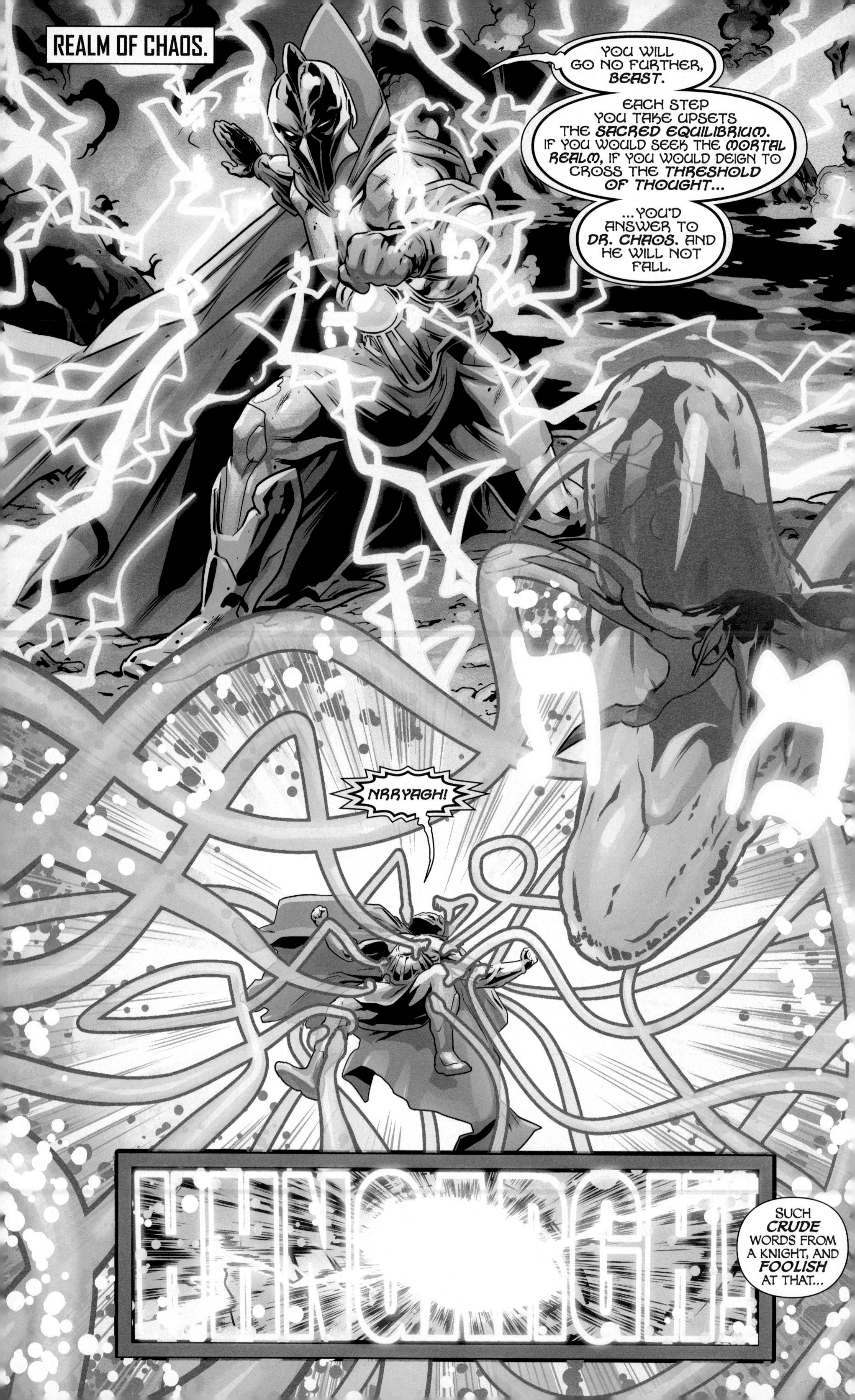
REALM OF CHAOS.
YOU WILL GO NO FURTHER, BEAST.
EACH STEP YOU TAKE UPSETS THE SACRED EQUILIBRIUM. IF YOU WOULD SEEK THE MORTAL REALM, IF YOU WOULD DEIGN TO CROSS THE THRESHOLD OF THOUGHT...
...YOU'D ANSWER TO DR. CHAOS. AND HE WILL NOT FALL.
NRRYAGH!
SUCH CRUDE WORDS FROM A KNIGHT, AND FOOLISH AT THAT...

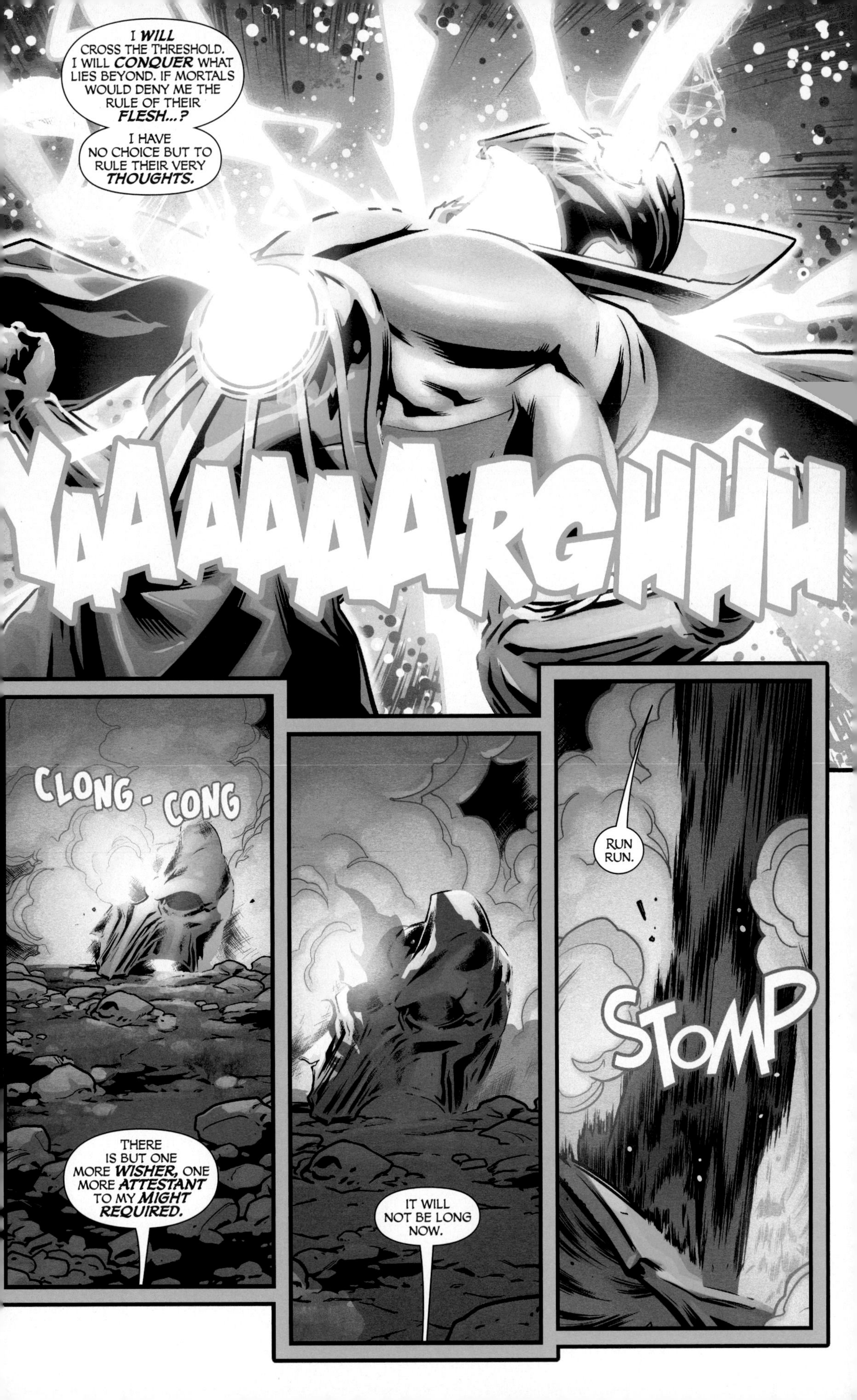
I WILL CROSS THE THRESHOLD. I WILL CONQUER WHAT LIES BEYOND. IF MORTALS WOULD DENY ME THE RULE OF THEIR FLESH...?
I HAVE NO CHOICE BUT TO RULE THEIR VERY THOUGHTS.
YAAAAAARGHHH
CLONG - CONG
THERE IS BUT ONE MORE WISHER, ONE MORE ATTESTANT TO MY MIGHT REQUIRED.
IT WILL NOT BE LONG NOW.
RUN RUN.
STOMP

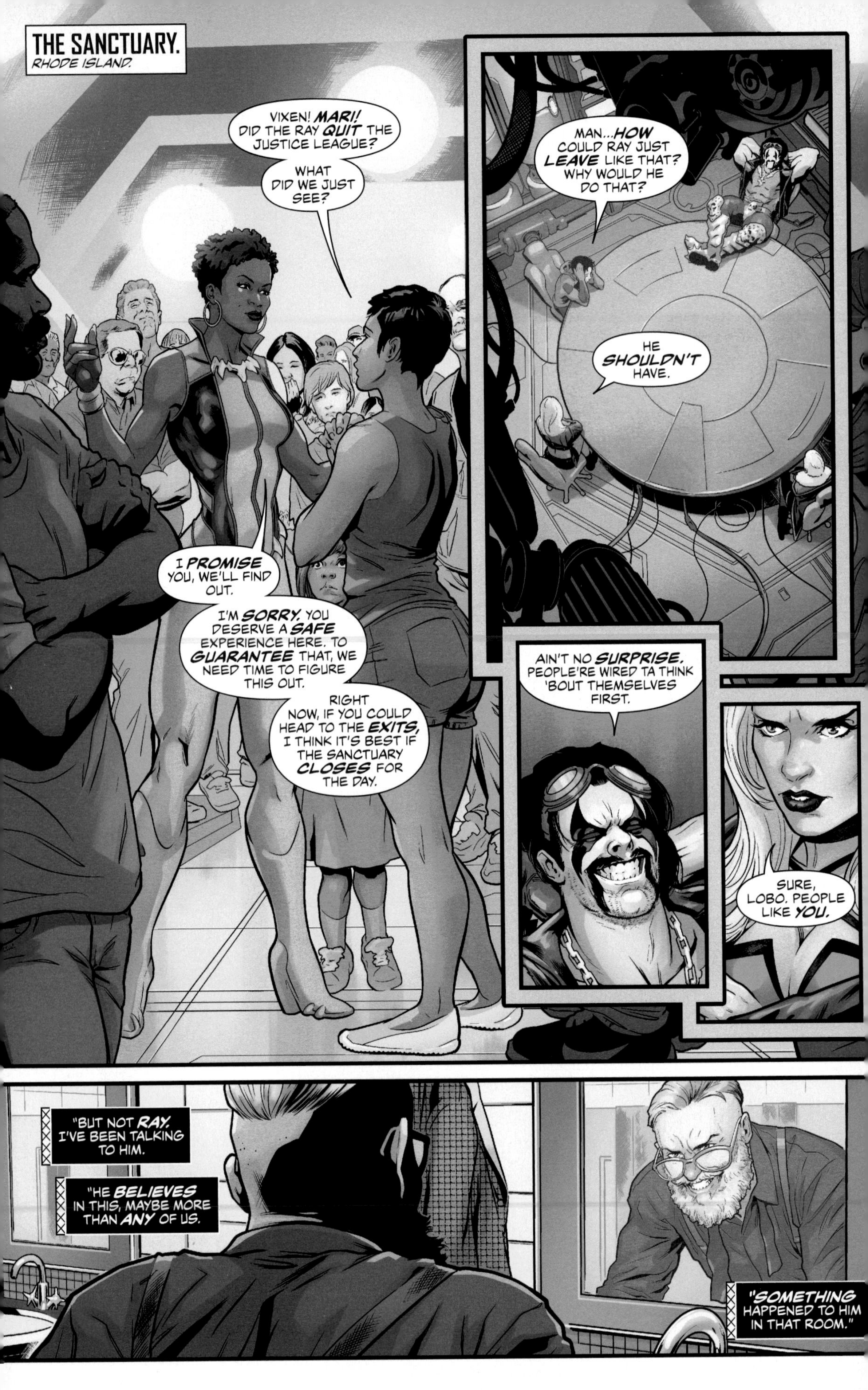
THE SANCTUARY.
RHODE ISLAND.
VIXEN! MARI! DID THE RAY QUIT THE JUSTICE LEAGUE?
WHAT DID WE JUST SEE?
I PROMISE YOU, WE'LL FIND OUT.
I'M SORRY. YOU DESERVE A SAFE EXPERIENCE HERE. TO GUARANTEE THAT, WE NEED TIME TO FIGURE THIS OUT.
RIGHT NOW, IF YOU COULD HEAD TO THE EXITS, I THINK IT'S BEST IF THE SANCTUARY CLOSES FOR THE DAY.
MAN...HOW COULD RAY JUST LEAVE LIKE THAT? WHY WOULD HE DO THAT?
HE SHOULDN'T HAVE.
AIN'T NO SURPRISE. PEOPLE'RE WIRED TA THINK 'BOUT THEMSELVES FIRST.
SURE, LOBO. PEOPLE LIKE YOU.
"BUT NOT RAY. I'VE BEEN TALKING TO HIM.
"HE BELIEVES IN THIS, MAYBE MORE THAN ANY OF US.
"SOMETHING HAPPENED TO HIM IN THAT ROOM."

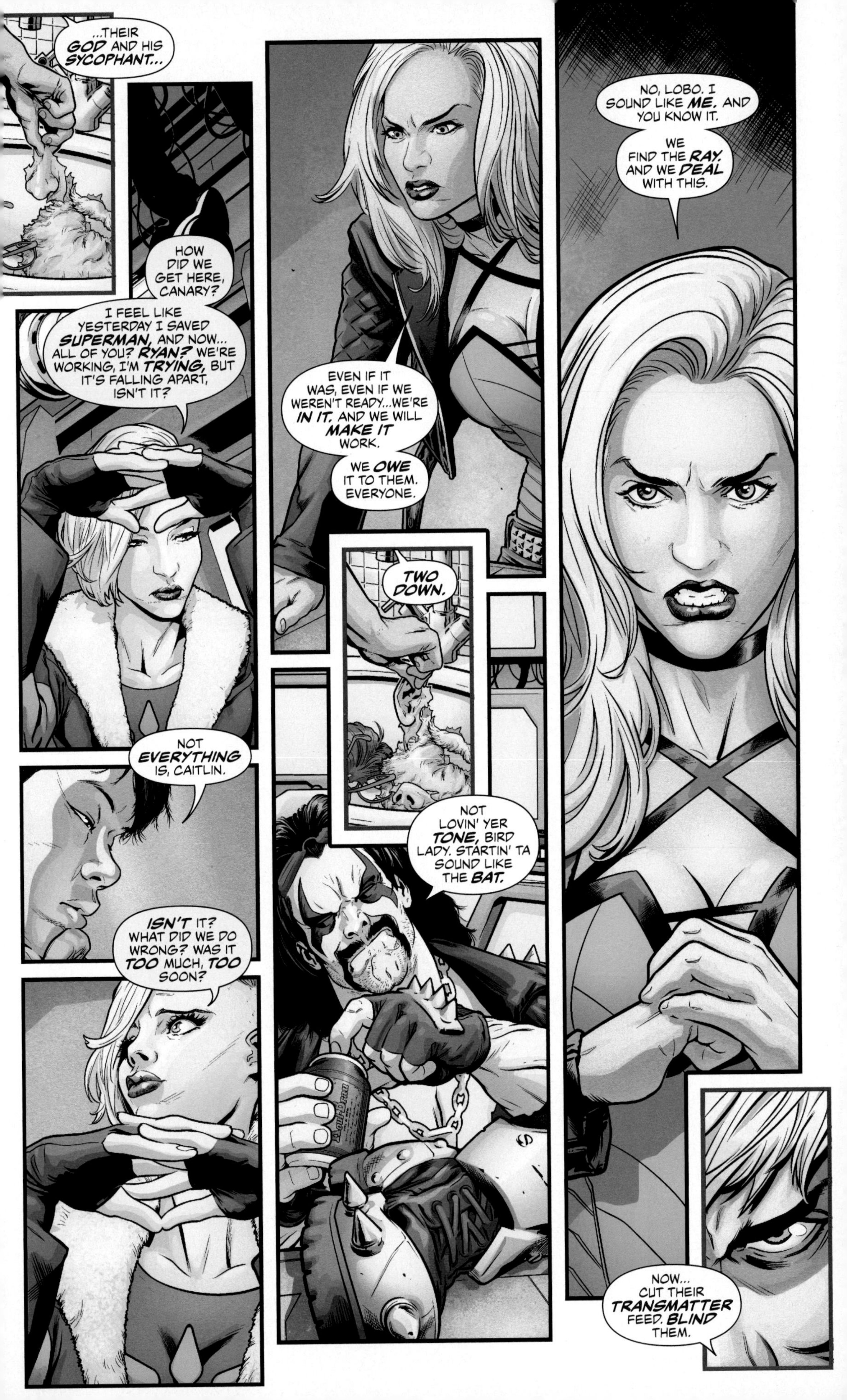
...THEIR GOD AND HIS SYCOPHANT...
HOW DID WE GET HERE, CANARY?
I FEEL LIKE YESTERDAY I SAVED SUPERMAN, AND NOW... ALL OF YOU? RYAN? WE'RE WORKING, I'M TRYING, BUT IT'S FALLING APART, ISN'T IT?
NOT EVERYTHING IS, CAITLIN.
ISN'T IT? WHAT DID WE DO WRONG? WAS IT TOO MUCH, TOO SOON?
EVEN IF IT WAS, EVEN IF WE WEREN'T READY...WE'RE IN IT. AND WE WILL MAKE IT WORK.
WE OWE IT TO THEM. EVERYONE.
TWO DOWN.
NOT LOVIN' YER TONE, BIRD LADY. STARTIN' TA SOUND LIKE THE BAT.
NO, LOBO. I SOUND LIKE ME. AND YOU KNOW IT.
WE FIND THE RAY. AND WE DEAL WITH THIS.
NOW... CUT THEIR TRANSMATTER FEED. BLIND THEM.

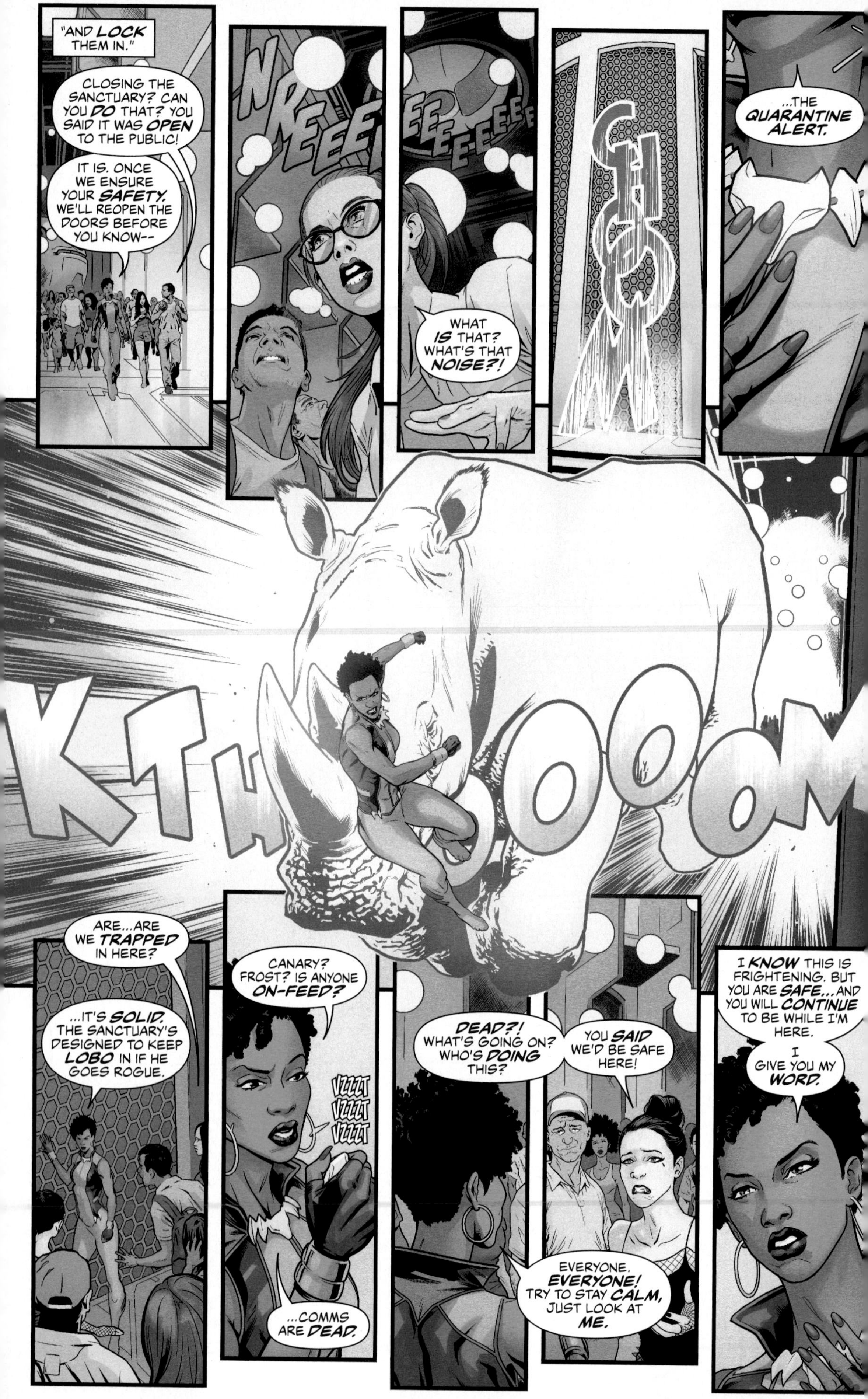
"AND LOCK THEM IN."
CLOSING THE SANCTUARY? CAN YOU DO THAT? YOU SAID IT WAS OPEN TO THE PUBLIC!
IT IS. ONCE WE ENSURE YOUR SAFETY. WE'LL REOPEN THE DOORS BEFORE YOU KNOW--
NREEEEEEEEEEEE
WHAT IS THAT? WHAT'S THAT NOISE?!
CHOOM
...THE QUARANTINE ALERT.
KTHOOOOM
ARE...ARE WE TRAPPED IN HERE?
...IT'S SOLID. THE SANCTUARY'S DESIGNED TO KEEP LOBO IN IF HE GOES ROGUE.
CANARY? FROST? IS ANYONE ON-FEED?
VZZZZT VZZZZT VZZZZT
...COMMS ARE DEAD.
DEAD?! WHAT'S GOING ON? WHO'S DOING THIS?
YOU SAID WE'D BE SAFE HERE!
EVERYONE. EVERYONE! TRY TO STAY CALM, JUST LOOK AT ME.
I KNOW THIS IS FRIGHTENING. BUT YOU ARE SAFE...AND YOU WILL CONTINUE TO BE WHILE I'M HERE.
I GIVE YOU MY WORD.

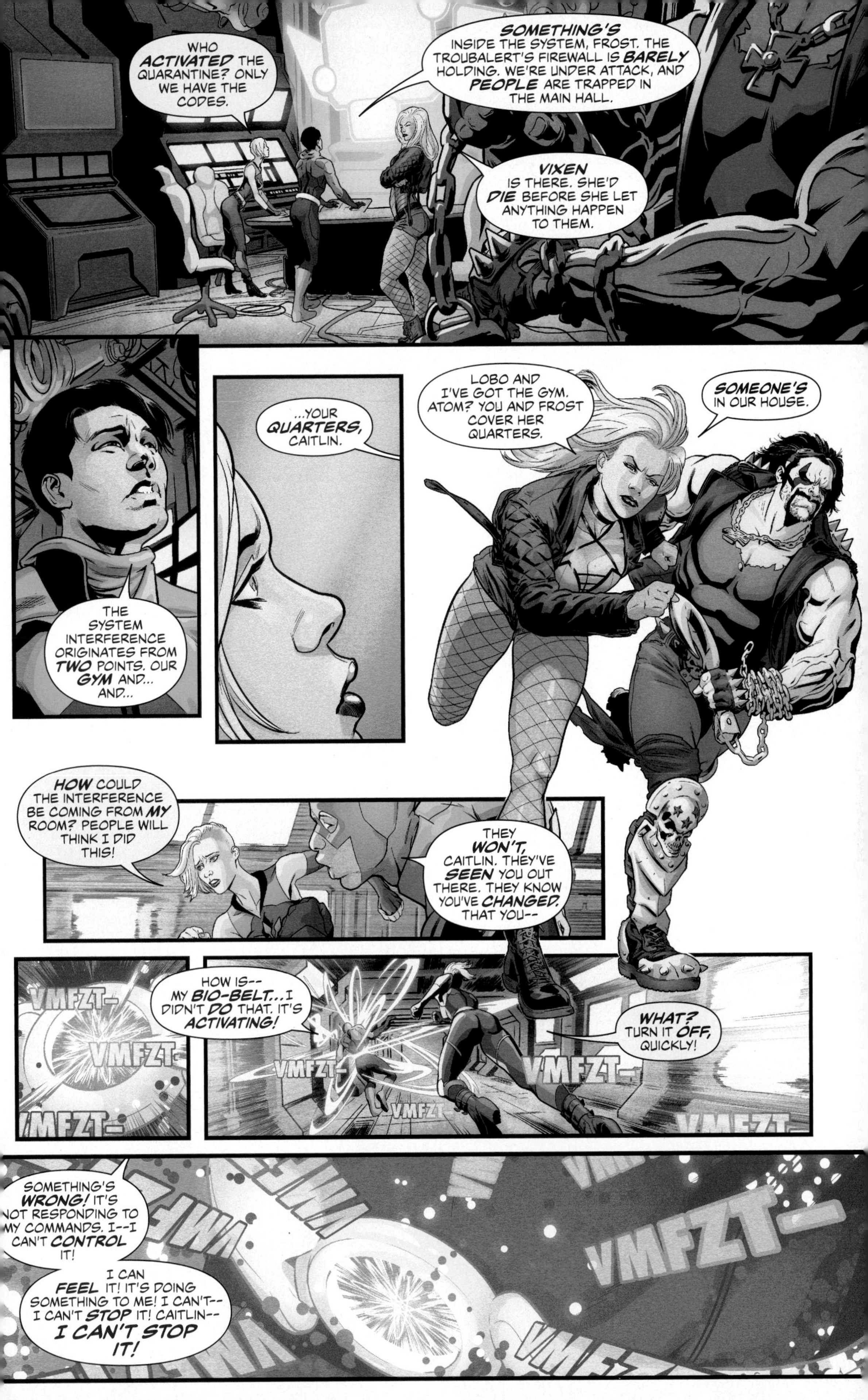
WHO ACTIVATED THE QUARANTINE? ONLY WE HAVE THE CODES.
SOMETHING'S INSIDE THE SYSTEM, FROST. THE TROUBALERT'S FIREWALL IS BARELY HOLDING. WE'RE UNDER ATTACK, AND PEOPLE ARE TRAPPED IN THE MAIN HALL.
VIXEN IS THERE. SHE'D DIE BEFORE SHE LET ANYTHING HAPPEN TO THEM.
THE SYSTEM INTERFERENCE ORIGINATES FROM TWO POINTS. OUR GYM AND... AND...
...YOUR QUARTERS, CAITLIN.
LOBO AND I'VE GOT THE GYM. ATOM? YOU AND FROST COVER HER QUARTERS.
SOMEONE'S IN OUR HOUSE.
HOW COULD THE INTERFERENCE BE COMING FROM MY ROOM? PEOPLE WILL THINK I DID THIS!
THEY WON'T, CAITLIN. THEY'VE SEEN YOU OUT THERE. THEY KNOW YOU'VE CHANGED. THAT YOU--
VMFZT-
VMFZT-
VMFZT-
HOW IS-- MY BIO-BELT... I DIDN'T DO THAT. IT'S ACTIVATING!
VMFZT-
VMFZT
WHAT? TURN IT OFF, QUICKLY!
VMFZT-
SOMETHING'S WRONG! IT'S NOT RESPONDING TO MY COMMANDS. I--I CAN'T CONTROL IT!
I CAN FEEL IT! IT'S DOING SOMETHING TO ME! I CAN'T-- I CAN'T STOP IT! CAITLIN-- I CAN'T STOP IT!
VMFZT-

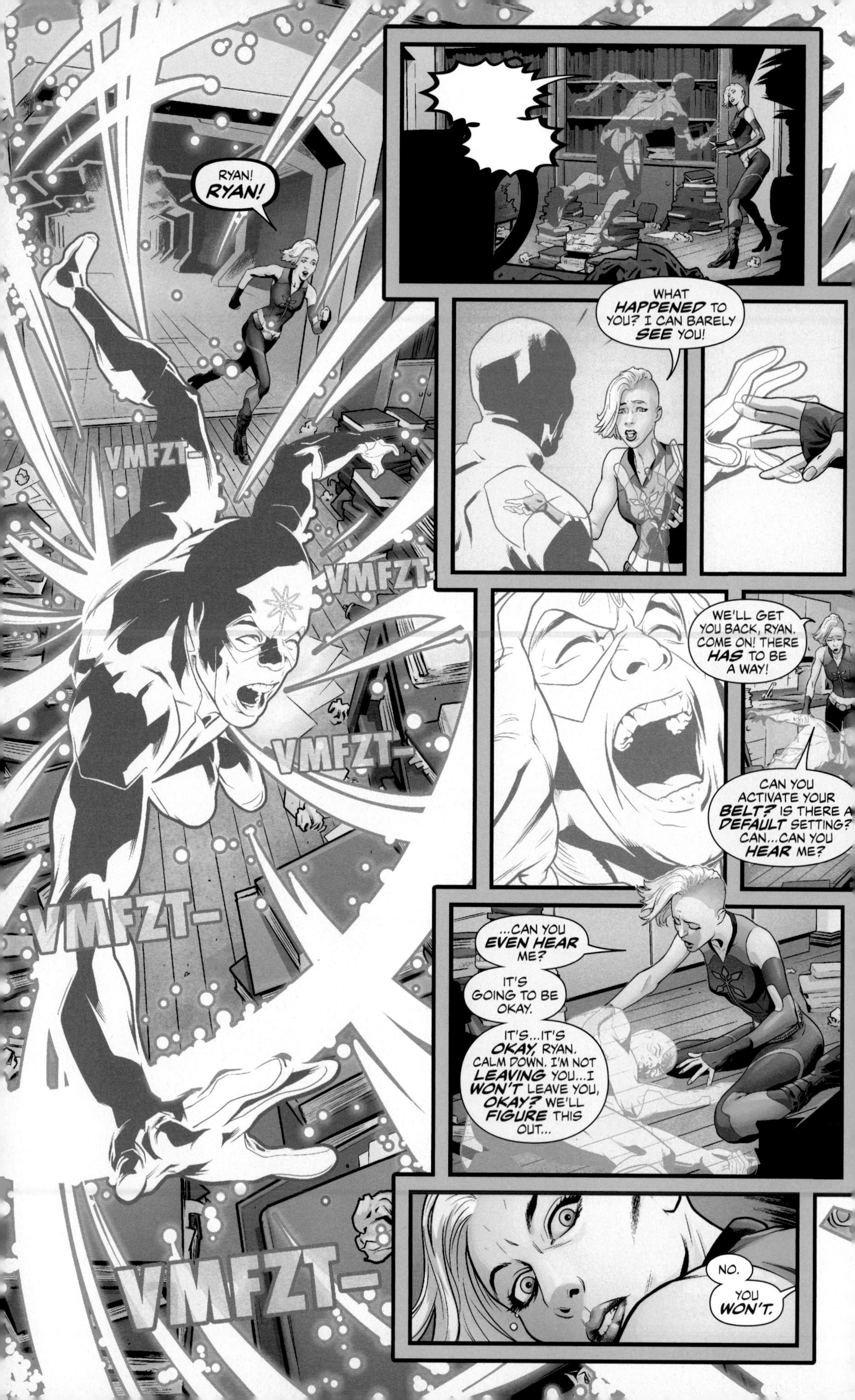
RYAN! RYAN!
VMFZT-
VMFZT-
VMFZT-
VMFZT-
VMFZT-
WHAT HAPPENED TO YOU? I CAN BARELY SEE YOU!
WE'LL GET YOU BACK, RYAN. COME ON! THERE HAS TO BE A WAY!
CAN YOU ACTIVATE YOUR BELT? IS THERE A DEFAULT SETTING? CAN...CAN YOU HEAR ME?
...CAN YOU EVEN HEAR ME?
IT'S GOING TO BE OKAY.
IT'S...IT'S OKAY, RYAN. CALM DOWN. I'M NOT LEAVING YOU...I WON'T LEAVE YOU, OKAY? WE'LL FIGURE THIS OUT...
NO.
YOU WON'T.

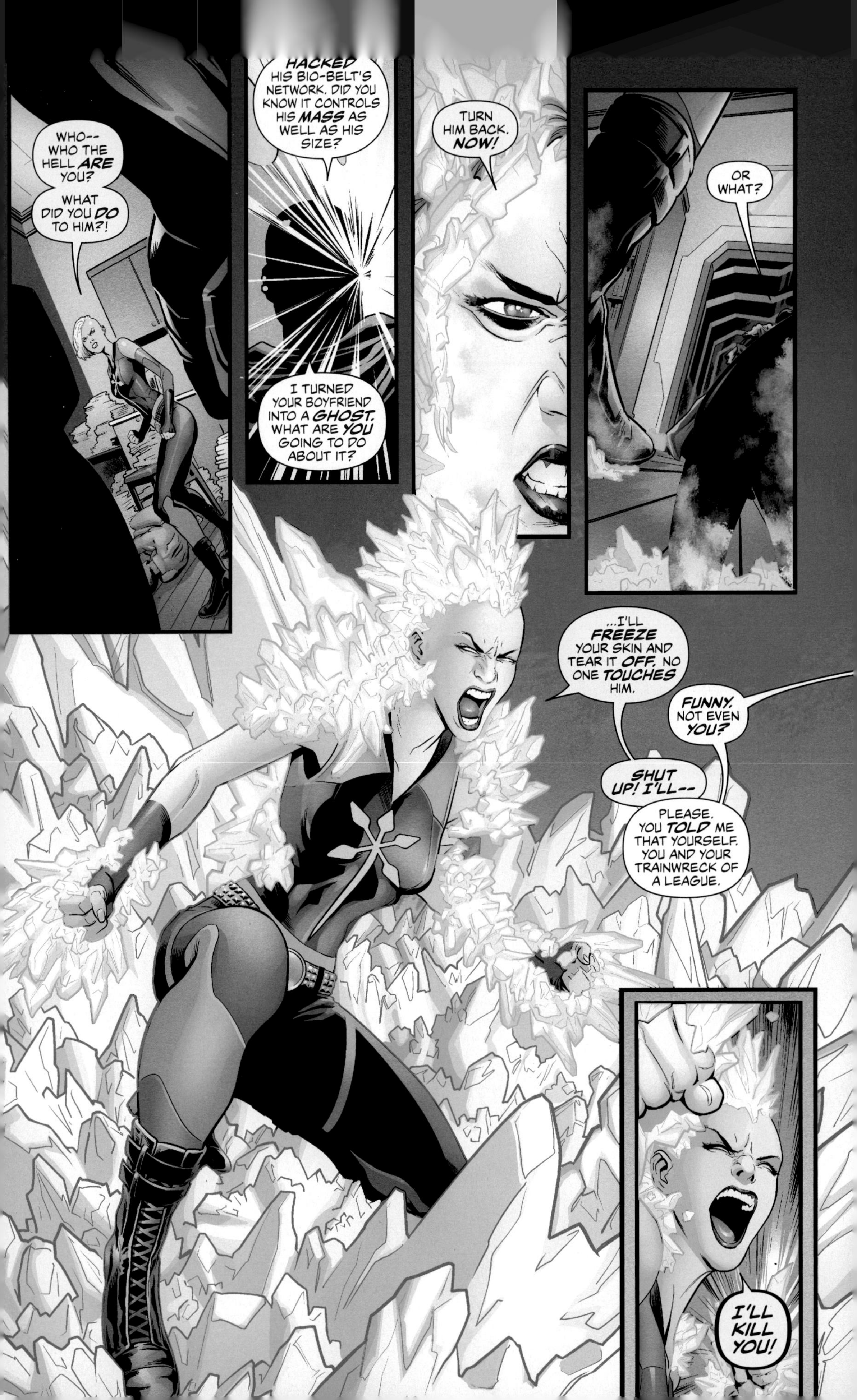
WHO-- WHO THE HELL ARE YOU?
WHAT DID YOU DO TO HIM?!
HACKED HIS BIO-BELT'S NETWORK. DID YOU KNOW IT CONTROLS HIS MASS AS WELL AS HIS SIZE?
I TURNED YOUR BOYFRIEND INTO A GHOST. WHAT ARE YOU GOING TO DO ABOUT IT?
TURN HIM BACK. NOW!
OR WHAT?
...I'LL FREEZE YOUR SKIN AND TEAR IT OFF. NO ONE TOUCHES HIM.
FUNNY. NOT EVEN YOU?
SHUT UP! I'LL--
PLEASE. YOU TOLD ME THAT YOURSELF. YOU AND YOUR TRAINWRECK OF A LEAGUE.
I'LL KILL YOU!

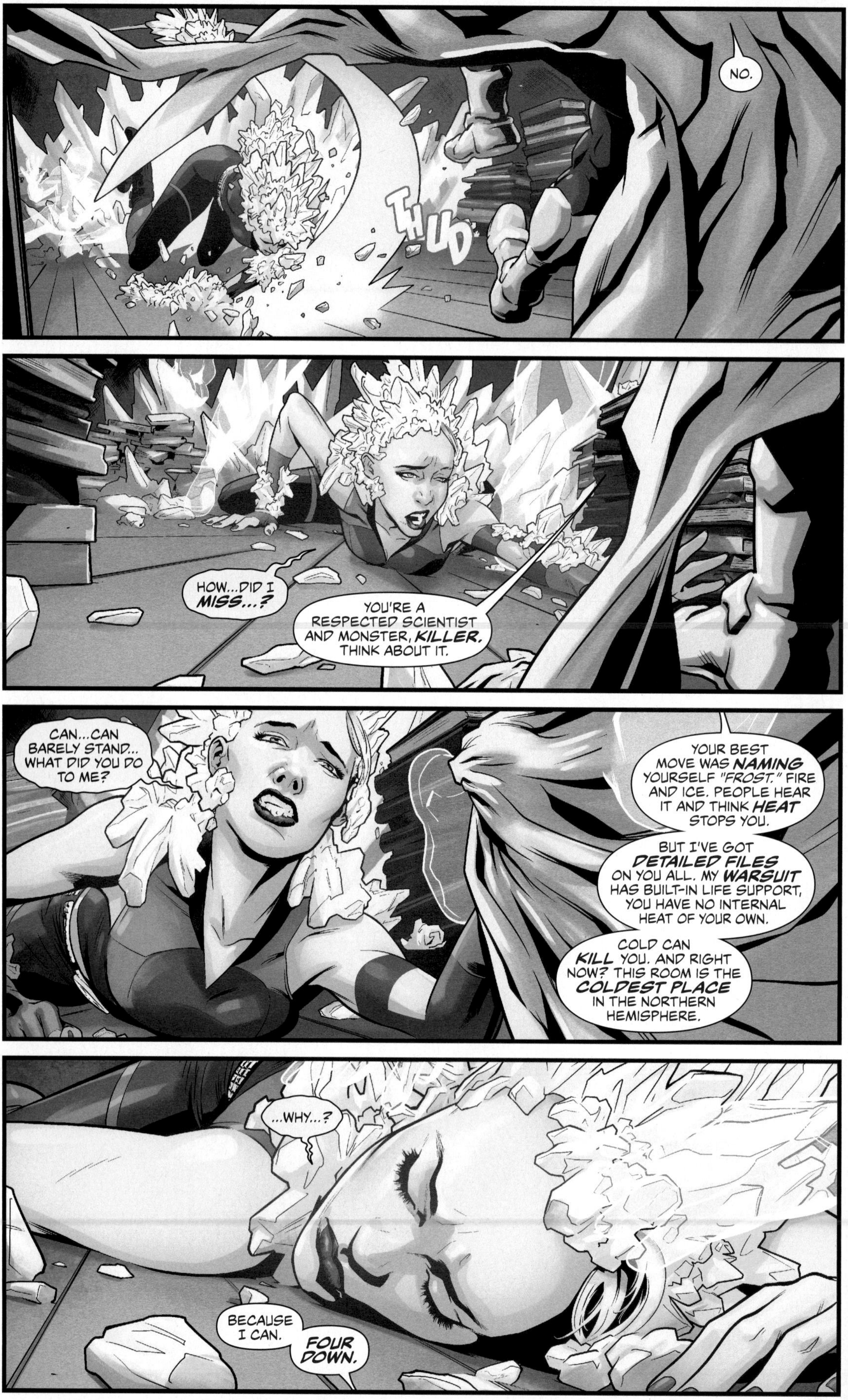
NO.
THUD
HOW...DID I MISS...?
YOU'RE A RESPECTED SCIENTIST AND MONSTER, KILLER. THINK ABOUT IT.
CAN...CAN BARELY STAND... WHAT DID YOU DO TO ME?
YOUR BEST MOVE WAS NAMING YOURSELF "FROST." FIRE AND ICE. PEOPLE HEAR IT AND THINK HEAT STOPS YOU.
BUT I'VE GOT DETAILED FILES ON YOU ALL. MY WARSUIT HAS BUILT-IN LIFE SUPPORT, YOU HAVE NO INTERNAL HEAT OF YOUR OWN.
COLD CAN KILL YOU. AND RIGHT NOW? THIS ROOM IS THE COLDEST PLACE IN THE NORTHERN HEMISPHERE.
...WHY...?
BECAUSE I CAN.
FOUR DOWN.

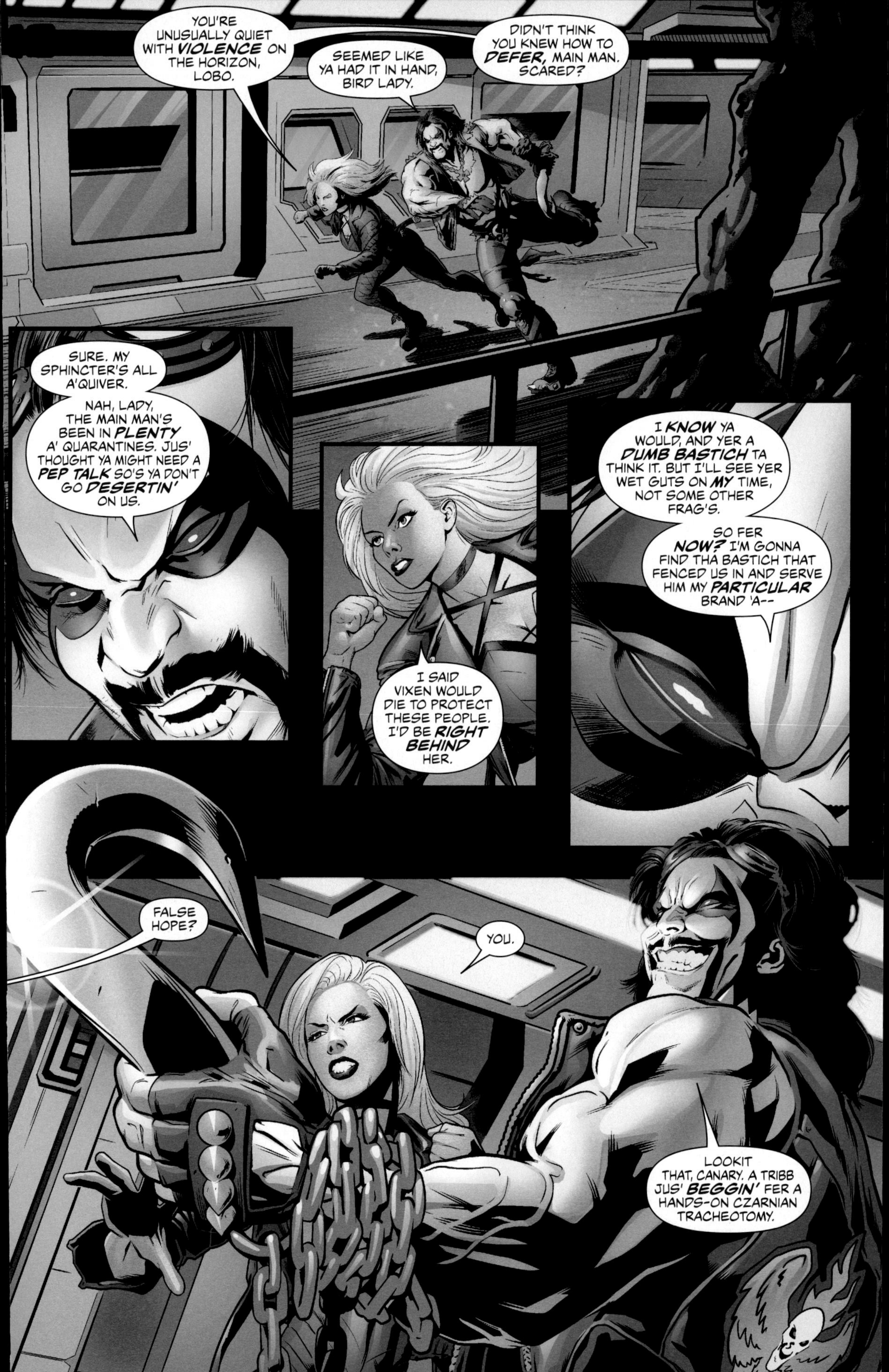
YOU'RE UNUSUALLY QUIET WITH VIOLENCE ON THE HORIZON, LOBO.
SEEMED LIKE YA HAD IT IN HAND, BIRD LADY.
DIDN'T THINK YOU KNEW HOW TO DEFER, MAIN MAN. SCARED?
SURE. MY SPHINCTER'S ALL A'QUIVER.
NAH, LADY, THE MAIN MAN'S BEEN IN PLENTY A' QUARANTINES. JUS' THOUGHT YA MIGHT NEED A PEP TALK SO'S YA DON'T GO DESERTIN' ON US.
I SAID VIXEN WOULD DIE TO PROTECT THESE PEOPLE. I'D BE RIGHT BEHIND HER.
I KNOW YA WOULD, AND YER A DUMB BASTICH TA THINK IT. BUT I'LL SEE YER WET GUTS ON MY TIME, NOT SOME OTHER FRAG'S.
SO FER NOW? I'M GONNA FIND THA BASTICH THAT FENCED US IN AND SERVE HIM MY PARTICULAR BRAND 'A--
FALSE HOPE?
YOU.
LOOKIT THAT, CANARY. A TRIBB JUS' BEGGIN' FER A HANDS-ON CZARNIAN TRACHEOTOMY.

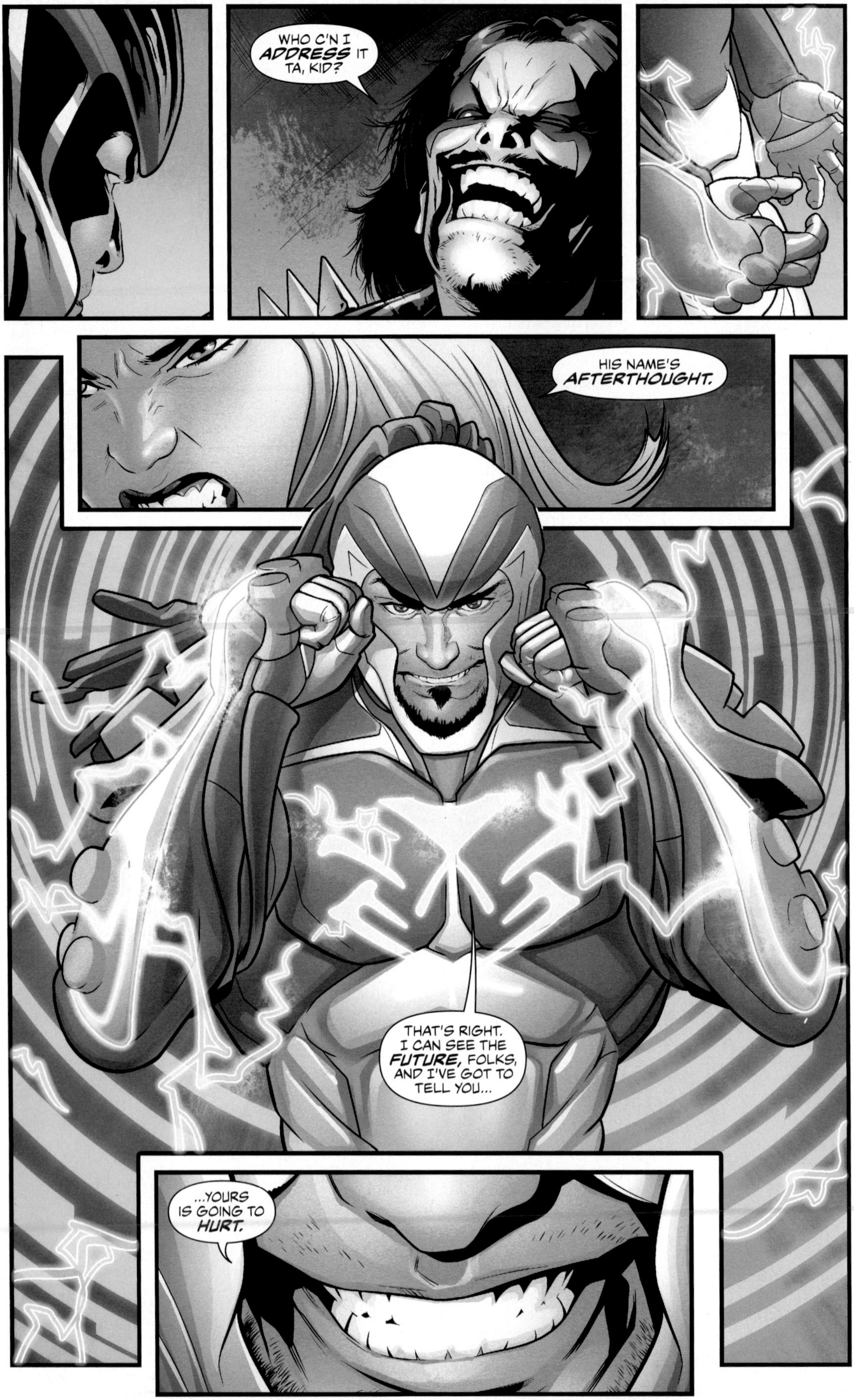
WHO C'N I ADDRESS IT TA, KID?
HIS NAME'S AFTERTHOUGHT.
THAT'S RIGHT. I CAN SEE THE FUTURE, FOLKS, AND I'VE GOT TO TELL YOU...
...YOURS IS GOING TO HURT.

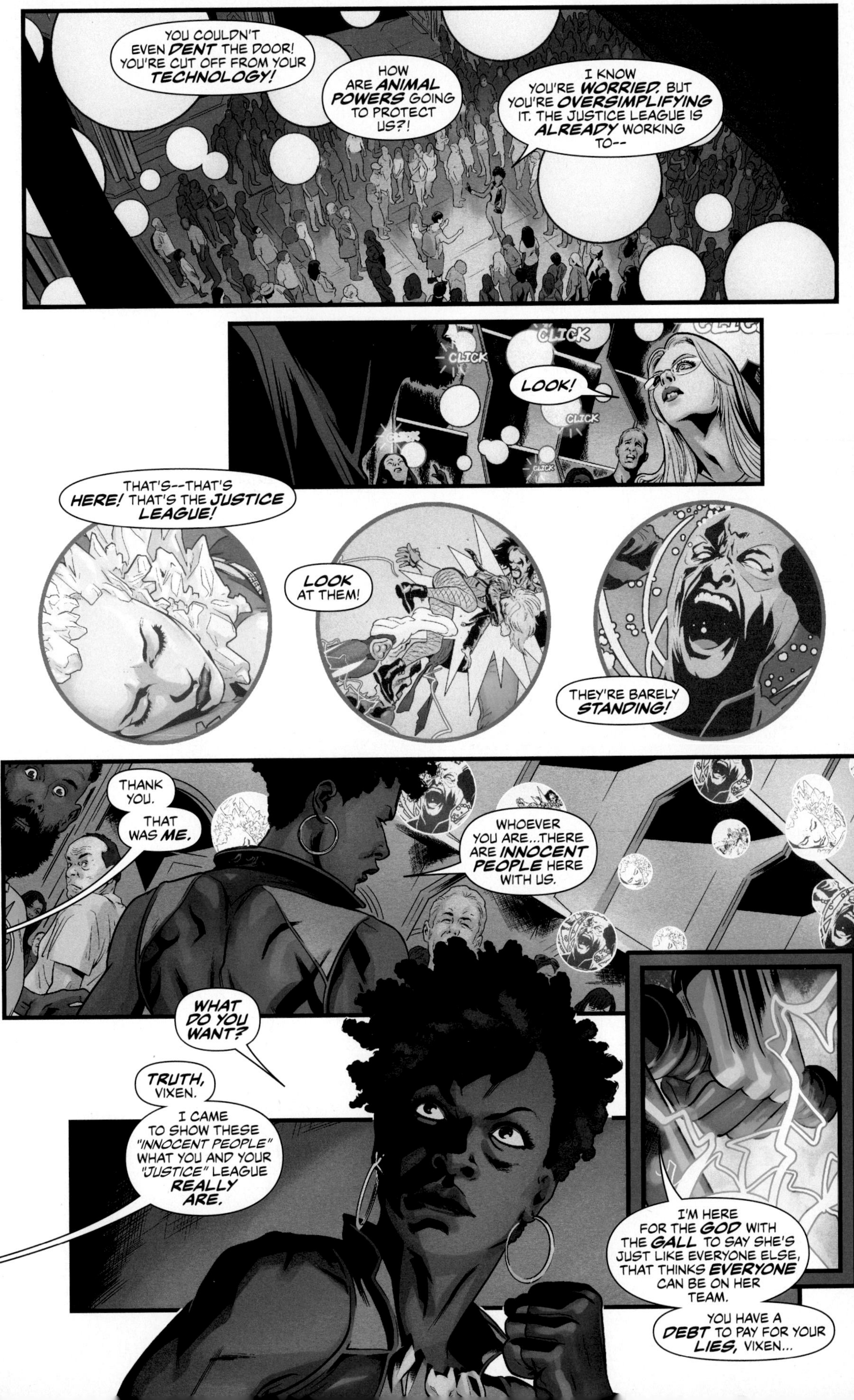
YOU COULDN'T EVEN DENT THE DOOR! YOU'RE CUT OFF FROM YOUR TECHNOLOGY!
HOW ARE ANIMAL POWERS GOING TO PROTECT US?!
I KNOW YOU'RE WORRIED, BUT YOU'RE OVERSIMPLIFYING IT. THE JUSTICE LEAGUE IS ALREADY WORKING TO--
CLICK
CLICK
LOOK!
CLICK
CLICK
THAT'S--THAT'S HERE! THAT'S THE JUSTICE LEAGUE!
LOOK AT THEM!
THEY'RE BARELY STANDING!
THANK YOU.
THAT WAS ME.
WHOEVER YOU ARE...THERE ARE INNOCENT PEOPLE HERE WITH US.
WHAT DO YOU WANT?
TRUTH, VIXEN.
I CAME TO SHOW THESE "INNOCENT PEOPLE" WHAT YOU AND YOUR "JUSTICE" LEAGUE REALLY ARE.
I'M HERE FOR THE GOD WITH THE GALL TO SAY SHE'S JUST LIKE EVERYONE ELSE, THAT THINKS EVERYONE CAN BE ON HER TEAM.
YOU HAVE A DEBT TO PAY FOR YOUR LIES, VIXEN...

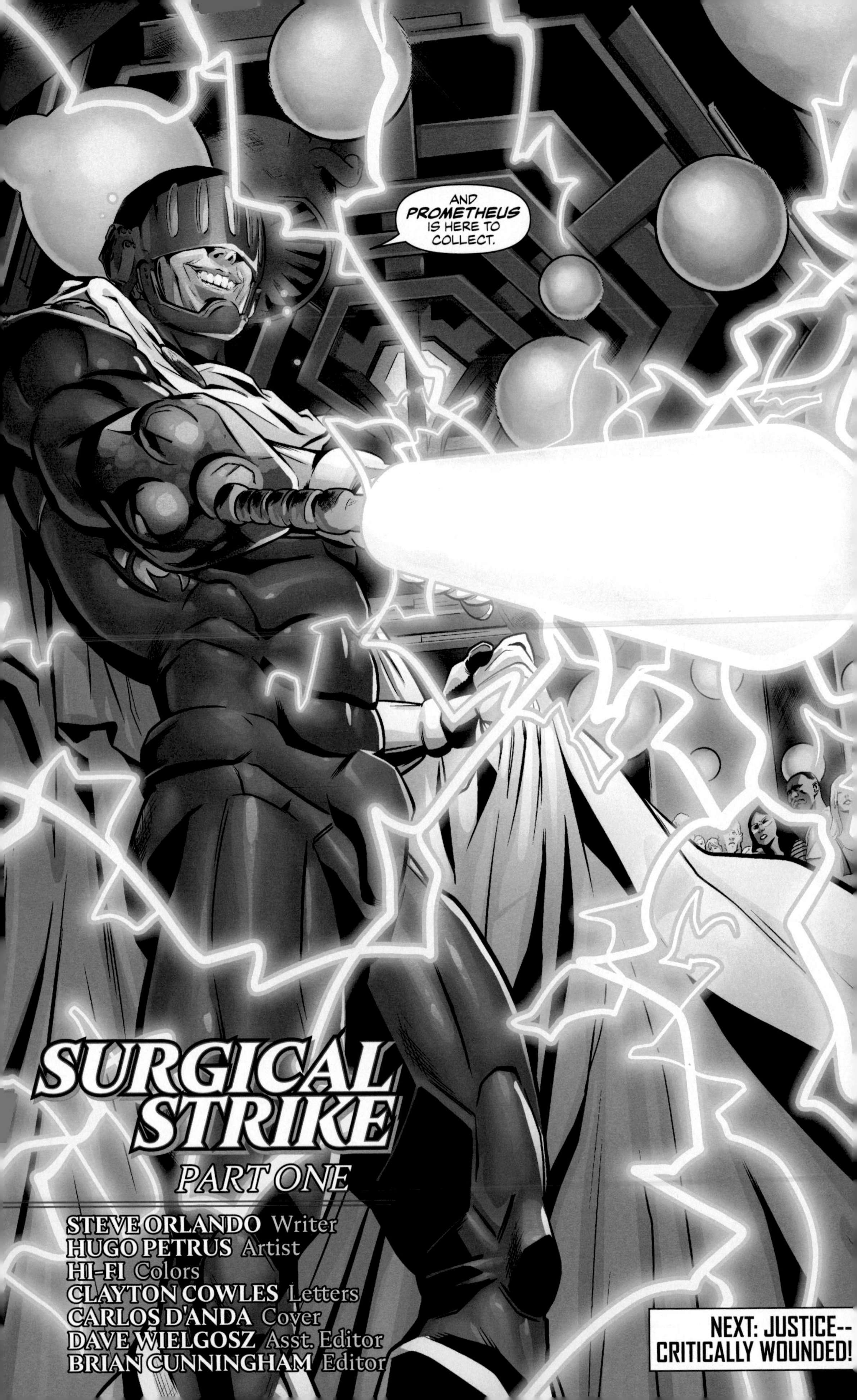
AND PROMETHEUS IS HERE TO COLLECT.
SURGICAL STRIKE
PART ONE
STEVE ORLANDO Writer
HUGO PETRUS Artist
HI-FI Colors
CLAYTON COWLES Letters
CARLOS D'ANDA Cover
DAVE WIELGOSZ Asst. Editor
BRIAN CUNNINGHAM Editor
NEXT: JUSTICE-- CRITICALLY WOUNDED!

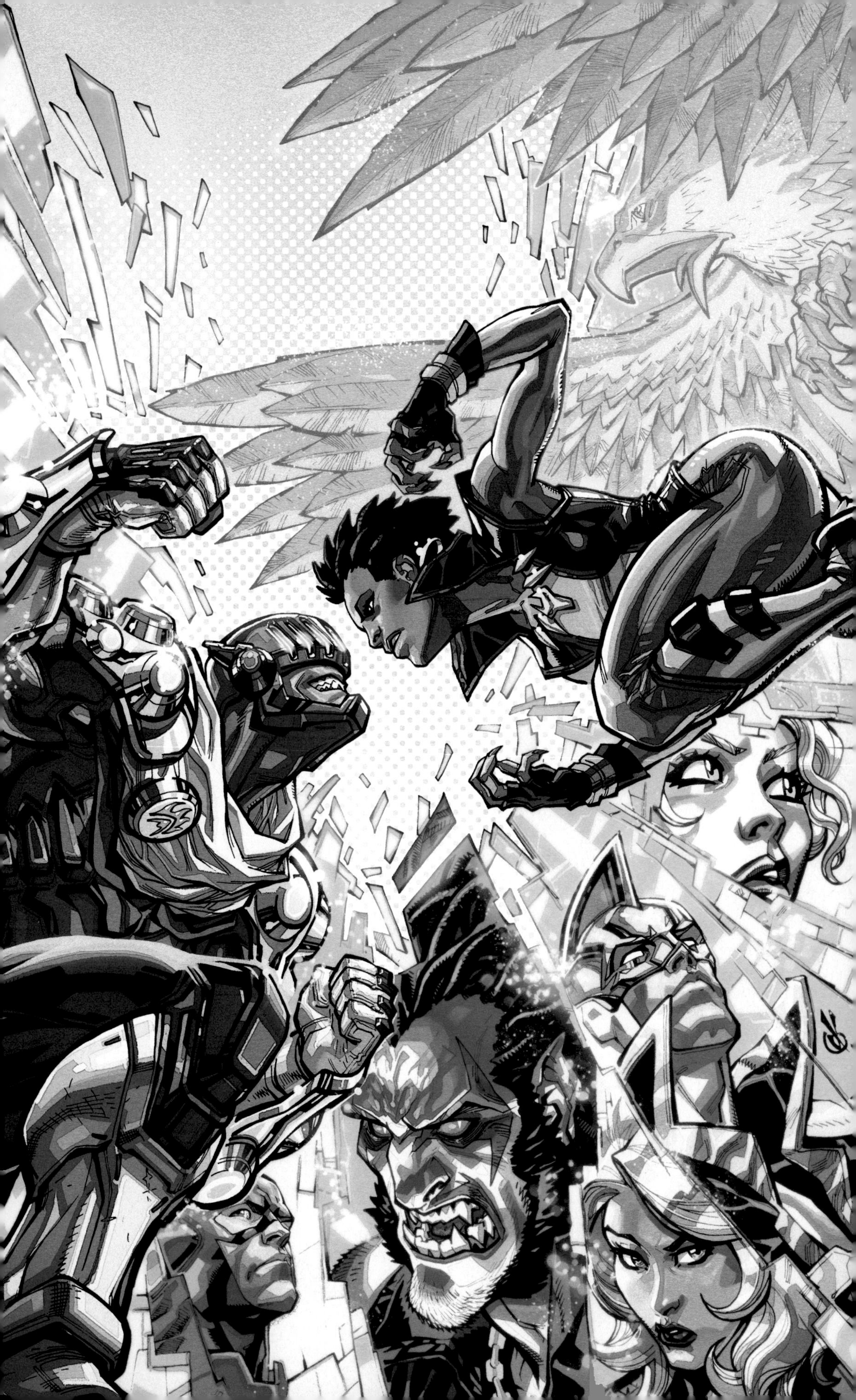

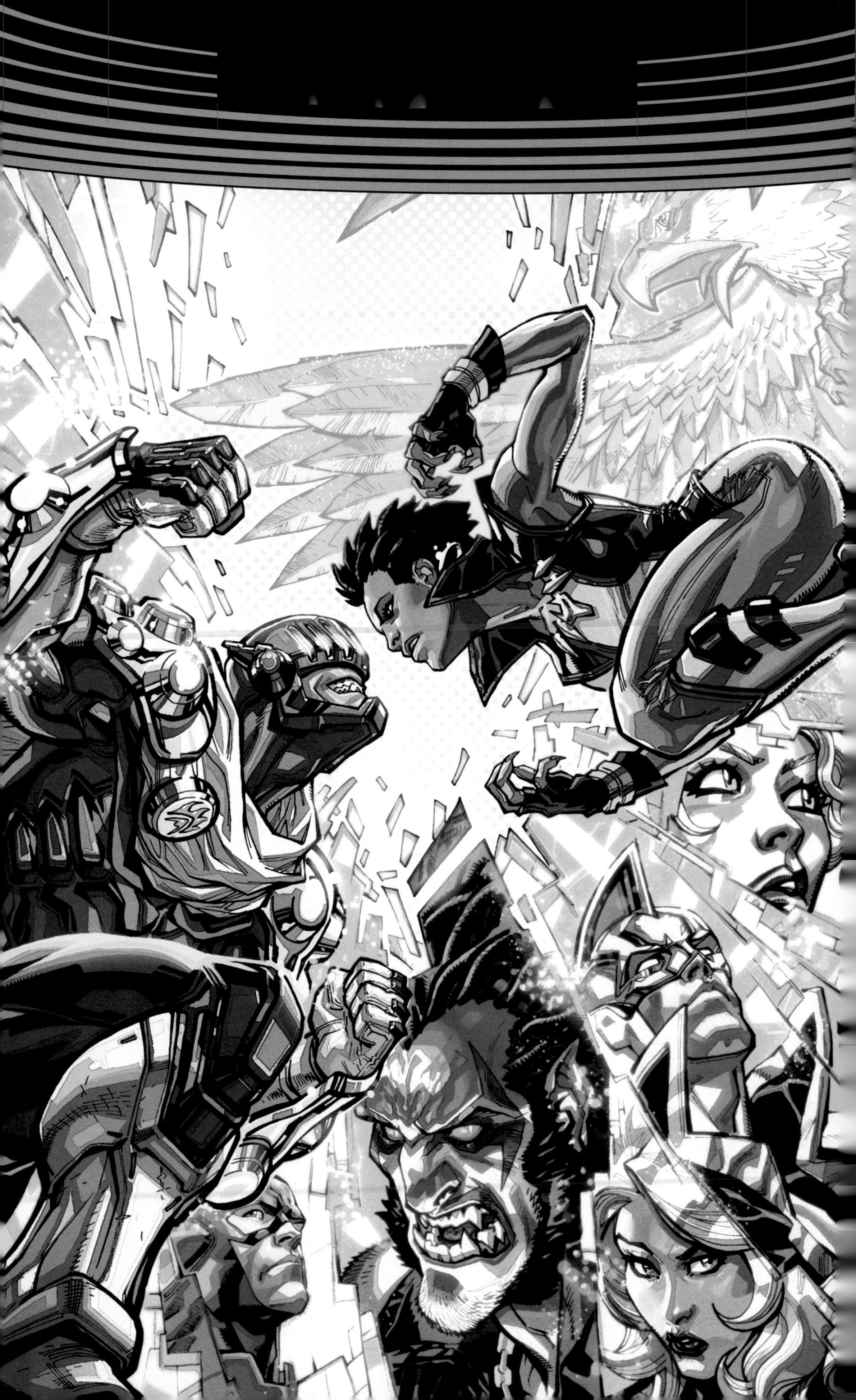

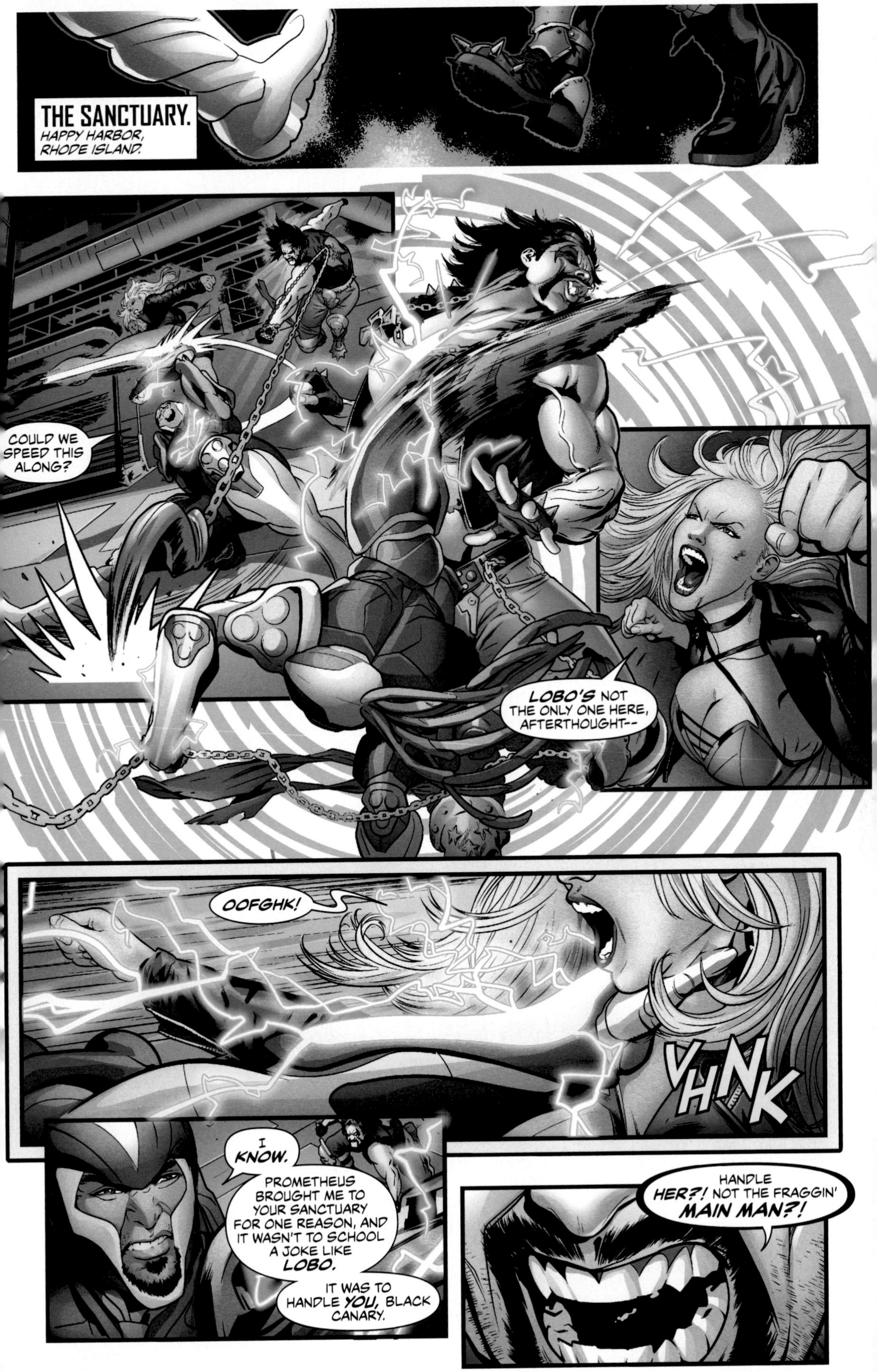
THE SANCTUARY.
HAPPY HARBOR, RHODE ISLAND.
COULD WE SPEED THIS ALONG?
LOBO'S NOT THE ONLY ONE HERE, AFTERTHOUGHT--
OOFGHK!
VHNK
I KNOW.
PROMETHEUS BROUGHT ME TO YOUR SANCTUARY FOR ONE REASON, AND IT WASN'T TO SCHOOL A JOKE LIKE LOBO.
IT WAS TO HANDLE YOU, BLACK CANARY.
HANDLE HER?! NOT THE FRAGGIN' MAIN MAN?!

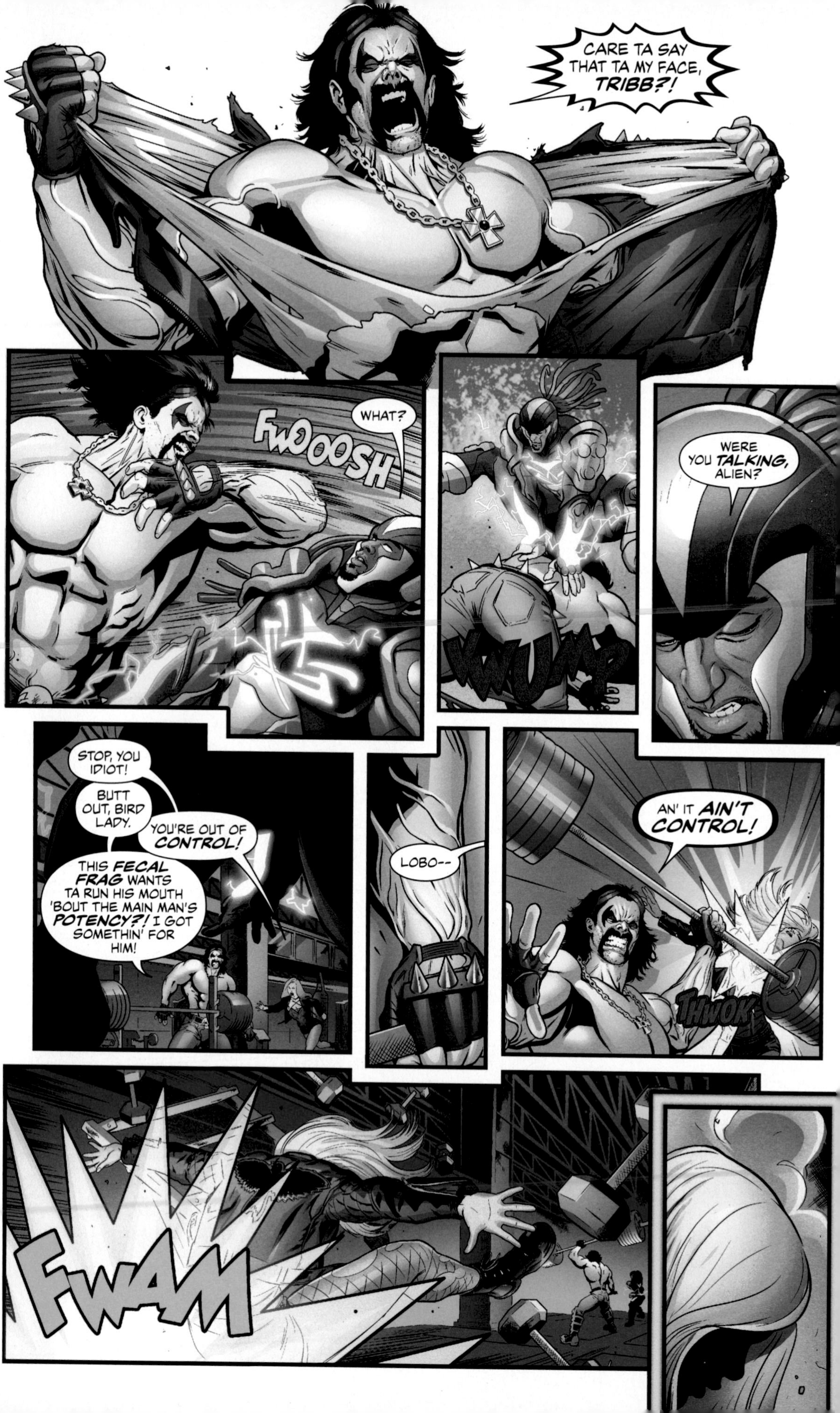
CARE TA SAY THAT TA MY FACE, TRIBB?!
WHAT?
FWOOOSH
KWUMP
WERE YOU TALKING, ALIEN?
STOP, YOU IDIOT!
BUTT OUT, BIRD LADY.
YOU'RE OUT OF CONTROL!
THIS FECAL FRAG WANTS TA RUN HIS MOUTH 'BOUT THE MAIN MAN'S POTENCY?! I GOT SOMETHIN' FOR HIM!
LOBO--
AN' IT AIN'T CONTROL!
THWOK
FWAM

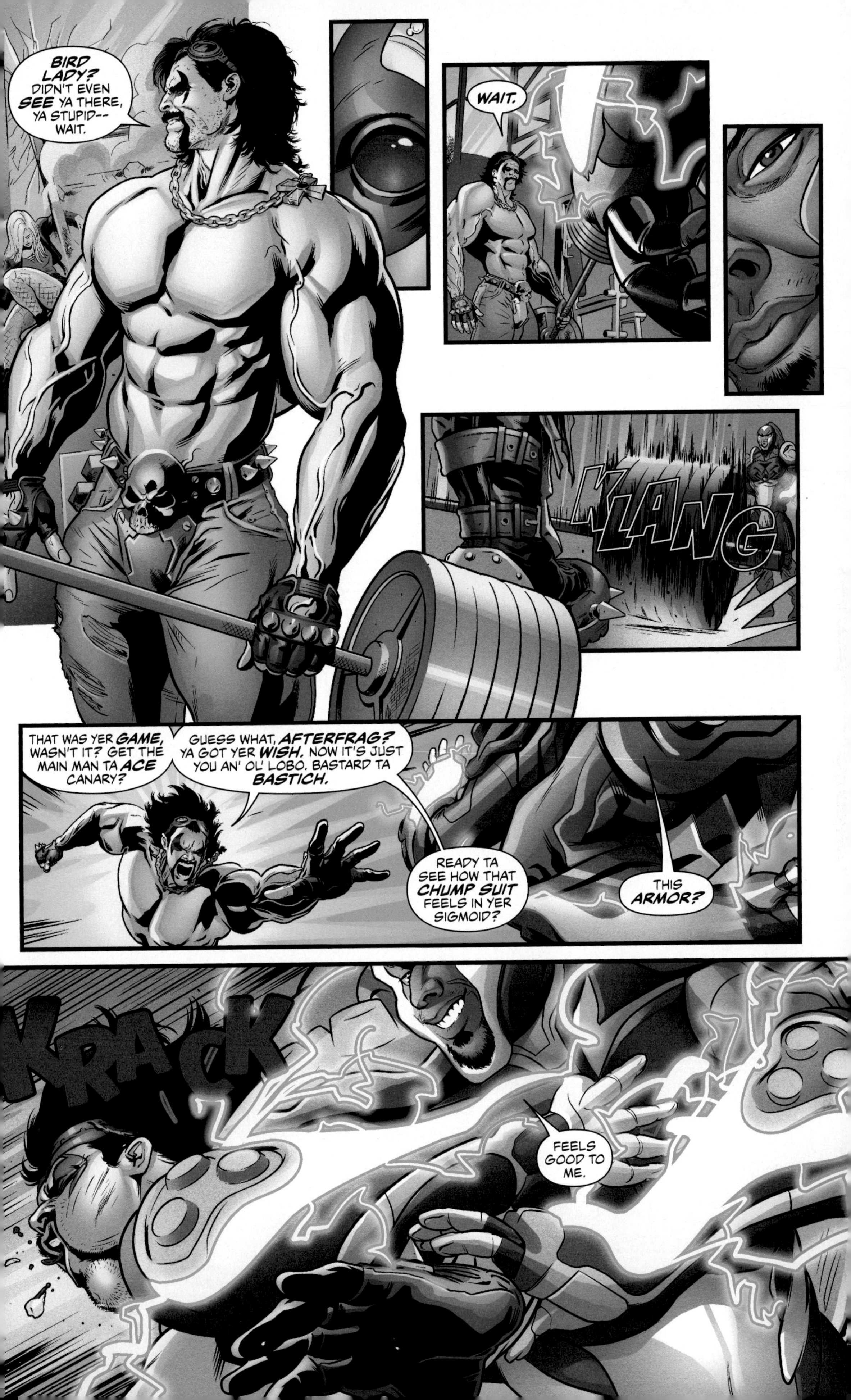
BIRD LADY? DIDN'T EVEN SEE YA THERE, YA STUPID-- WAIT.
WAIT.
KLANG
THAT WAS YER GAME, WASN'T IT? GET THE MAIN MAN TA ACE CANARY?
GUESS WHAT, AFTERFRAG? YA GOT YER WISH. NOW IT'S JUST YOU AN' OL' LOBO. BASTARD TA BASTICH.
READY TA SEE HOW THAT CHUMP SUIT FEELS IN YER SIGMOID?
THIS ARMOR?
KRACK
FEELS GOOD TO ME.

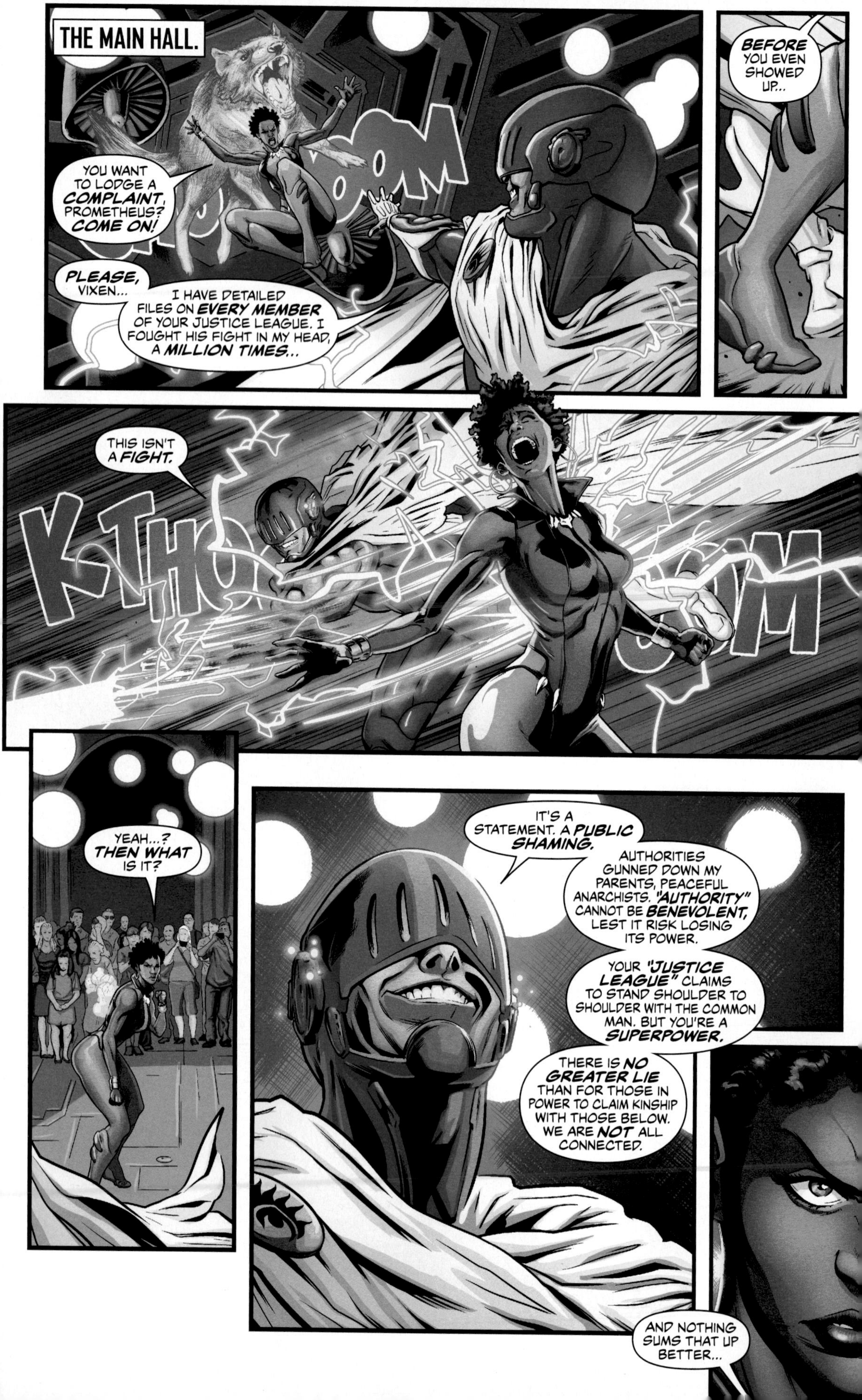
THE MAIN HALL.
YOU WANT TO LODGE A COMPLAINT, PROMETHEUS? COME ON!
PLEASE, VIXEN...
I HAVE DETAILED FILES ON EVERY MEMBER OF YOUR JUSTICE LEAGUE. I FOUGHT HIS FIGHT IN MY HEAD, A MILLION TIMES...
BEFORE YOU EVEN SHOWED UP...
THIS ISN'T A FIGHT.
K-THOOOOOM
YEAH...? THEN WHAT IS IT?
IT'S A STATEMENT. A PUBLIC SHAMING.
AUTHORITIES GUNNED DOWN MY PARENTS, PEACEFUL ANARCHISTS. "AUTHORITY" CANNOT BE BENEVOLENT, LEST IT RISK LOSING ITS POWER.
YOUR "JUSTICE LEAGUE" CLAIMS TO STAND SHOULDER TO SHOULDER WITH THE COMMON MAN. BUT YOU'RE A SUPERPOWER.
THERE IS NO GREATER LIE THAN FOR THOSE IN POWER TO CLAIM KINSHIP WITH THOSE BELOW. WE ARE NOT ALL CONNECTED.
AND NOTHING SUMS THAT UP BETTER...

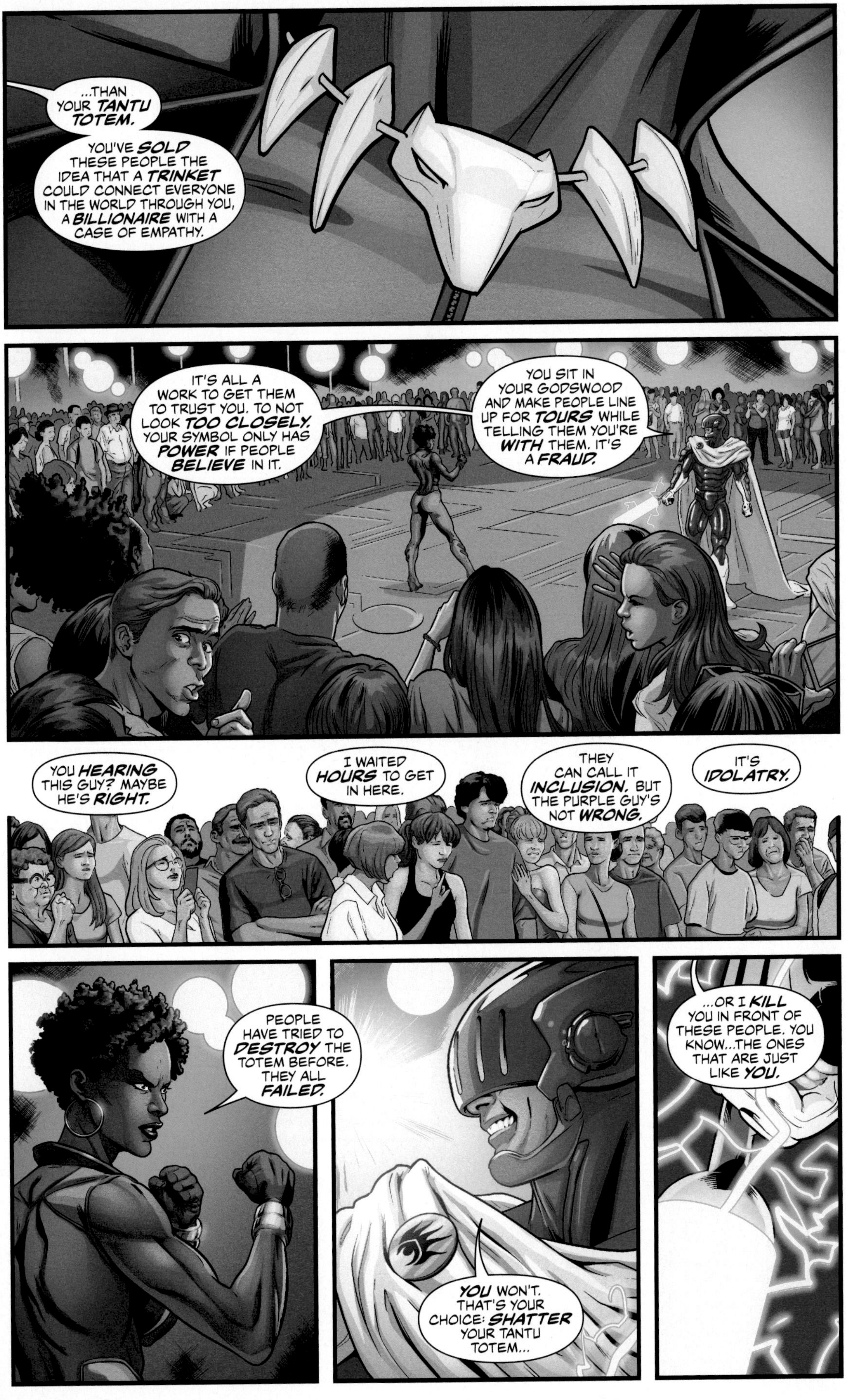
...THAN YOUR TANTU TOTEM.
YOU'VE SOLD THESE PEOPLE THE IDEA THAT A TRINKET COULD CONNECT EVERYONE IN THE WORLD THROUGH YOU, A BILLIONAIRE WITH A CASE OF EMPATHY.
IT'S ALL A WORK TO GET THEM TO TRUST YOU. TO NOT LOOK TOO CLOSELY. YOUR SYMBOL ONLY HAS POWER IF PEOPLE BELIEVE IN IT.
YOU SIT IN YOUR GODSWOOD AND MAKE PEOPLE LINE UP FOR TOURS WHILE TELLING THEM YOU'RE WITH THEM. IT'S A FRAUD.
YOU HEARING THIS GUY? MAYBE HE'S RIGHT.
I WAITED HOURS TO GET IN HERE.
THEY CAN CALL IT INCLUSION, BUT THE PURPLE GUY'S NOT WRONG.
IT'S IDOLATRY.
PEOPLE HAVE TRIED TO DESTROY THE TOTEM BEFORE. THEY ALL FAILED.
YOU WON'T. THAT'S YOUR CHOICE: SHATTER YOUR TANTU TOTEM...
...OR I KILL YOU IN FRONT OF THESE PEOPLE. YOU KNOW...THE ONES THAT ARE JUST LIKE YOU.

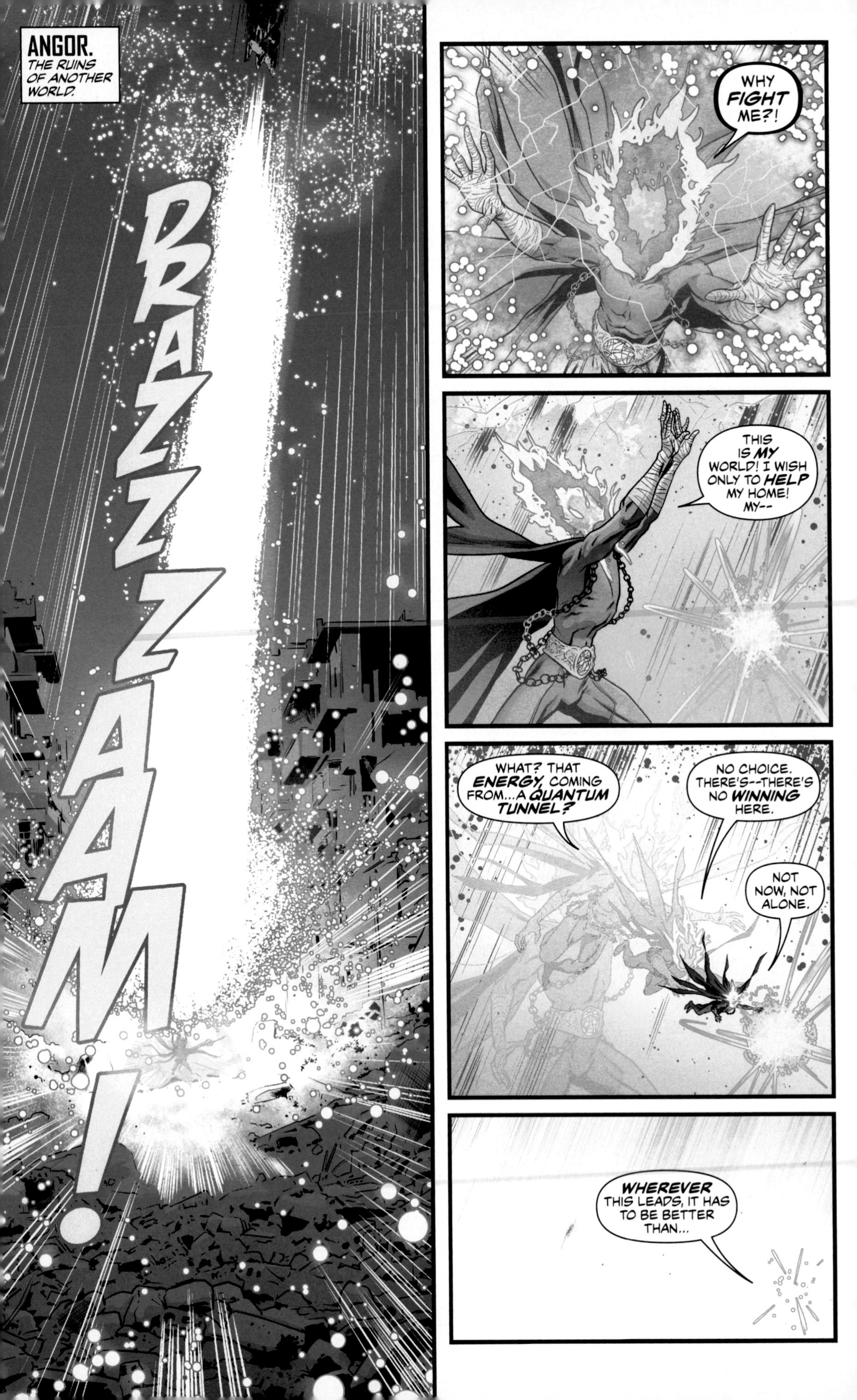

ANGOR. THE RUINS OF ANOTHER WORLD.
BRAZZZAAM!
WHY FIGHT ME?!
THIS IS MY WORLD! I WISH ONLY TO HELP MY HOME! MY--
WHAT? THAT ENERGY, COMING FROM...A QUANTUM TUNNEL?
NO CHOICE. THERE'S--THERE'S NO WINNING HERE.
NOT NOW, NOT ALONE.
WHEREVER THIS LEADS, IT HAS TO BE BETTER THAN...

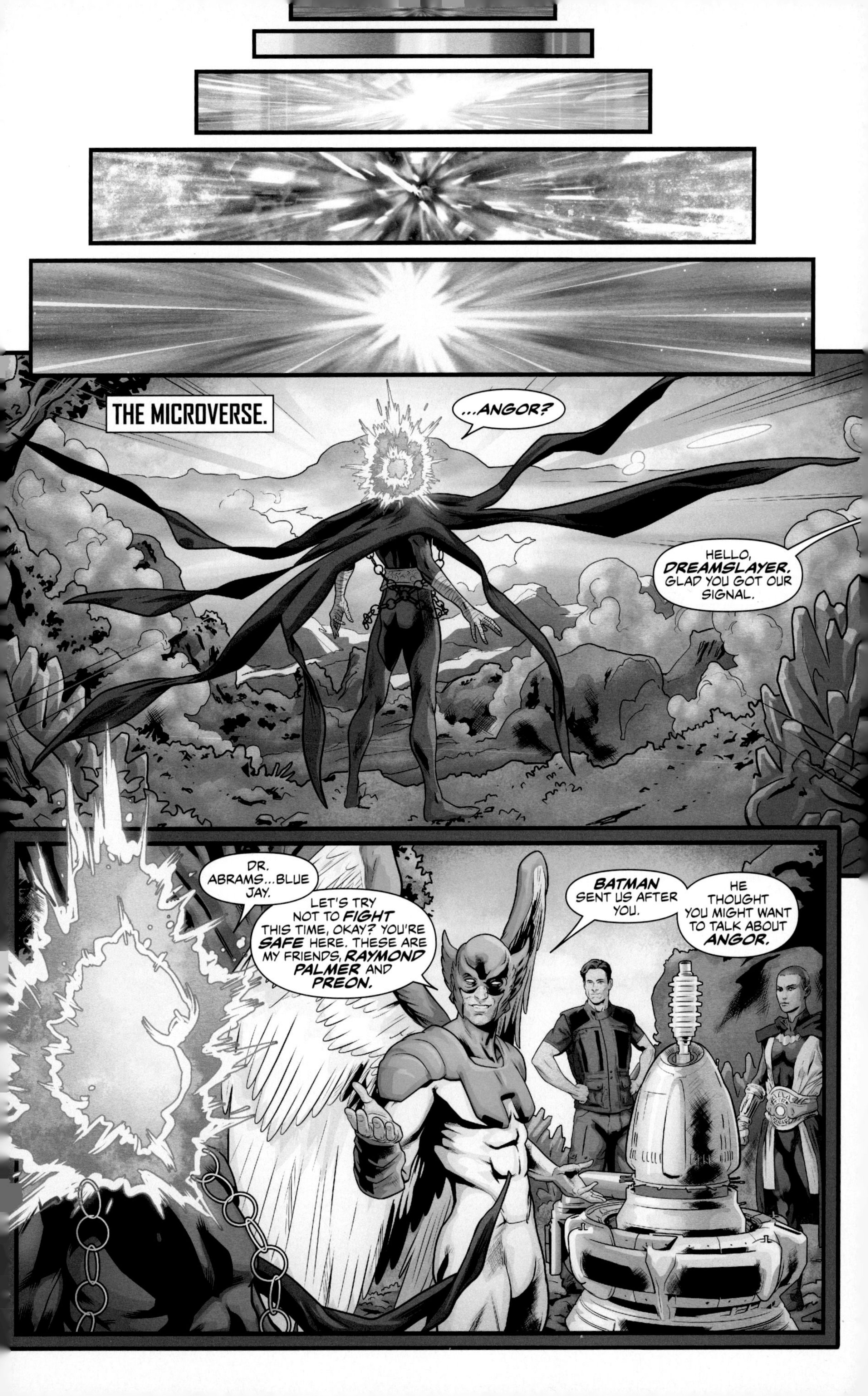
THE MICROVERSE.
...ANGOR?
HELLO, DREAMSLAYER. GLAD YOU GOT OUR SIGNAL.
DR. ABRAMS...BLUE JAY.
LET'S TRY NOT TO FIGHT THIS TIME, OKAY? YOU'RE SAFE HERE. THESE ARE MY FRIENDS, RAYMOND PALMER AND PREON.
BATMAN SENT US AFTER YOU.
HE THOUGHT YOU MIGHT WANT TO TALK ABOUT ANGOR.

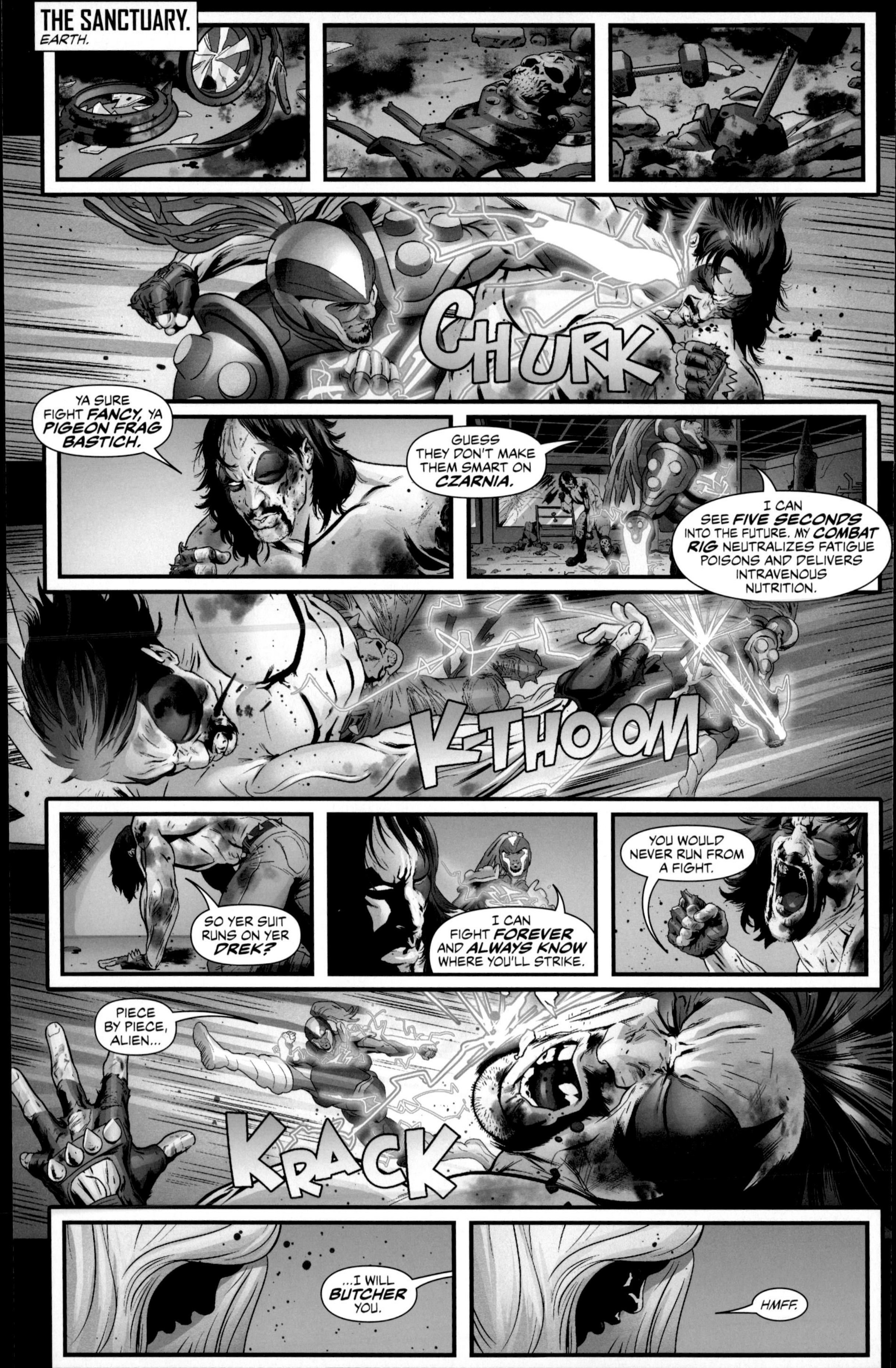
THE SANCTUARY.
EARTH.
CHURK
YA SURE FIGHT FANCY, YA PIGEON FRAG BASTICH.
GUESS THEY DON'T MAKE THEM SMART ON CZARNIA.
I CAN SEE FIVE SECONDS INTO THE FUTURE. MY COMBAT RIG NEUTRALIZES FATIGUE POISONS AND DELIVERS INTRAVENOUS NUTRITION.
K-THOOM
SO YER SUIT RUNS ON YER DREK?
I CAN FIGHT FOREVER AND ALWAYS KNOW WHERE YOU'LL STRIKE.
YOU WOULD NEVER RUN FROM A FIGHT.
PIECE BY PIECE, ALIEN...
KRACK
...I WILL BUTCHER YOU.
HMFF.

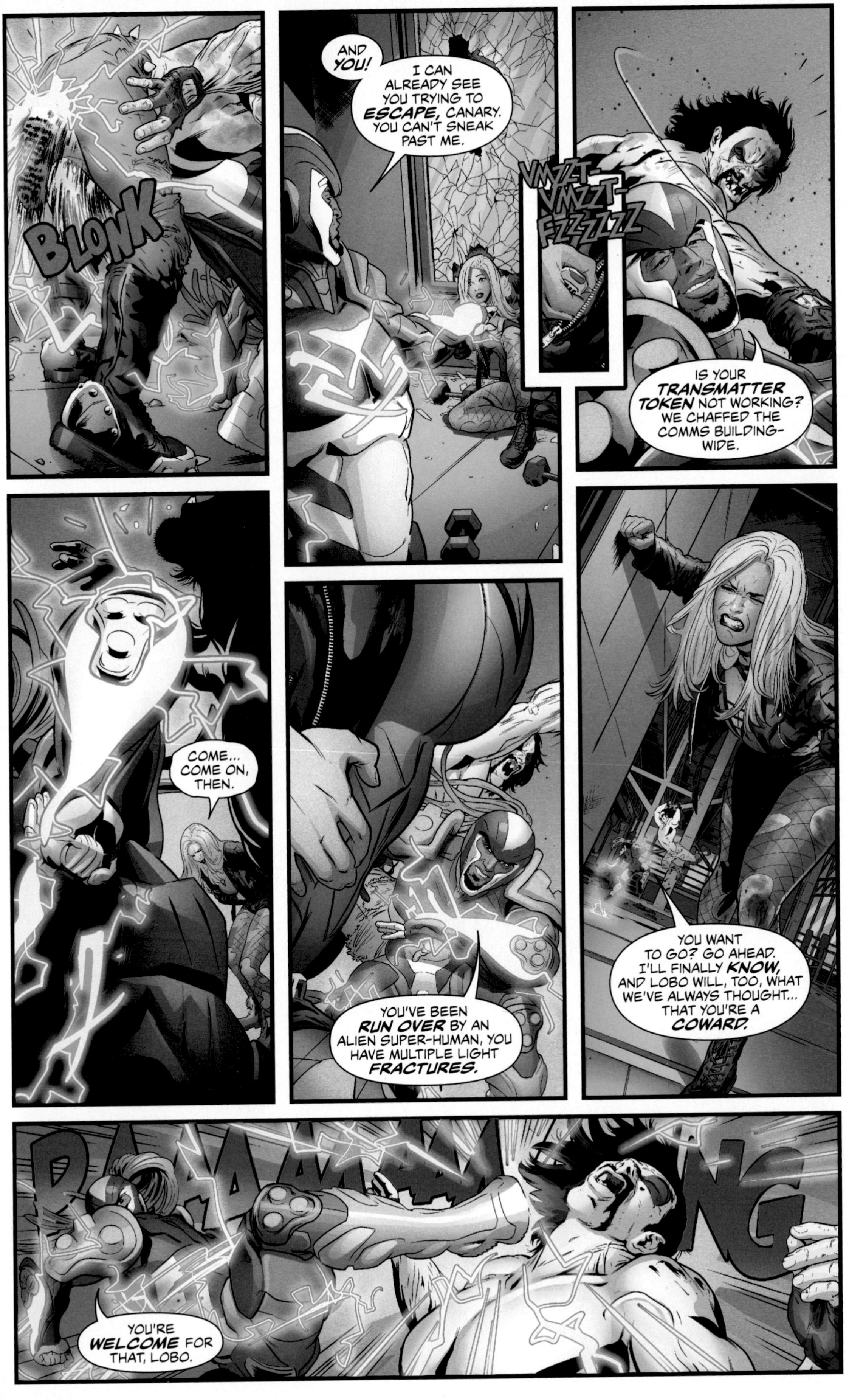

BLONK
AND YOU!
I CAN ALREADY SEE YOU TRYING TO ESCAPE, CANARY. YOU CAN'T SNEAK PAST ME.
VMZZT-VMZZT-FZZZZZZ
IS YOUR TRANSMATTER TOKEN NOT WORKING? WE CHAFFED THE COMMS BUILDING-WIDE.
COME... COME ON, THEN.
YOU'VE BEEN RUN OVER BY AN ALIEN SUPER-HUMAN, YOU HAVE MULTIPLE LIGHT FRACTURES.
YOU WANT TO GO? GO AHEAD. I'LL FINALLY KNOW, AND LOBO WILL, TOO, WHAT WE'VE ALWAYS THOUGHT... THAT YOU'RE A COWARD.
YOU'RE WELCOME FOR THAT, LOBO.

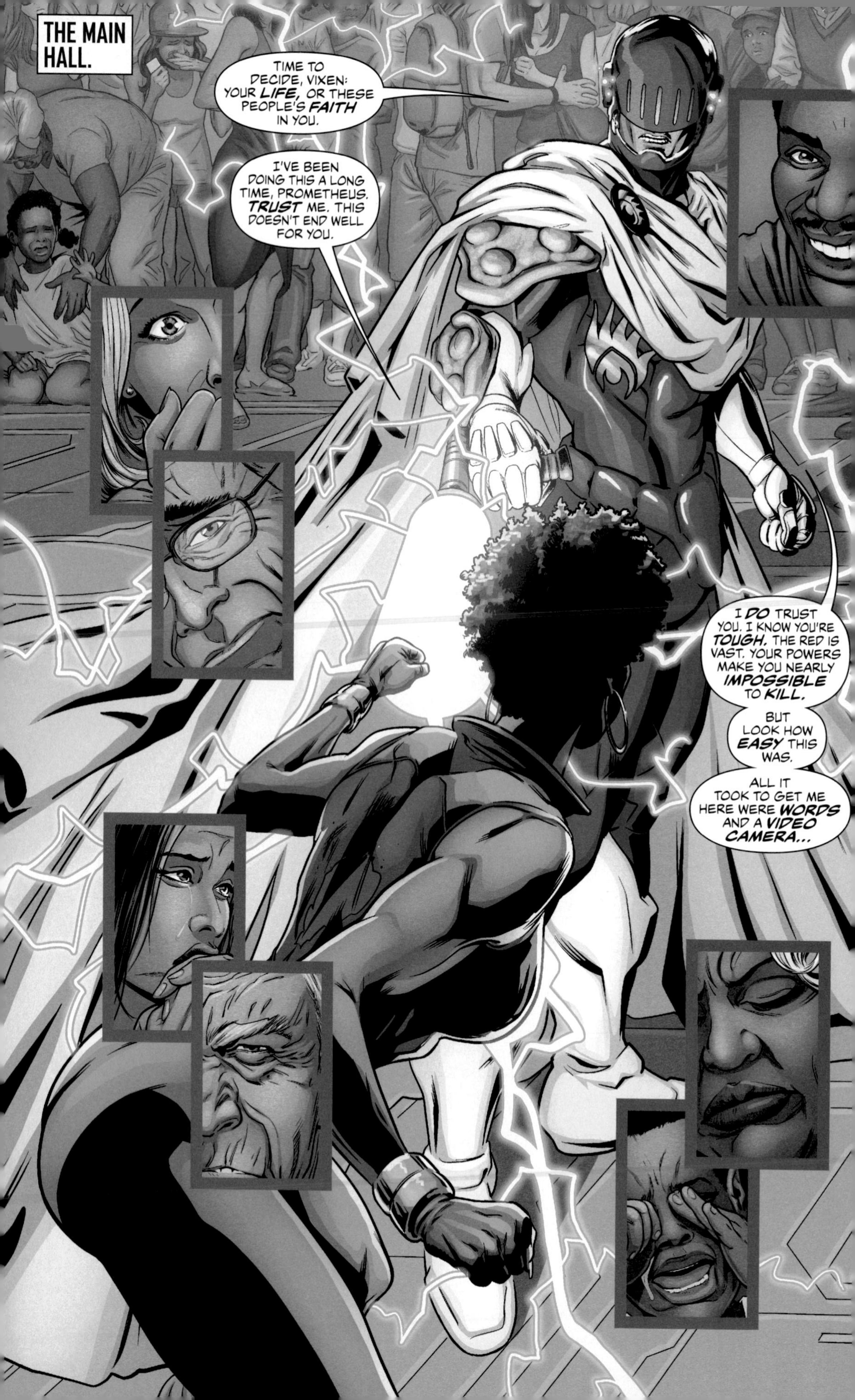
THE MAIN HALL.
TIME TO DECIDE, VIXEN: YOUR LIFE, OR THESE PEOPLE'S FAITH IN YOU.
I'VE BEEN DOING THIS A LONG TIME, PROMETHEUS. TRUST ME. THIS DOESN'T END WELL FOR YOU.
I DO TRUST YOU. I KNOW YOU'RE TOUGH. THE RED IS VAST. YOUR POWERS MAKE YOU NEARLY IMPOSSIBLE TO KILL.
BUT LOOK HOW EASY THIS WAS.
ALL IT TOOK TO GET ME HERE WERE WORDS AND A VIDEO CAMERA...

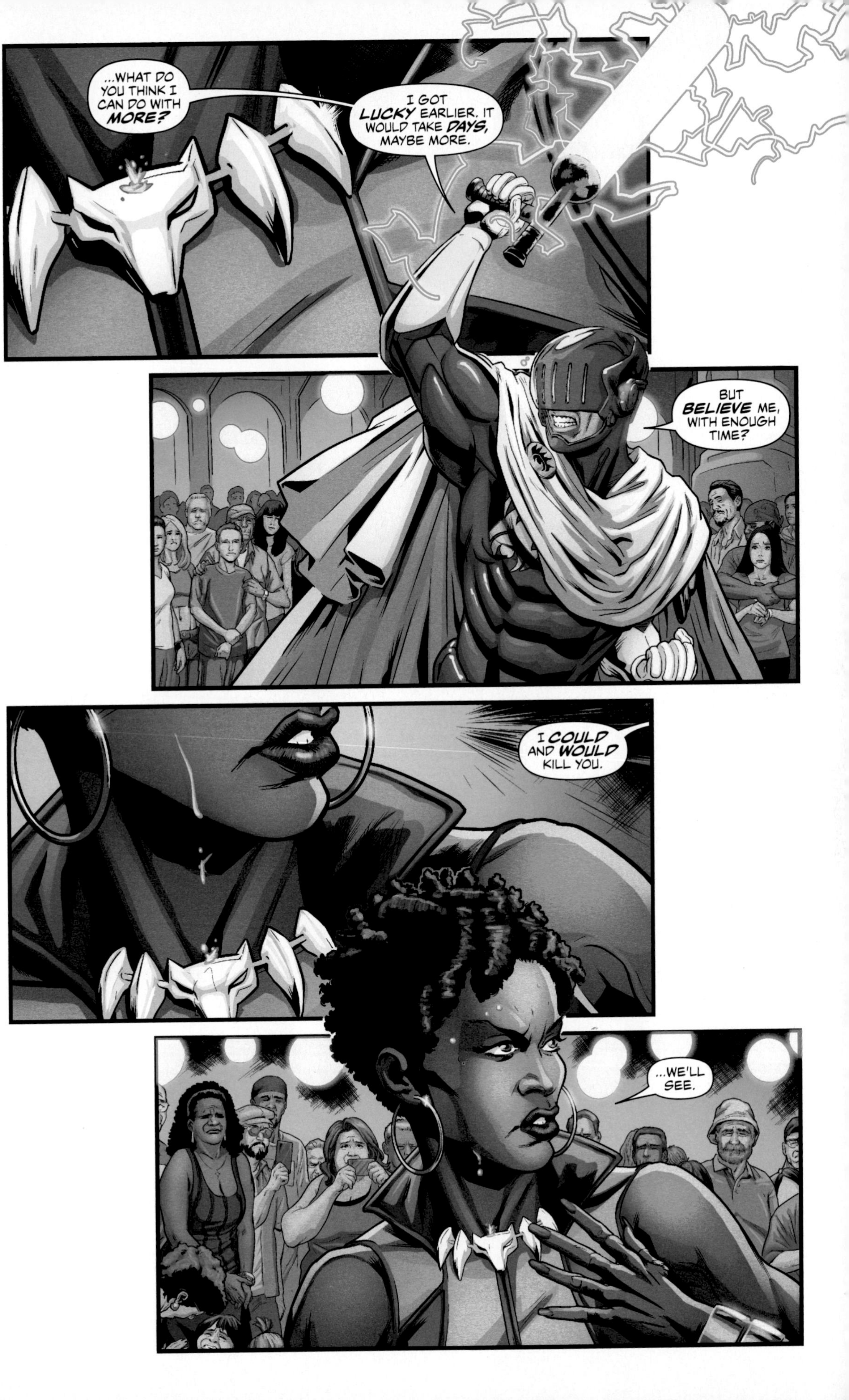
...WHAT DO YOU THINK I CAN DO WITH MORE?
I GOT LUCKY EARLIER. IT WOULD TAKE DAYS, MAYBE MORE.
BUT BELIEVE ME, WITH ENOUGH TIME?
I COULD AND WOULD KILL YOU.
...WE'LL SEE.

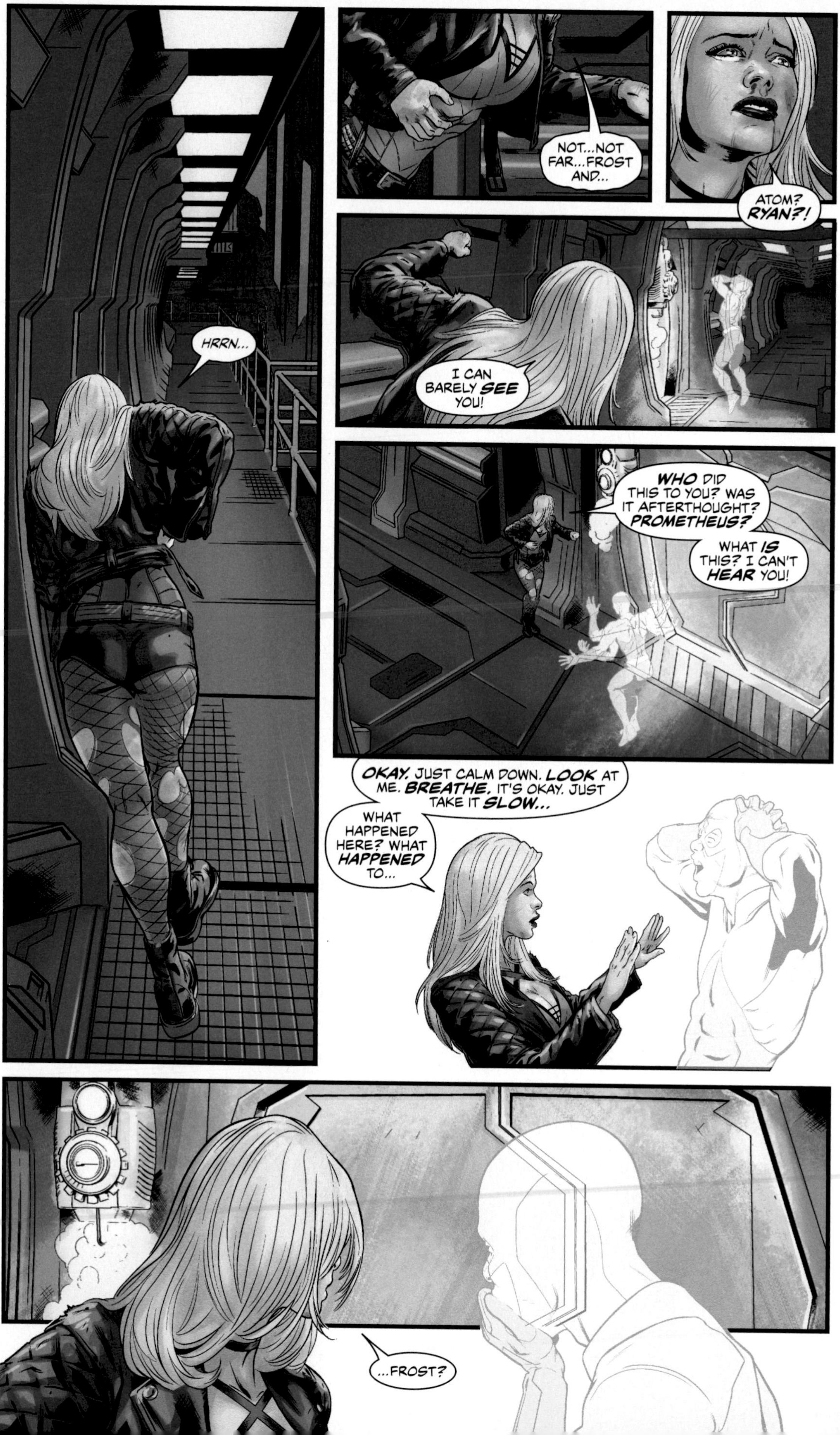
HRRN...
NOT...NOT FAR...FROST AND...
ATOM? RYAN?!
I CAN BARELY SEE YOU!
WHO DID THIS TO YOU? WAS IT AFTERTHOUGHT? PROMETHEUS?
WHAT IS THIS? I CAN'T HEAR YOU!
OKAY. JUST CALM DOWN. LOOK AT ME. BREATHE. IT'S OKAY. JUST TAKE IT SLOW...
WHAT HAPPENED HERE? WHAT HAPPENED TO...
...FROST?

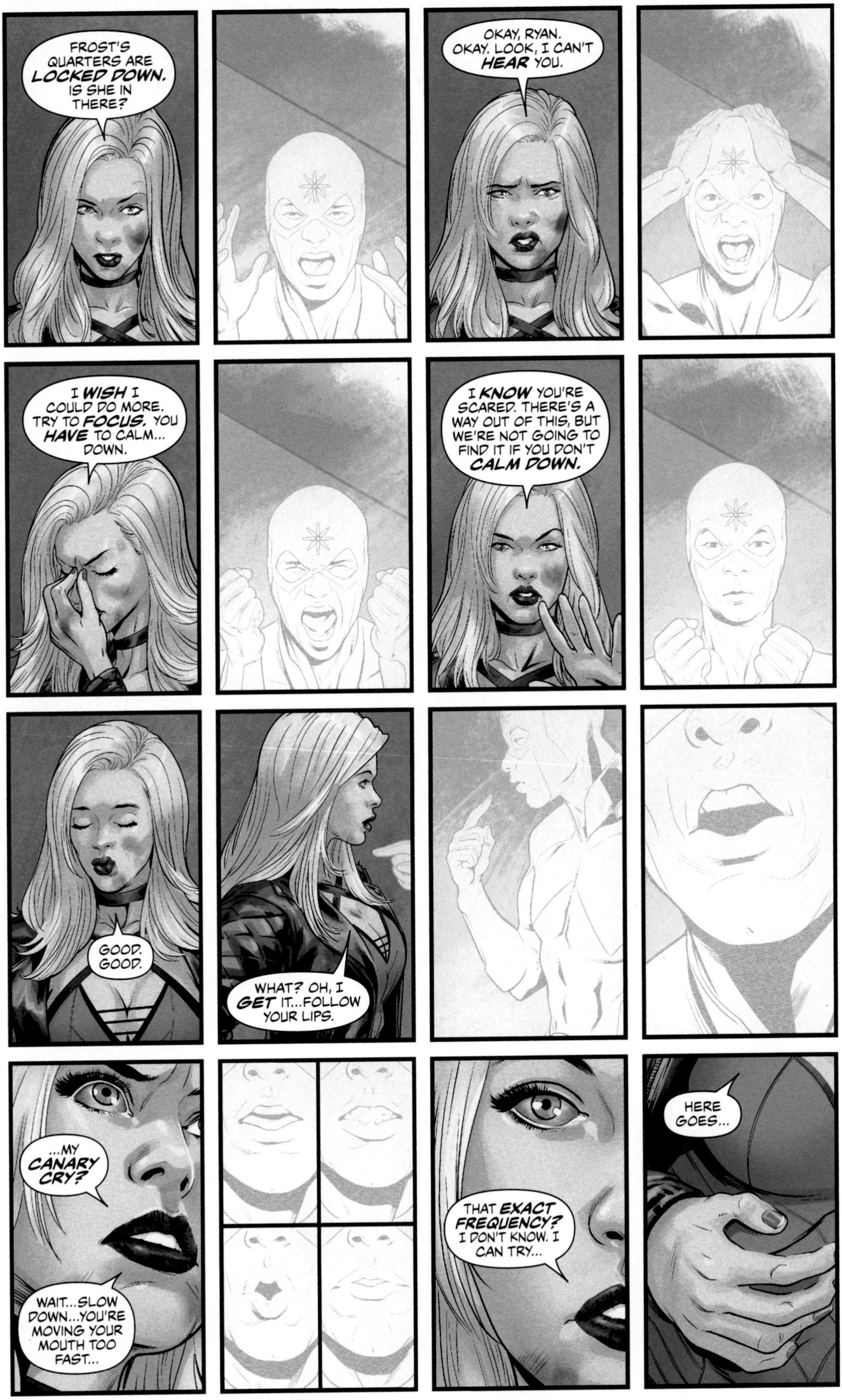

FROST'S QUARTERS ARE LOCKED DOWN. IS SHE IN THERE?
OKAY, RYAN. OKAY. LOOK, I CAN'T HEAR YOU.
I WISH I COULD DO MORE. TRY TO FOCUS. YOU HAVE TO CALM... DOWN.
I KNOW YOU'RE SCARED. THERE'S A WAY OUT OF THIS, BUT WE'RE NOT GOING TO FIND IT IF YOU DON'T CALM DOWN.
GOOD. GOOD.
WHAT? OH, I GET IT...FOLLOW YOUR LIPS.
...MY CANARY CRY?
WAIT...SLOW DOWN...YOU'RE MOVING YOUR MOUTH TOO FAST...
THAT EXACT FREQUENCY? I DON'T KNOW. I CAN TRY...
HERE GOES...

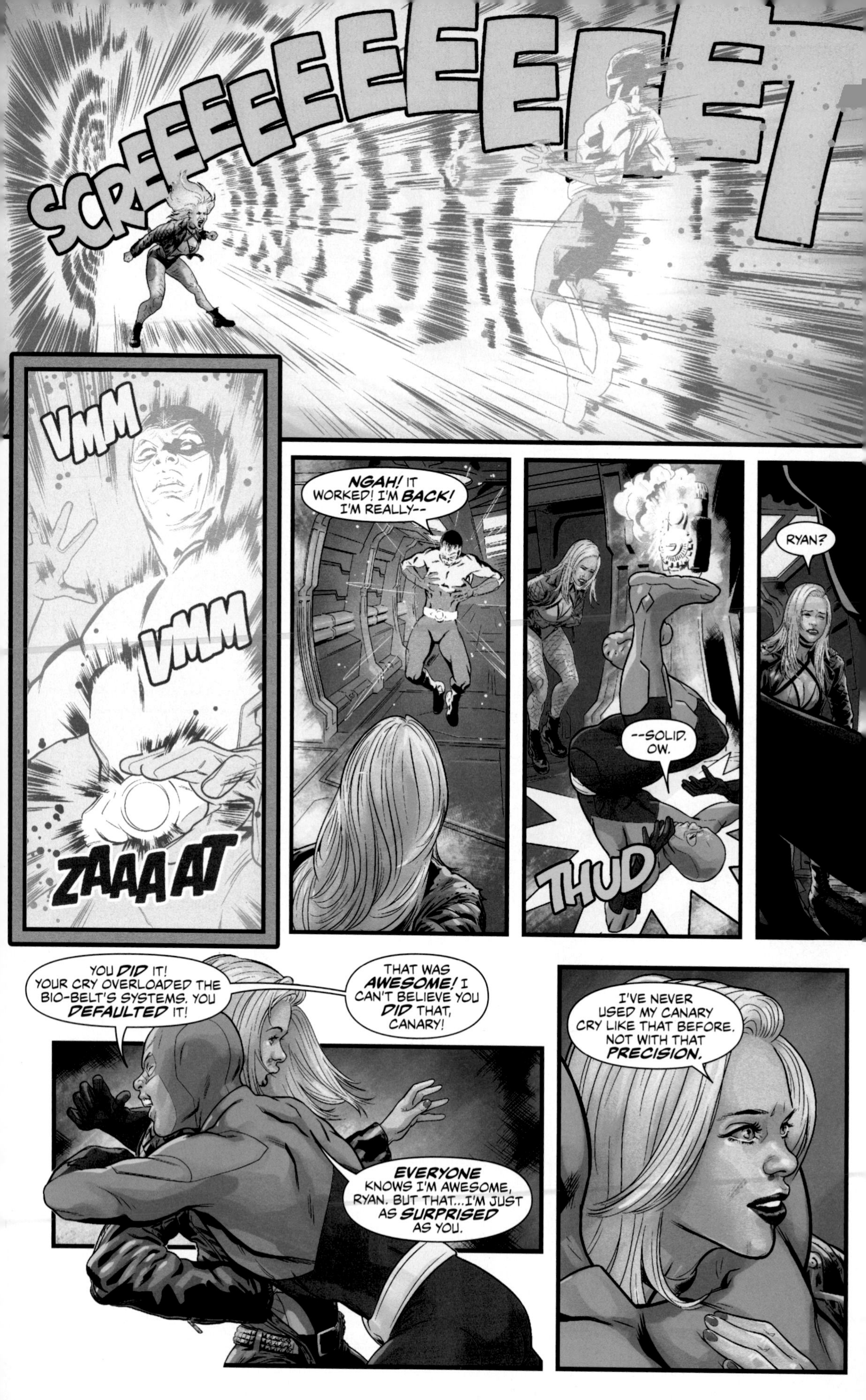
SCREEEEEEEEEET
VMM
VMM
ZAAAAT
NGAH! IT WORKED! I'M BACK! I'M REALLY--
--SOLID. OW.
THUD
RYAN?
YOU DID IT! YOUR CRY OVERLOADED THE BIO-BELT'S SYSTEMS. YOU DEFAULTED IT!
THAT WAS AWESOME! I CAN'T BELIEVE YOU DID THAT, CANARY!
EVERYONE KNOWS I'M AWESOME, RYAN. BUT THAT...I'M JUST AS SURPRISED AS YOU.
I'VE NEVER USED MY CANARY CRY LIKE THAT BEFORE. NOT WITH THAT PRECISION.

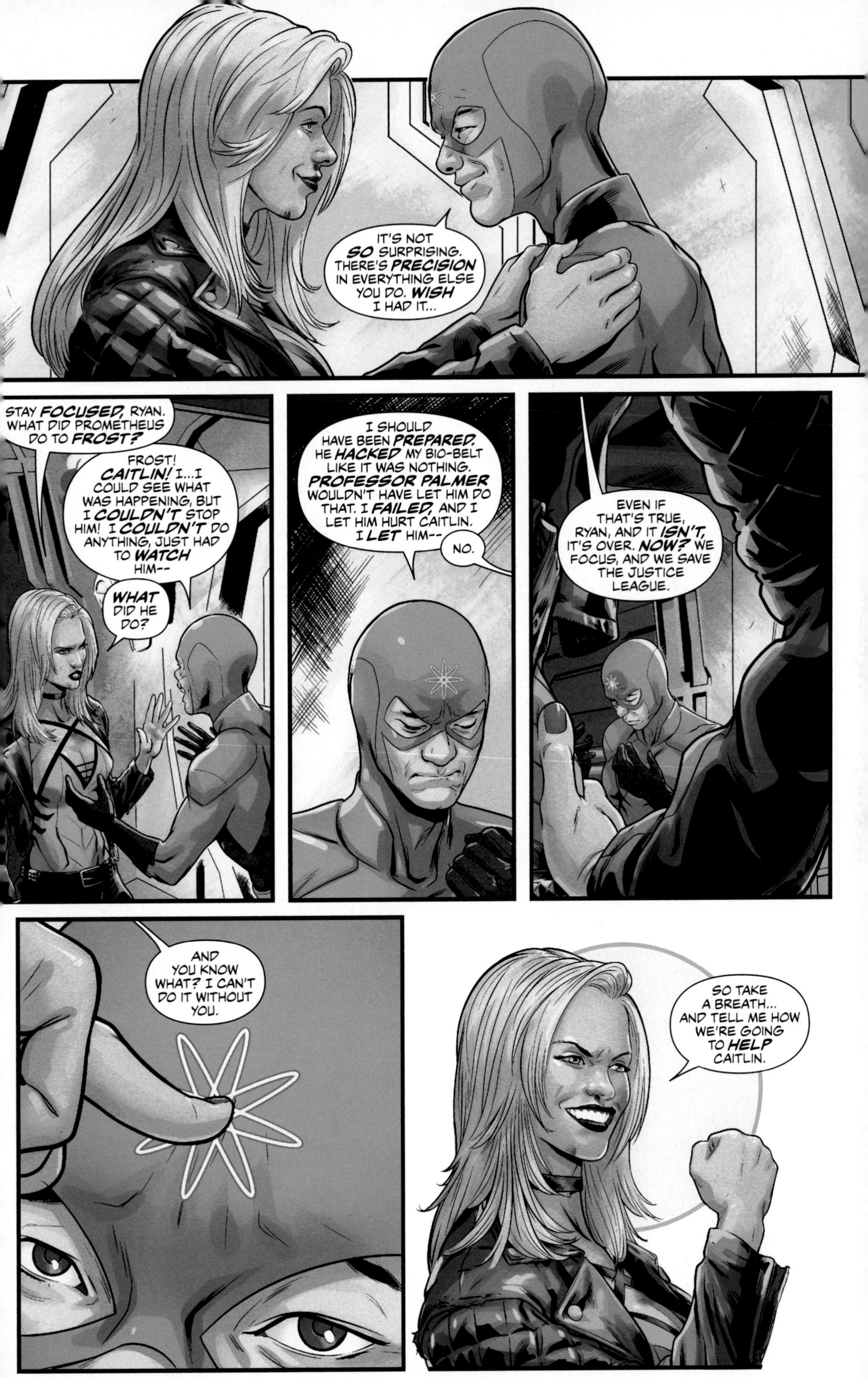
IT'S NOT SO SURPRISING. THERE'S PRECISION IN EVERYTHING ELSE YOU DO. WISH I HAD IT...
STAY FOCUSED, RYAN. WHAT DID PROMETHEUS DO TO FROST?
FROST! CAITLIN! I...I COULD SEE WHAT WAS HAPPENING, BUT I COULDN'T STOP HIM! I COULDN'T DO ANYTHING, JUST HAD TO WATCH HIM--
WHAT DID HE DO?
I SHOULD HAVE BEEN PREPARED. HE HACKED MY BIO-BELT LIKE IT WAS NOTHING. PROFESSOR PALMER WOULDN'T HAVE LET HIM DO THAT. I FAILED, AND I LET HIM HURT CAITLIN. I LET HIM--
NO.
EVEN IF THAT'S TRUE, RYAN, AND IT ISN'T, IT'S OVER. NOW? WE FOCUS, AND WE SAVE THE JUSTICE LEAGUE.
AND YOU KNOW WHAT? I CAN'T DO IT WITHOUT YOU.
SO TAKE A BREATH... AND TELL ME HOW WE'RE GOING TO HELP CAITLIN.

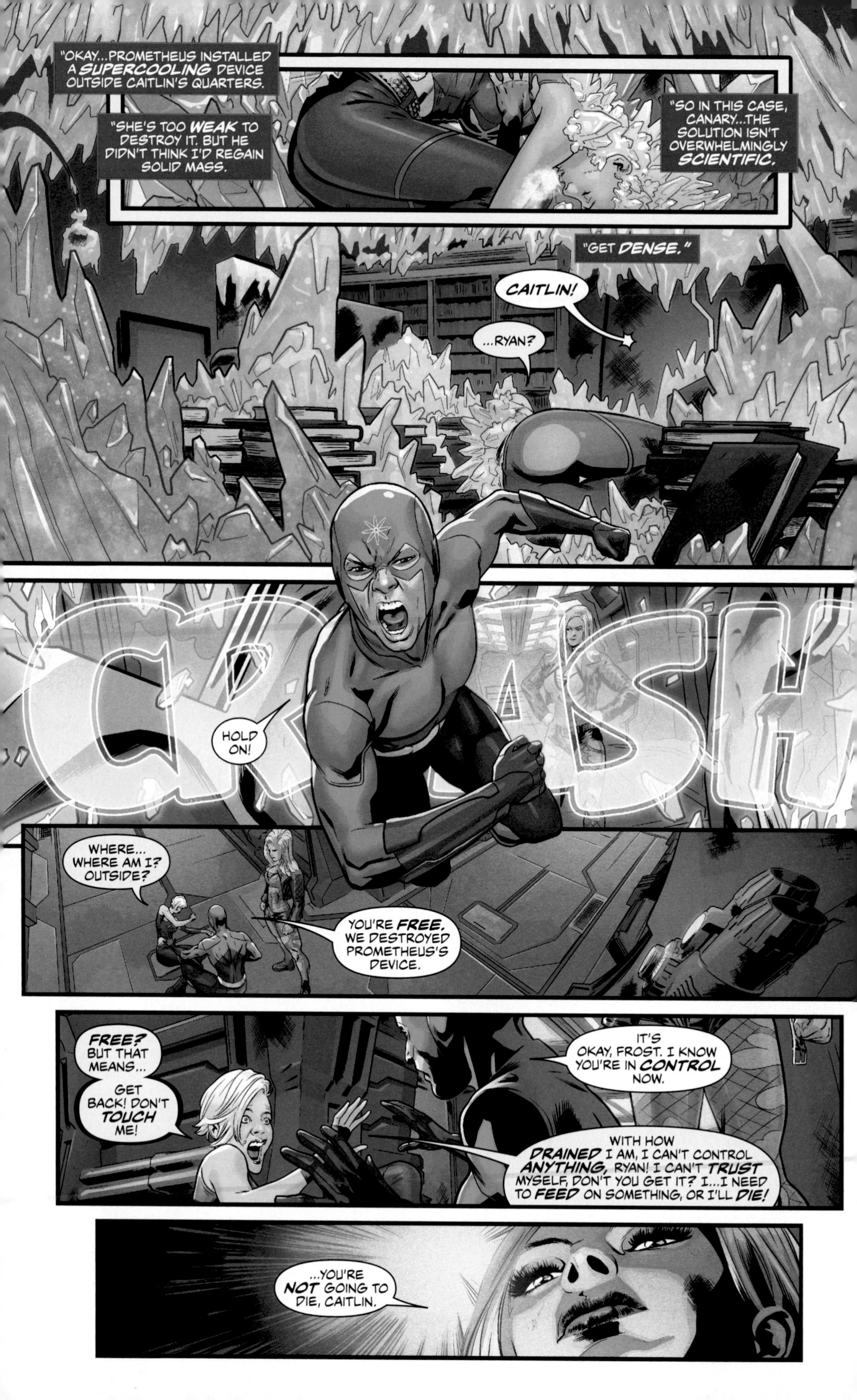
"OKAY...PROMETHEUS INSTALLED A SUPERCOOLING DEVICE OUTSIDE CAITLIN'S QUARTERS.
"SHE'S TOO WEAK TO DESTROY IT. BUT HE DIDN'T THINK I'D REGAIN SOLID MASS.
"SO IN THIS CASE, CANARY...THE SOLUTION ISN'T OVERWHELMINGLY SCIENTIFIC.
"GET DENSE."
CAITLIN!
...RYAN?
CRASH
HOLD ON!
WHERE... WHERE AM I? OUTSIDE?
YOU'RE FREE. WE DESTROYED PROMETHEUS'S DEVICE.
FREE? BUT THAT MEANS...
GET BACK! DON'T TOUCH ME!
IT'S OKAY, FROST. I KNOW YOU'RE IN CONTROL NOW.
WITH HOW DRAINED I AM, I CAN'T CONTROL ANYTHING, RYAN! I CAN'T TRUST MYSELF, DON'T YOU GET IT? I...I NEED TO FEED ON SOMETHING, OR I'LL DIE!
...YOU'RE NOT GOING TO DIE, CAITLIN.

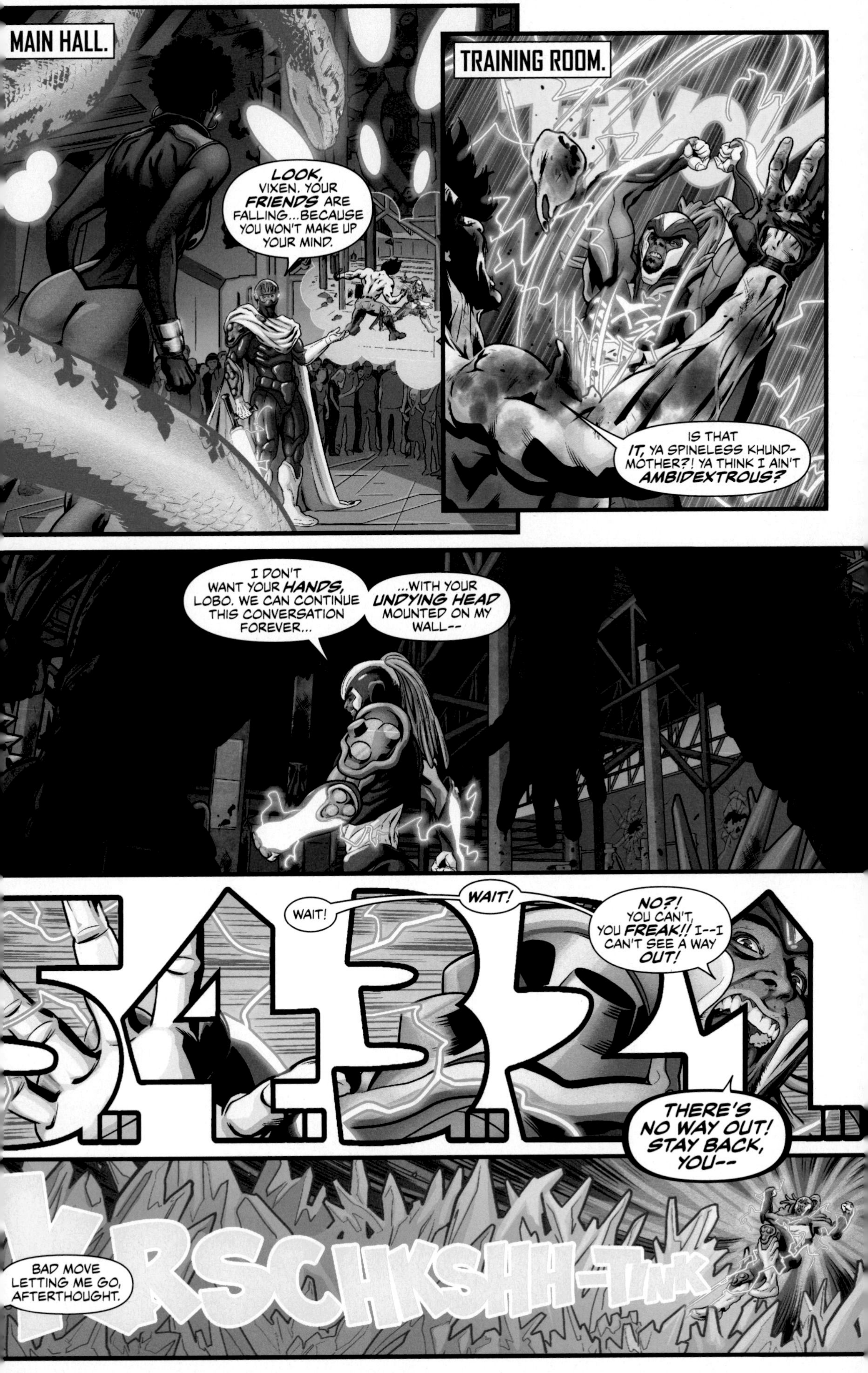
MAIN HALL.
LOOK, VIXEN. YOUR FRIENDS ARE FALLING...BECAUSE YOU WON'T MAKE UP YOUR MIND.
TRAINING ROOM.
IS THAT IT, YA SPINELESS KHUND-MOTHER?! YA THINK I AIN'T AMBIDEXTROUS?
I DON'T WANT YOUR HANDS, LOBO. WE CAN CONTINUE THIS CONVERSATION FOREVER...
...WITH YOUR UNDYING HEAD MOUNTED ON MY WALL--
5...4...3...2...1...
WAIT!
WAIT!
NO?! YOU CAN'T, YOU FREAK!! I--I CAN'T SEE A WAY OUT!
THERE'S NO WAY OUT! STAY BACK, YOU--
KRSCHKSHH-TINK
BAD MOVE LETTING ME GO, AFTERTHOUGHT.

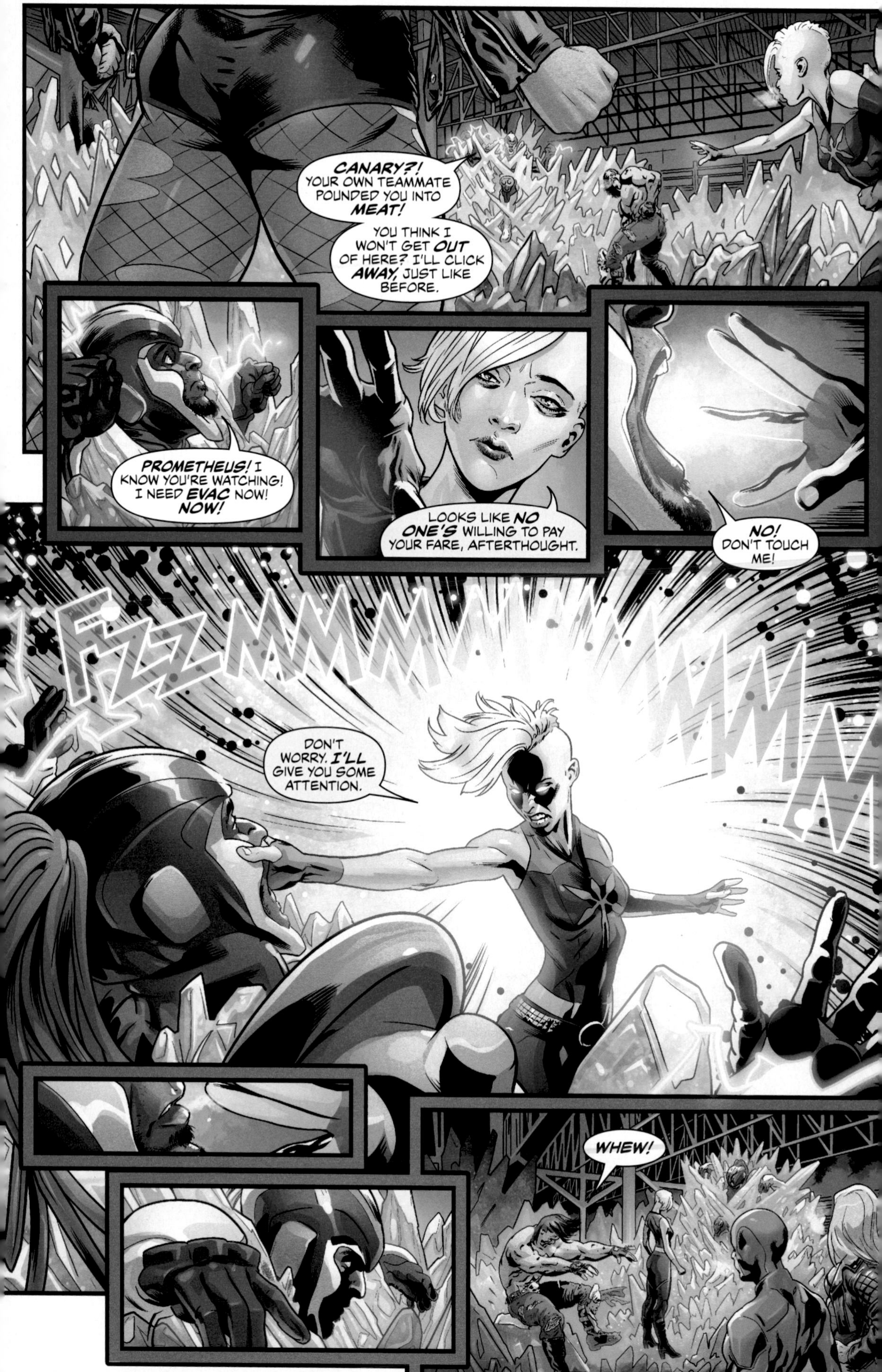
CANARY?! YOUR OWN TEAMMATE POUNDED YOU INTO MEAT!
YOU THINK I WON'T GET OUT OF HERE? I'LL CLICK AWAY, JUST LIKE BEFORE.
PROMETHEUS! I KNOW YOU'RE WATCHING! I NEED EVAC NOW! NOW!
LOOKS LIKE NO ONE'S WILLING TO PAY YOUR FARE, AFTERTHOUGHT.
NO! DON'T TOUCH ME!
FZZZMMMMMMMMMMMMM
DON'T WORRY. I'LL GIVE YOU SOME ATTENTION.
WHEW!

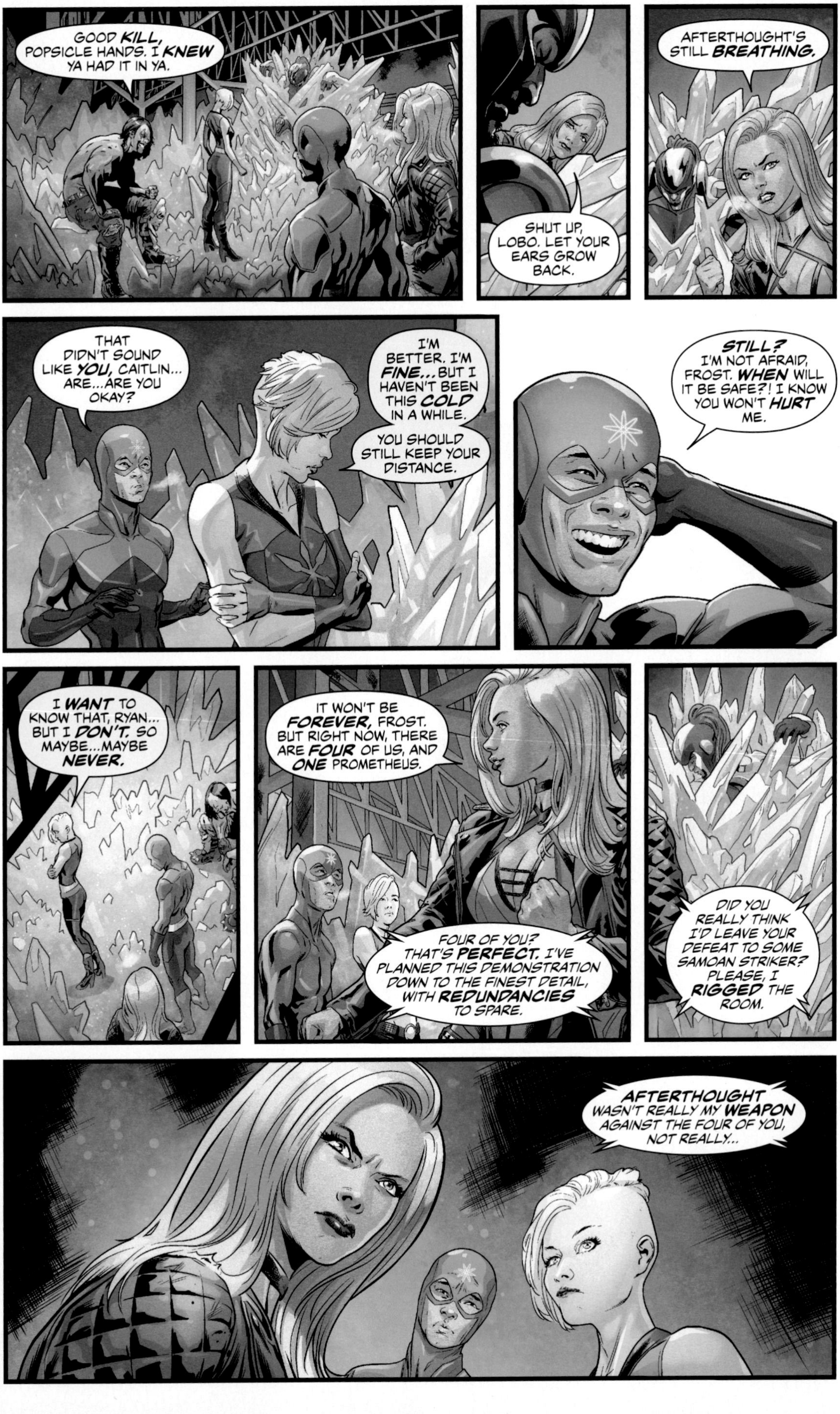
GOOD KILL, POPSICLE HANDS. I KNEW YA HAD IT IN YA.
SHUT UP, LOBO. LET YOUR EARS GROW BACK.
AFTERTHOUGHT'S STILL BREATHING.
THAT DIDN'T SOUND LIKE YOU, CAITLIN... ARE...ARE YOU OKAY?
I'M BETTER. I'M FINE... BUT I HAVEN'T BEEN THIS COLD IN A WHILE.
YOU SHOULD STILL KEEP YOUR DISTANCE.
STILL? I'M NOT AFRAID, FROST. WHEN WILL IT BE SAFE?! I KNOW YOU WON'T HURT ME.
I WANT TO KNOW THAT, RYAN... BUT I DON'T. SO MAYBE...MAYBE NEVER.
IT WON'T BE FOREVER, FROST. BUT RIGHT NOW, THERE ARE FOUR OF US, AND ONE PROMETHEUS.
FOUR OF YOU? THAT'S PERFECT. I'VE PLANNED THIS DEMONSTRATION DOWN TO THE FINEST DETAIL, WITH REDUNDANCIES TO SPARE.
DID YOU REALLY THINK I'D LEAVE YOUR DEFEAT TO SOME SAMOAN STRIKER? PLEASE, I RIGGED THE ROOM.
AFTERTHOUGHT WASN'T REALLY MY WEAPON AGAINST THE FOUR OF YOU, NOT REALLY...

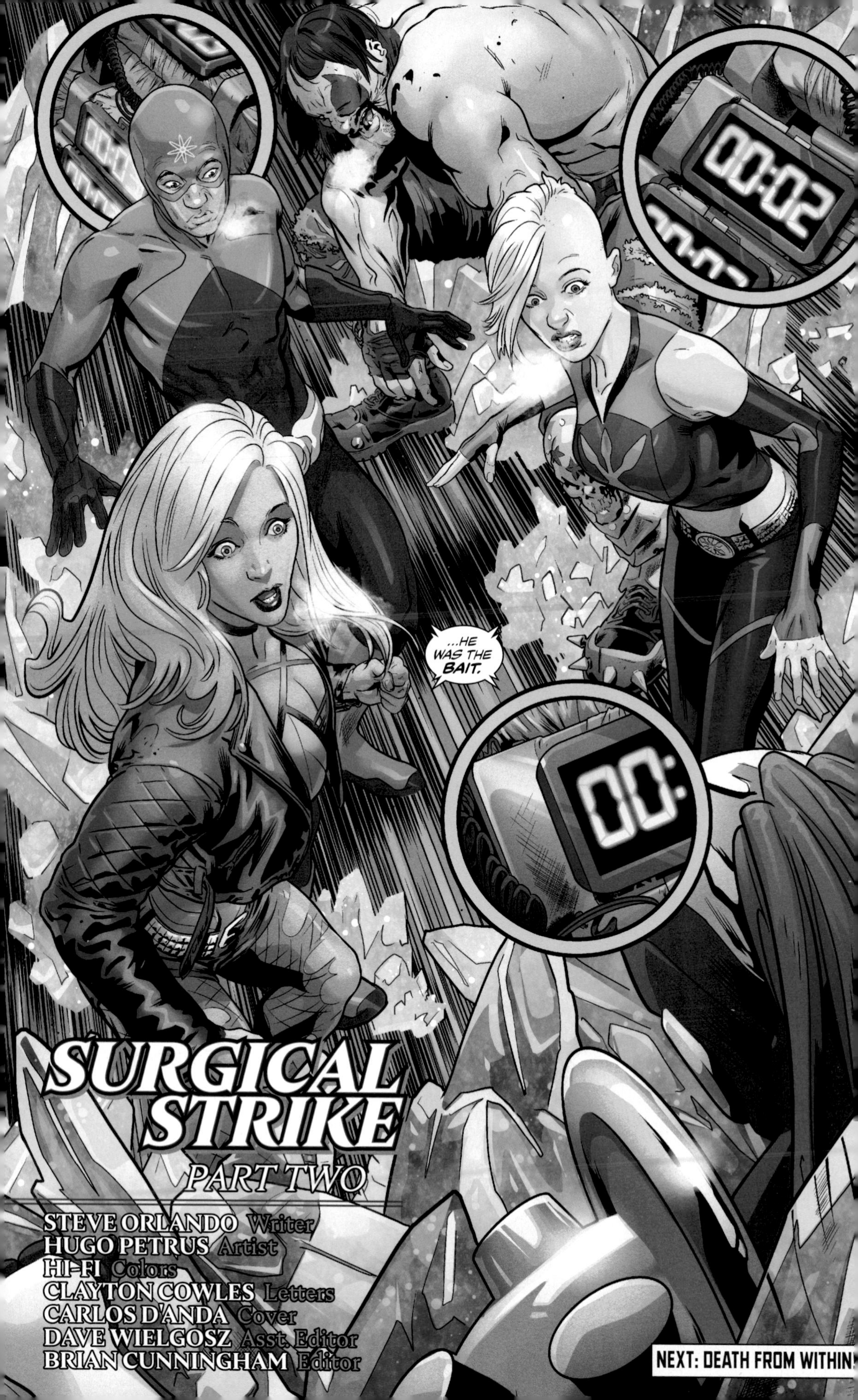
00:02
...HE WAS THE BAIT.
00:
SURGICAL STRIKE
PART TWO
STEVE ORLANDO Writer
HUGO PETRUS Artist
HI-FI Colors
CLAYTON COWLES Letters
CARLOS D'ANDA Cover
DAVE WIELGOSZ Asst. Editor
BRIAN CUNNINGHAM Editor
NEXT: DEATH FROM WITHIN!

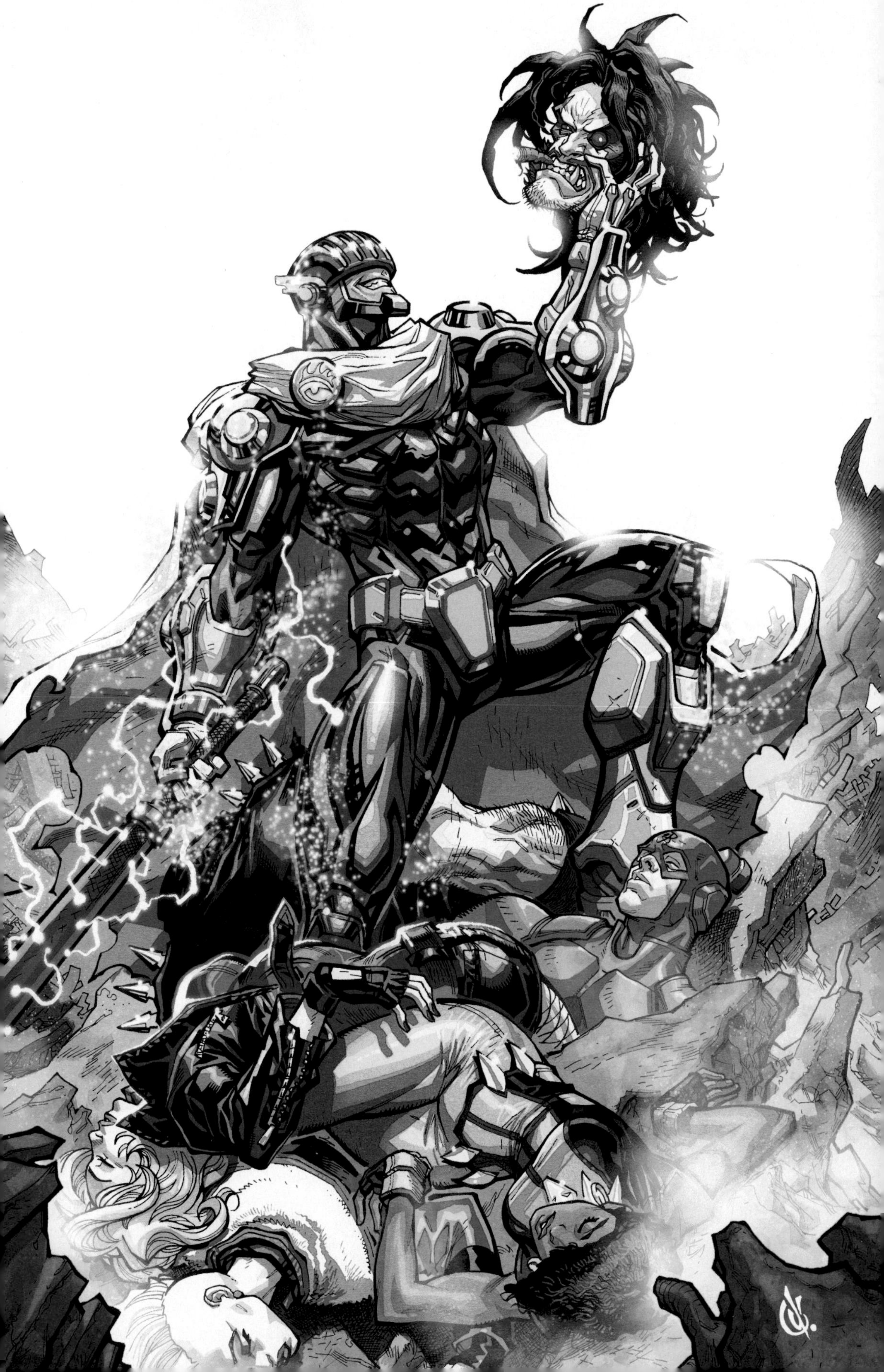

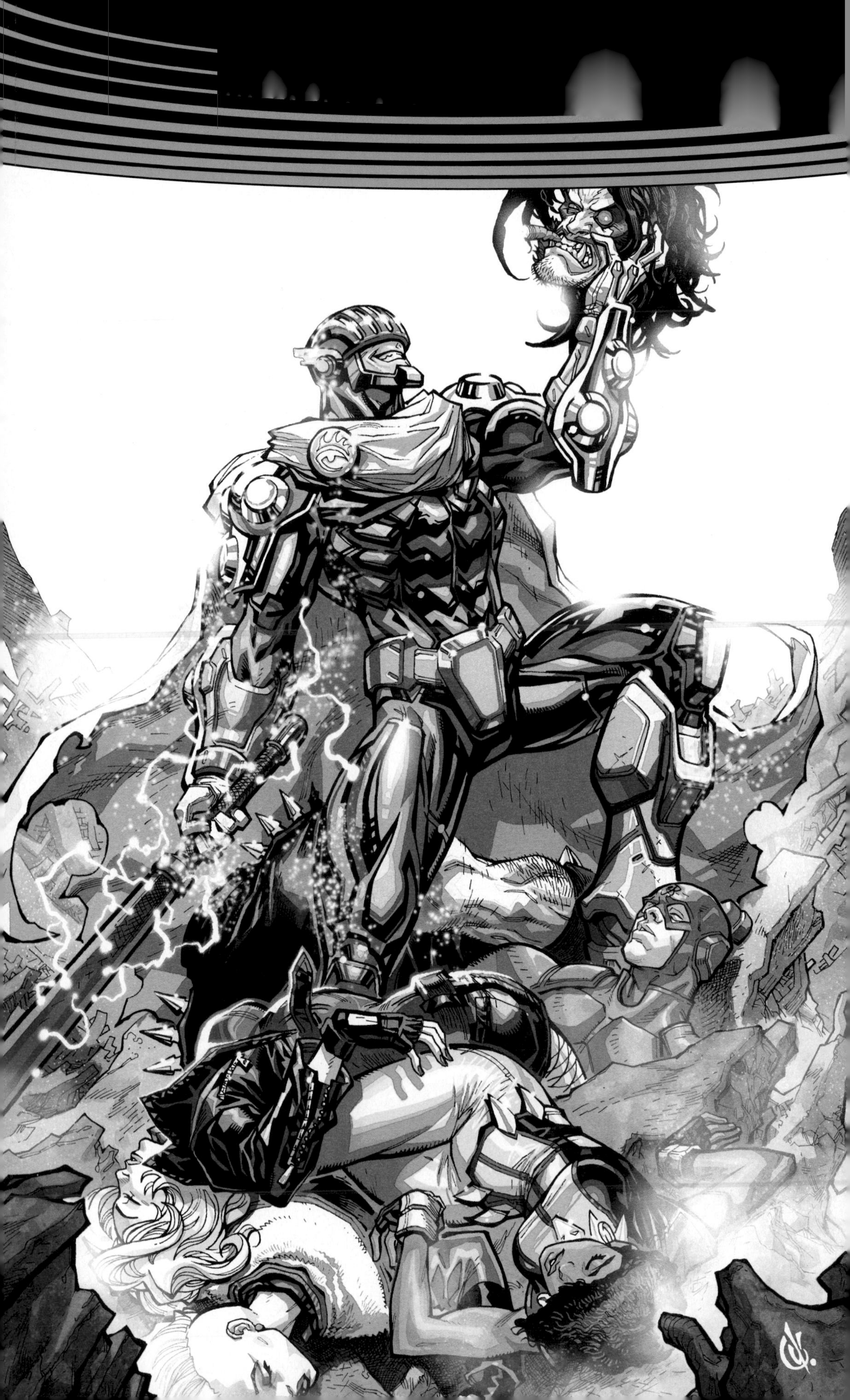

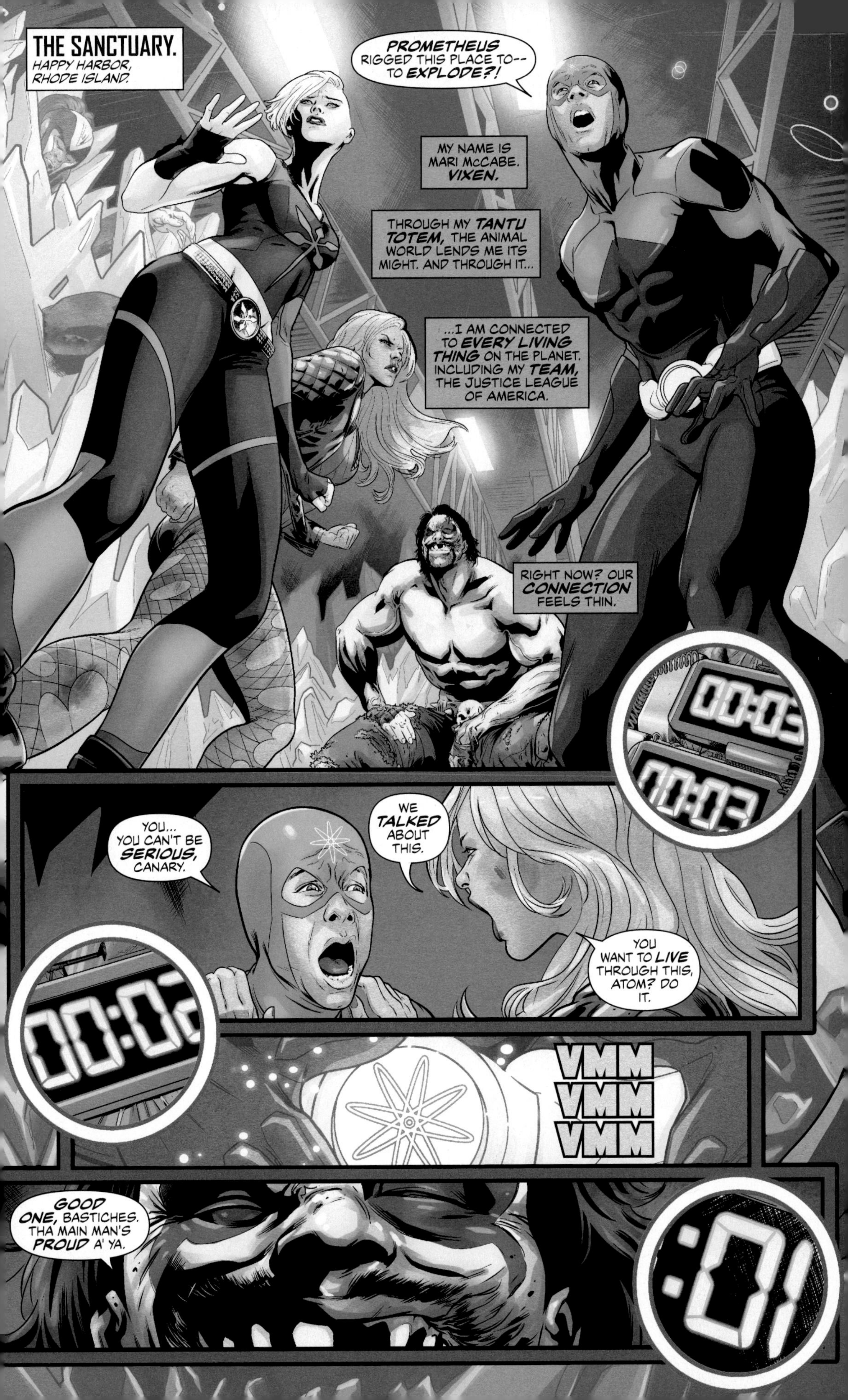
THE SANCTUARY.
HAPPY HARBOR, RHODE ISLAND.
PROMETHEUS RIGGED THIS PLACE TO-- TO EXPLODE?!
MY NAME IS MARI McCABE. VIXEN.
THROUGH MY TANTU TOTEM, THE ANIMAL WORLD LENDS ME ITS MIGHT. AND THROUGH IT...
...I AM CONNECTED TO EVERY LIVING THING ON THE PLANET. INCLUDING MY TEAM, THE JUSTICE LEAGUE OF AMERICA.
RIGHT NOW? OUR CONNECTION FEELS THIN.
00:03
00:03
YOU... YOU CAN'T BE SERIOUS, CANARY.
WE TALKED ABOUT THIS.
YOU WANT TO LIVE THROUGH THIS, ATOM? DO IT.
00:02
VMM VMM VMM
GOOD ONE, BASTICHES. THA MAIN MAN'S PROUD A' YA.
:01

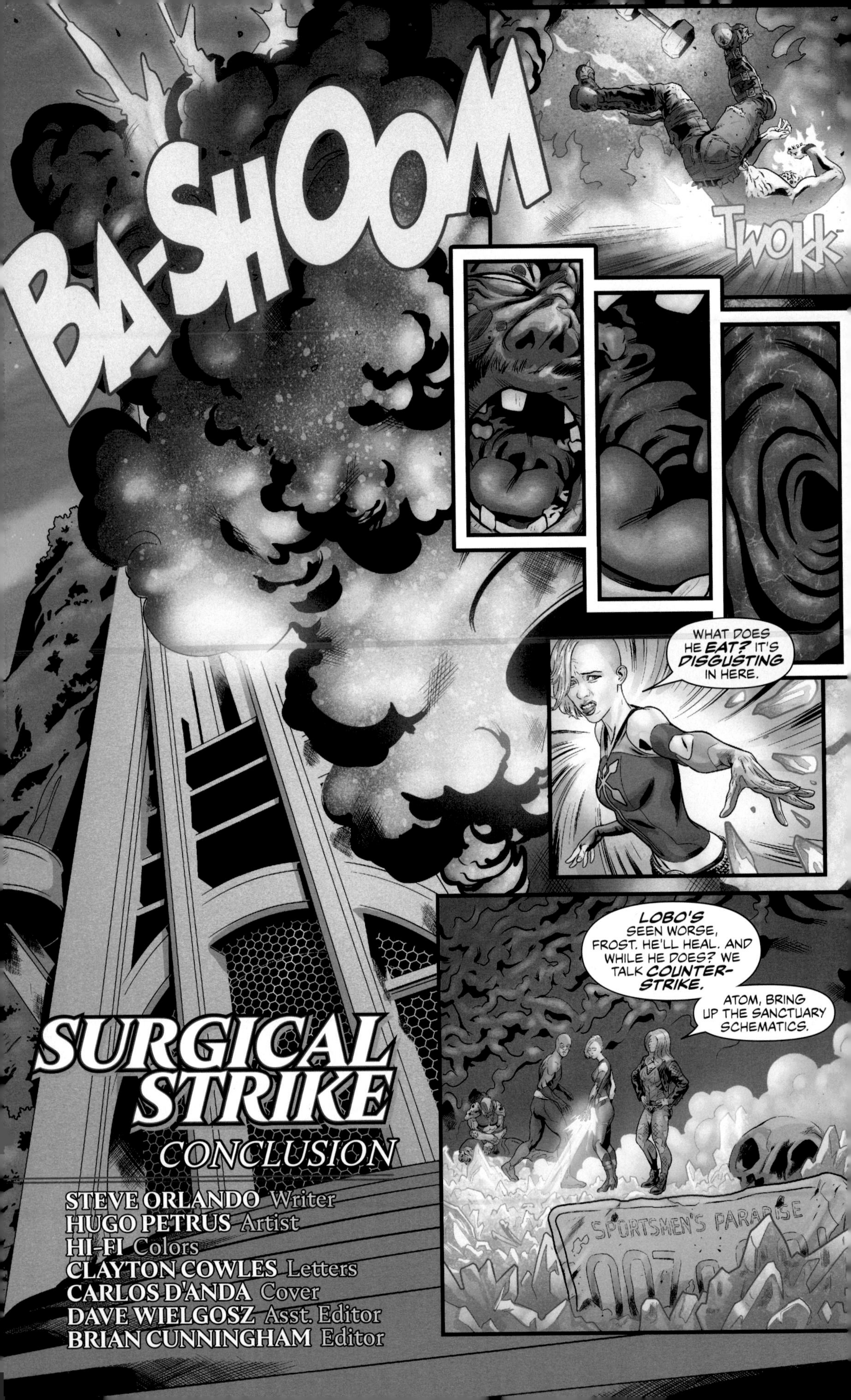
BA-SHOOM
TWOKK
WHAT DOES HE EAT? IT'S DISGUSTING IN HERE.
LOBO'S SEEN WORSE, FROST. HE'LL HEAL. AND WHILE HE DOES? WE TALK COUNTER-STRIKE.
ATOM, BRING UP THE SANCTUARY SCHEMATICS.
SPORTSMEN'S PARADISE
SURGICAL STRIKE
CONCLUSION
STEVE ORLANDO Writer
HUGO PETRUS Artist
HI-FI Colors
CLAYTON COWLES Letters
CARLOS D'ANDA Cover
DAVE WIELGOSZ Asst. Editor
BRIAN CUNNINGHAM Editor

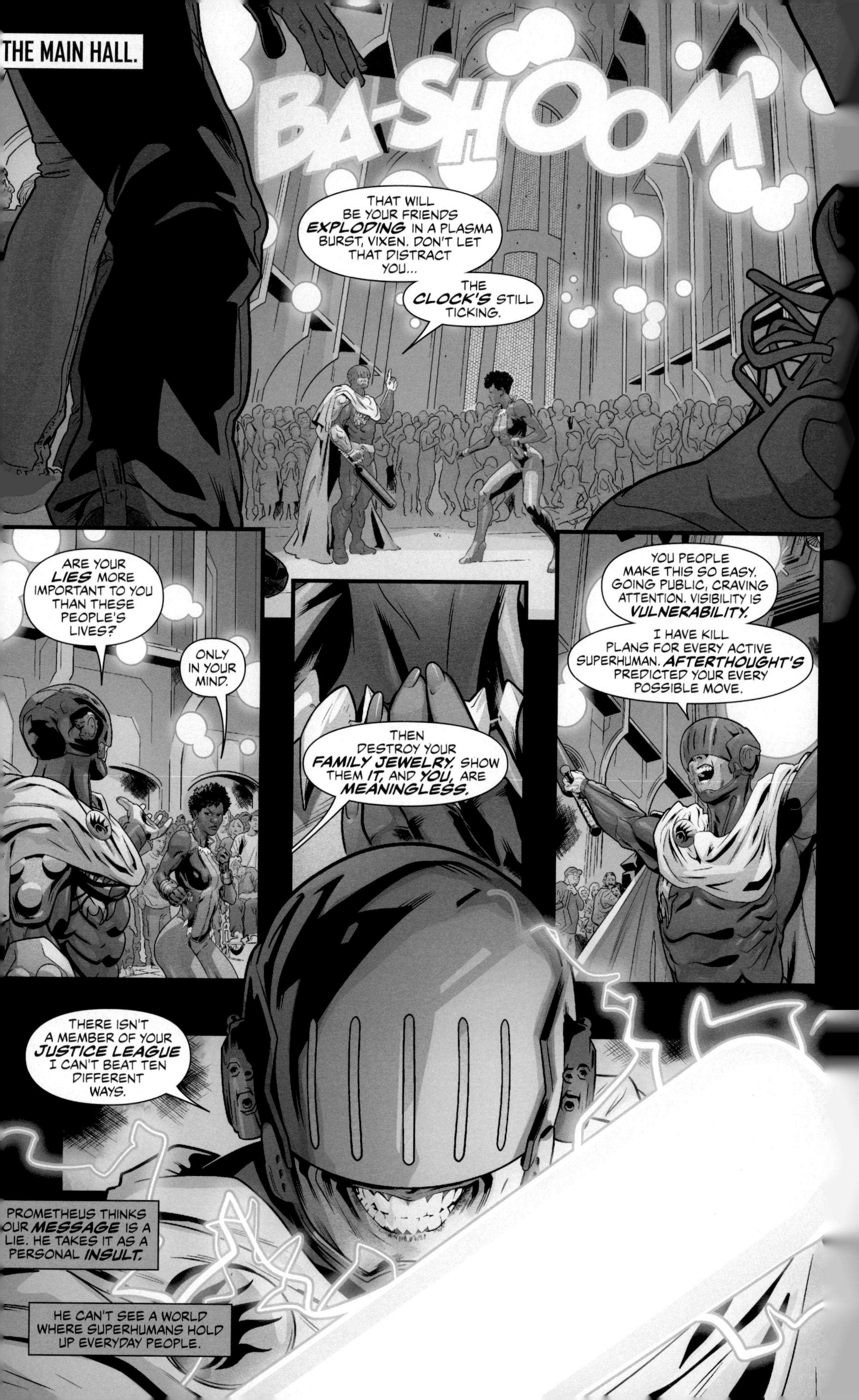
THE MAIN HALL.
BA-SHOOM
THAT WILL BE YOUR FRIENDS EXPLODING IN A PLASMA BURST, VIXEN. DON'T LET THAT DISTRACT YOU...
THE CLOCK'S STILL TICKING.
ARE YOUR LIES MORE IMPORTANT TO YOU THAN THESE PEOPLE'S LIVES?
ONLY IN YOUR MIND.
THEN DESTROY YOUR FAMILY JEWELRY. SHOW THEM IT, AND YOU, ARE MEANINGLESS.
YOU PEOPLE MAKE THIS SO EASY. GOING PUBLIC, CRAVING ATTENTION. VISIBILITY IS VULNERABILITY.
I HAVE KILL PLANS FOR EVERY ACTIVE SUPERHUMAN. AFTERTHOUGHT'S PREDICTED YOUR EVERY POSSIBLE MOVE.
THERE ISN'T A MEMBER OF YOUR JUSTICE LEAGUE I CAN'T BEAT TEN DIFFERENT WAYS.
PROMETHEUS THINKS OUR MESSAGE IS A LIE. HE TAKES IT AS A PERSONAL INSULT.
HE CAN'T SEE A WORLD WHERE SUPERHUMANS HOLD UP EVERYDAY PEOPLE.

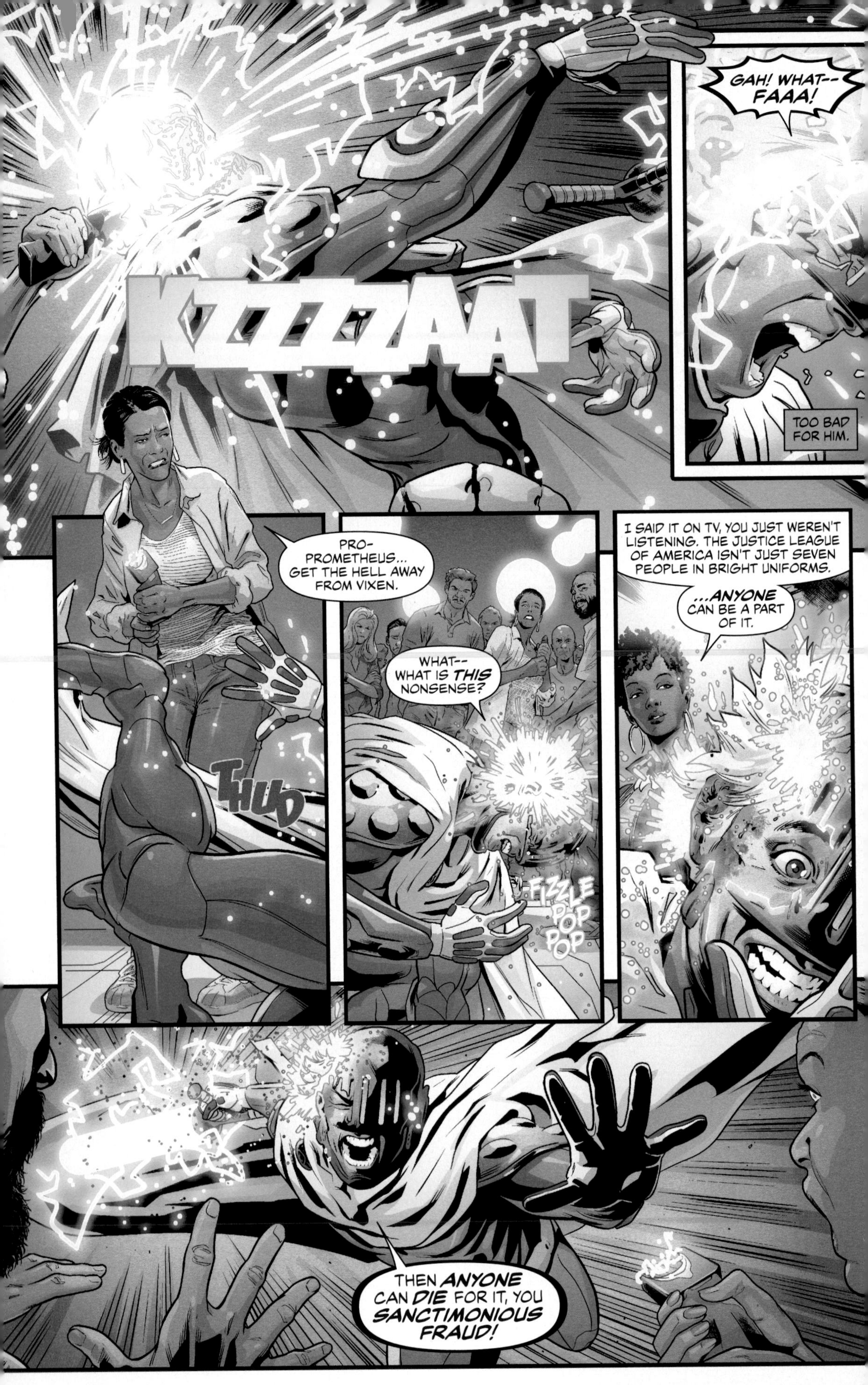
KZZZZAAT
GAH! WHAT--
FAAA!
TOO BAD FOR HIM.
PRO-
PROMETHEUS...
GET THE HELL AWAY
FROM VIXEN.
THUD
WHAT--
WHAT IS THIS
NONSENSE?
FIZZLE
POP
POP
I SAID IT ON TV, YOU JUST WEREN'T LISTENING. THE JUSTICE LEAGUE OF AMERICA ISN'T JUST SEVEN PEOPLE IN BRIGHT UNIFORMS.
...ANYONE CAN BE A PART OF IT.
THEN ANYONE CAN DIE FOR IT, YOU SANCTIMONIOUS FRAUD!

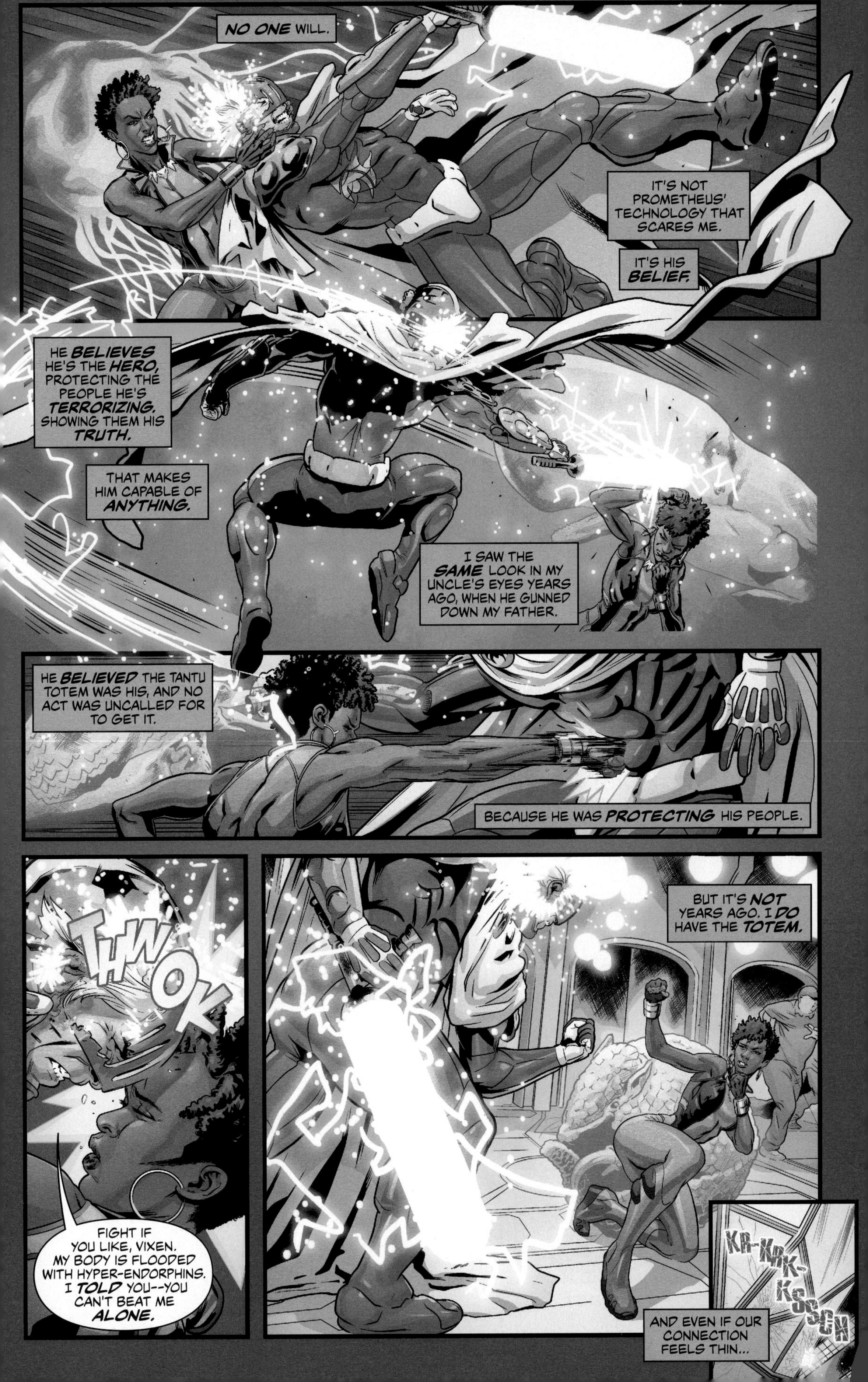
NO ONE WILL.
IT'S NOT PROMETHEUS' TECHNOLOGY THAT SCARES ME.
IT'S HIS BELIEF.
HE BELIEVES HE'S THE HERO, PROTECTING THE PEOPLE HE'S TERRORIZING, SHOWING THEM HIS TRUTH.
THAT MAKES HIM CAPABLE OF ANYTHING.
I SAW THE SAME LOOK IN MY UNCLE'S EYES YEARS AGO, WHEN HE GUNNED DOWN MY FATHER.
HE BELIEVED THE TANTU TOTEM WAS HIS, AND NO ACT WAS UNCALLED FOR TO GET IT.
BECAUSE HE WAS PROTECTING HIS PEOPLE.
THWOK
FIGHT IF YOU LIKE, VIXEN. MY BODY IS FLOODED WITH HYPER-ENDORPHINS. I TOLD YOU--YOU CAN'T BEAT ME ALONE.
BUT IT'S NOT YEARS AGO. I DO HAVE THE TOTEM.
KR-KRK-KSSCH
AND EVEN IF OUR CONNECTION FEELS THIN...

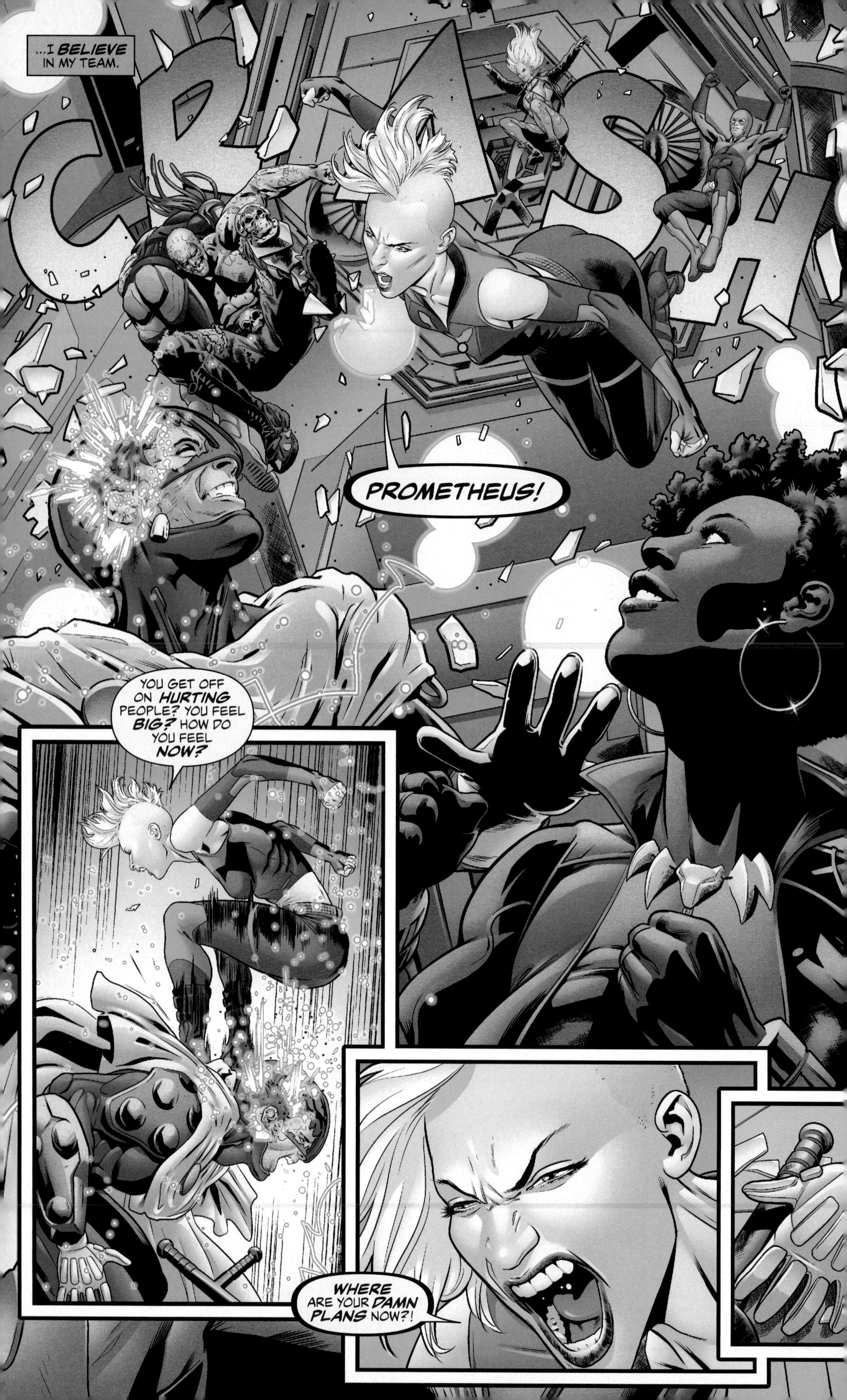
...I BELIEVE IN MY TEAM.
CRASH
PROMETHEUS!
YOU GET OFF ON HURTING PEOPLE? YOU FEEL BIG? HOW DO YOU FEEL NOW?
WHERE ARE YOUR DAMN PLANS NOW?!

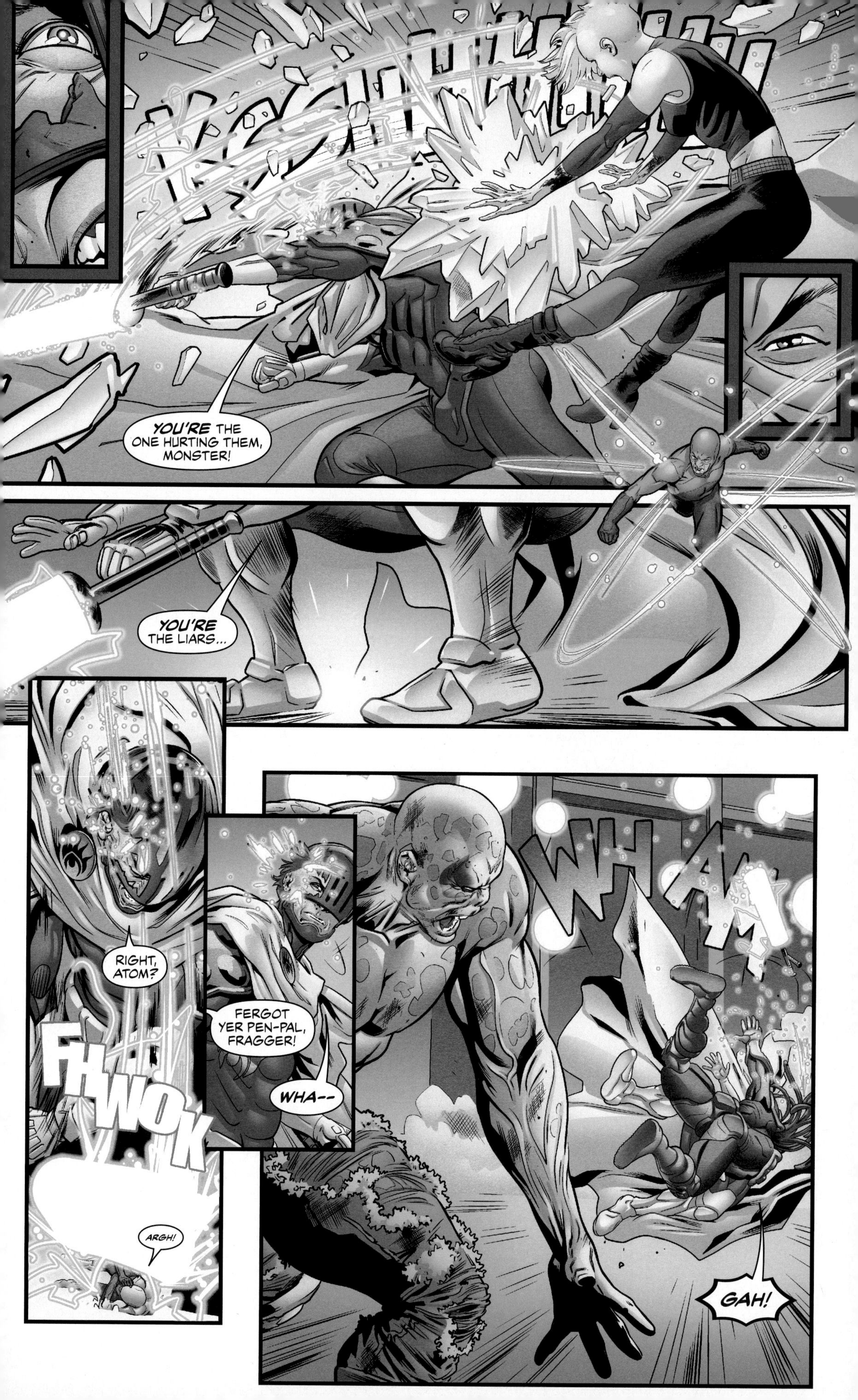
YOU'RE THE ONE HURTING THEM, MONSTER!
YOU'RE THE LIARS...
RIGHT, ATOM?
FHWOK
ARGH!
FERGOT YER PEN-PAL, FRAGGER!
WHA--
WHAM
GAH!

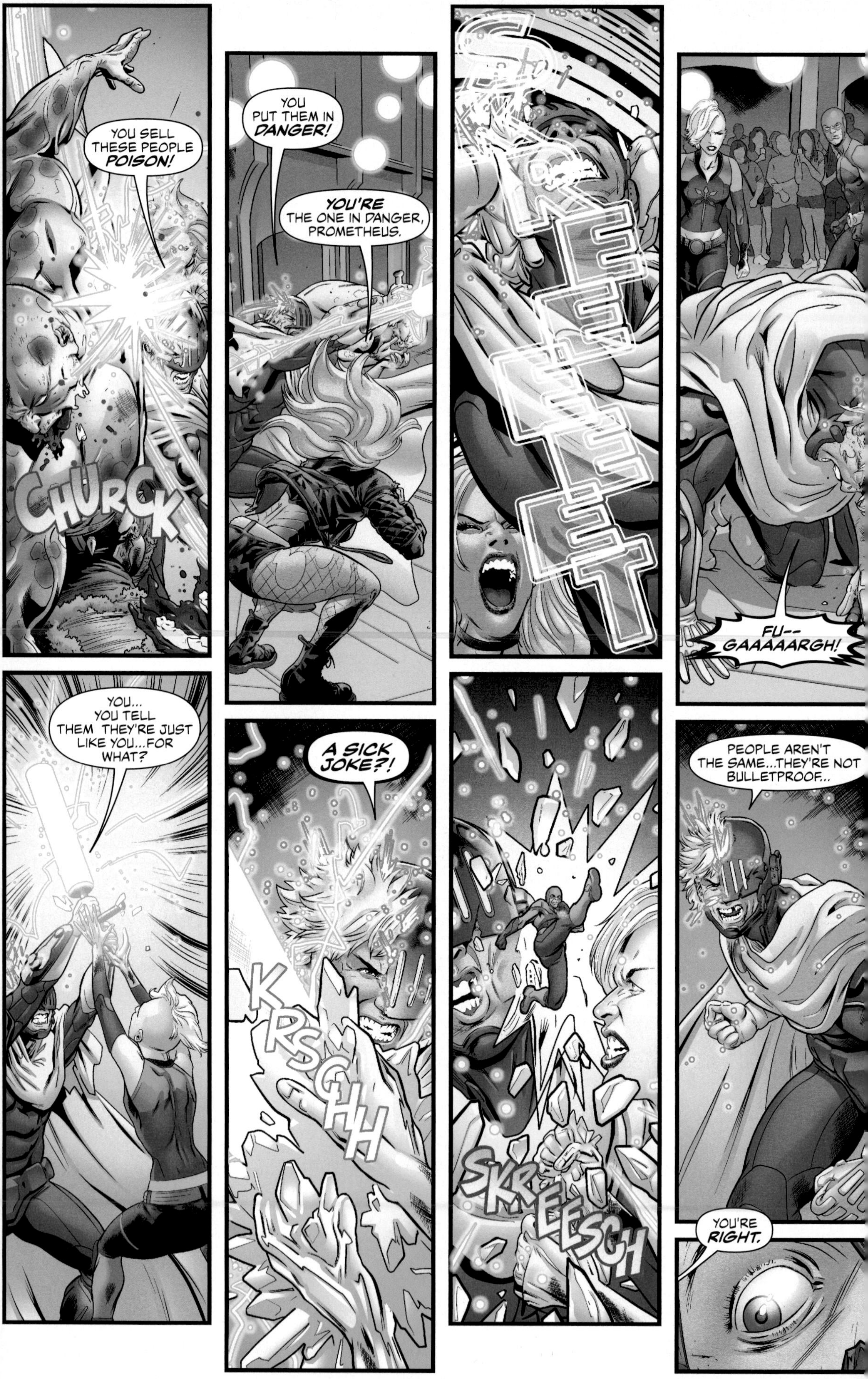
YOU SELL THESE PEOPLE POISON!
CHURCK
YOU PUT THEM IN DANGER!
YOU'RE THE ONE IN DANGER, PROMETHEUS.
FU-- GAAAAARGH!
YOU... YOU TELL THEM THEY'RE JUST LIKE YOU...FOR WHAT?
A SICK JOKE?!
KRSCHH
SKREESCH
PEOPLE AREN'T THE SAME...THEY'RE NOT BULLETPROOF...
YOU'RE RIGHT.

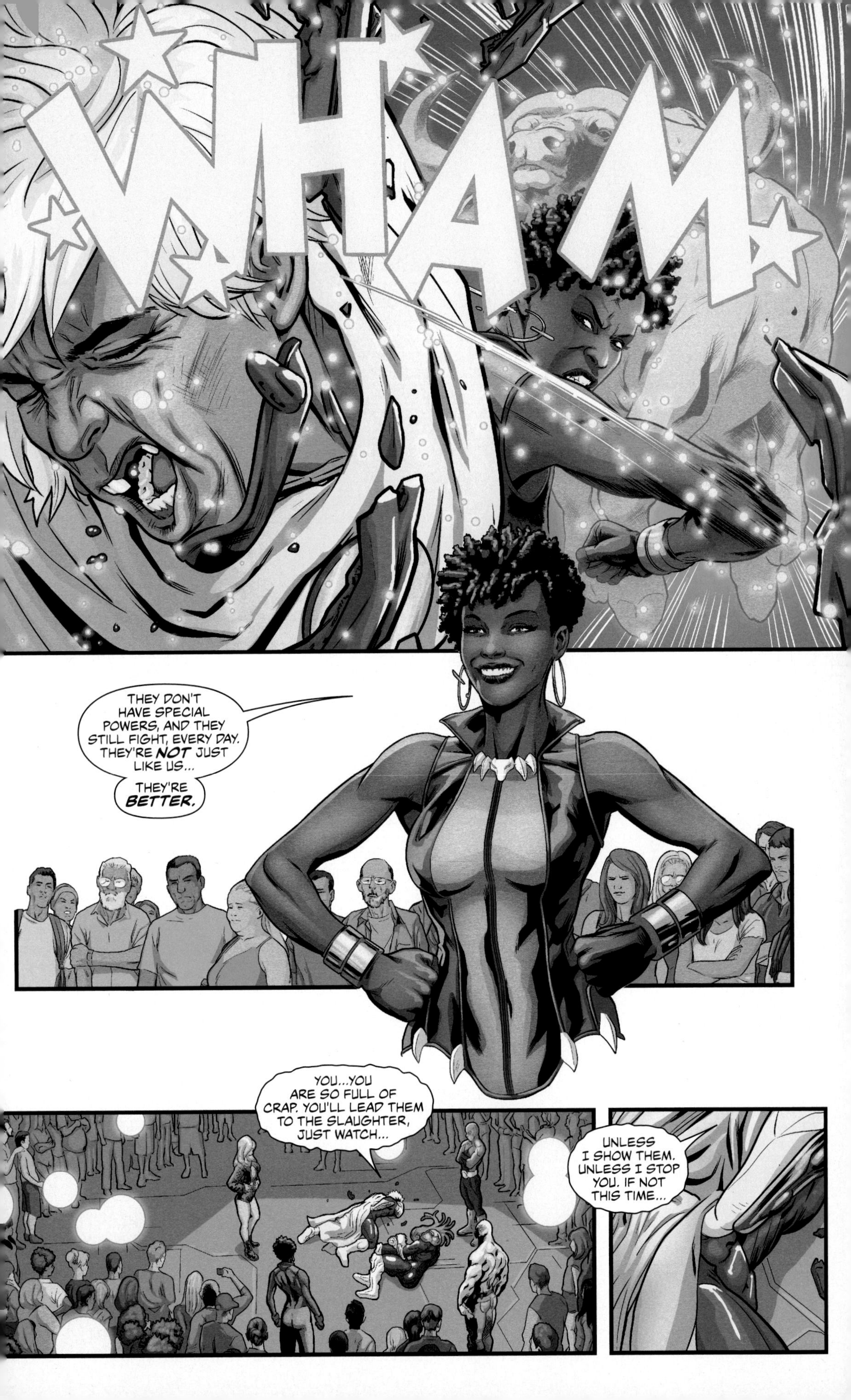
WHAM
THEY DON'T HAVE SPECIAL POWERS, AND THEY STILL FIGHT, EVERY DAY. THEY'RE NOT JUST LIKE US...
THEY'RE BETTER.
YOU...YOU ARE SO FULL OF CRAP. YOU'LL LEAD THEM TO THE SLAUGHTER, JUST WATCH...
UNLESS I SHOW THEM. UNLESS I STOP YOU. IF NOT THIS TIME...

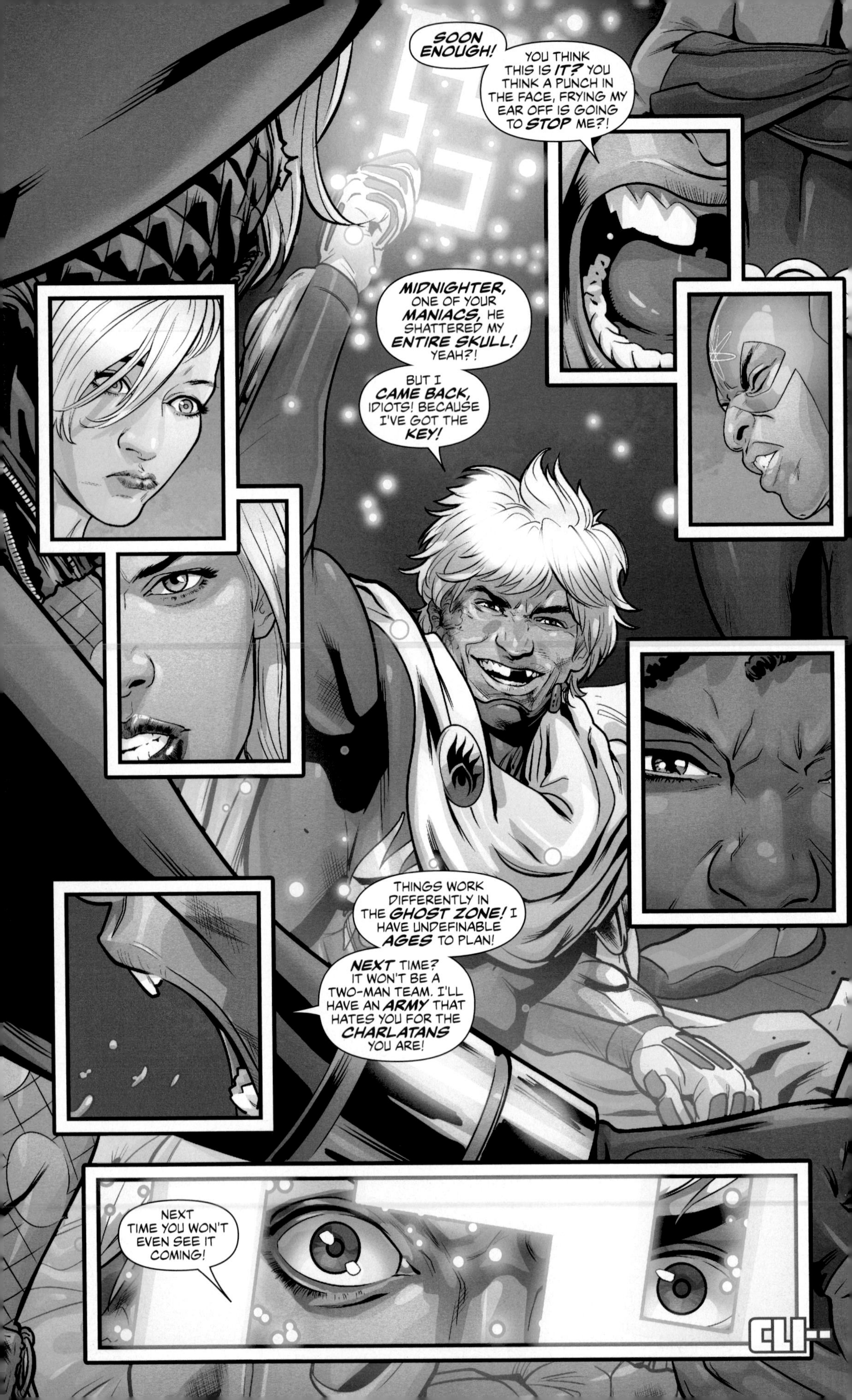
SOON ENOUGH!
YOU THINK THIS IS IT? YOU THINK A PUNCH IN THE FACE, FRYING MY EAR OFF IS GOING TO STOP ME?!
MIDNIGHTER, ONE OF YOUR MANIACS, HE SHATTERED MY ENTIRE SKULL! YEAH?!
BUT I CAME BACK, IDIOTS! BECAUSE I'VE GOT THE KEY!
THINGS WORK DIFFERENTLY IN THE GHOST ZONE! I HAVE UNDEFINABLE AGES TO PLAN!
NEXT TIME? IT WON'T BE A TWO-MAN TEAM. I'LL HAVE AN ARMY THAT HATES YOU FOR THE CHARLATANS YOU ARE!
NEXT TIME YOU WON'T EVEN SEE IT COMING!
CLI--

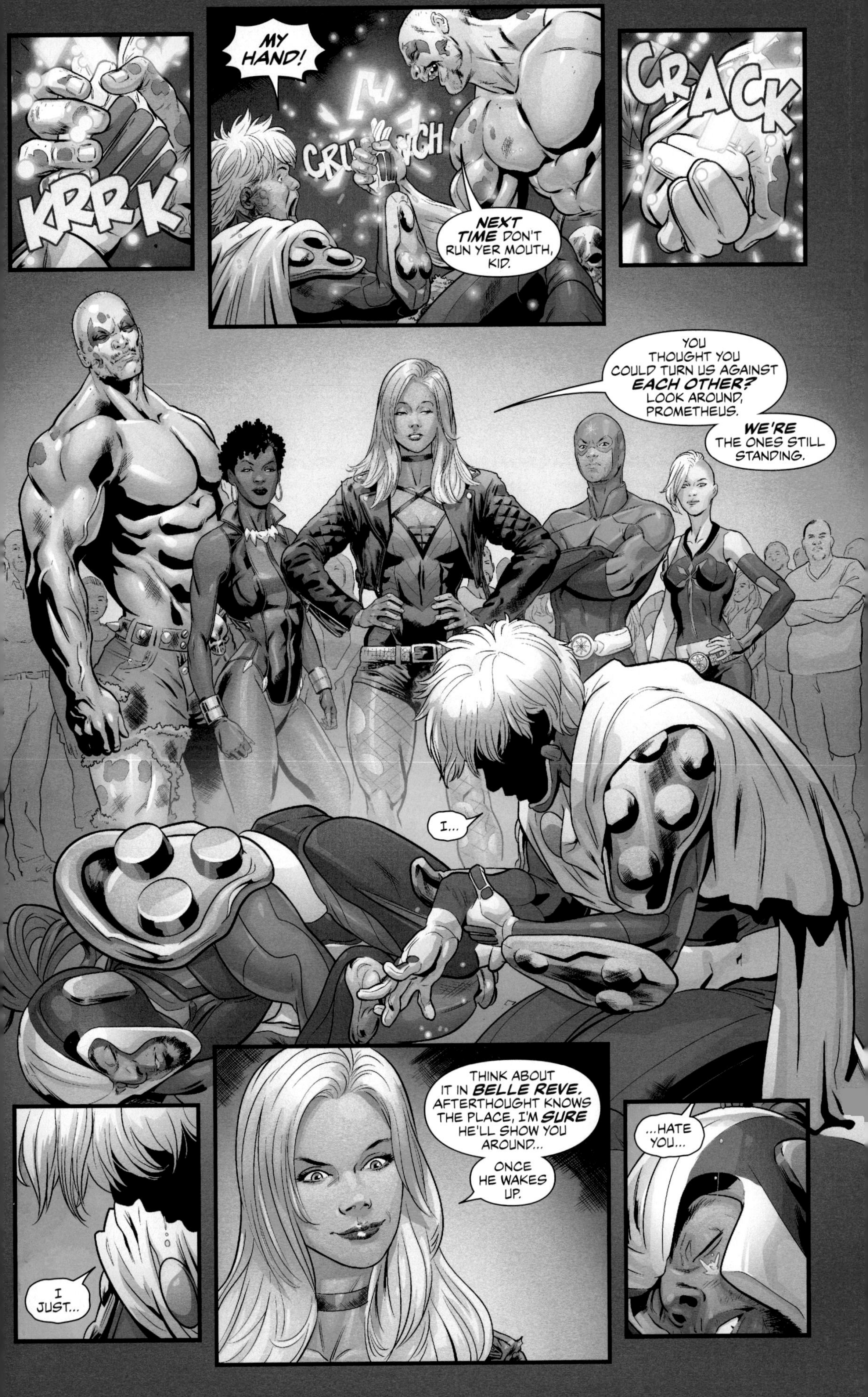
KRRK
MY HAND!
CRUNCH
NEXT TIME DON'T RUN YER MOUTH, KID.
CRACK
YOU THOUGHT YOU COULD TURN US AGAINST EACH OTHER? LOOK AROUND, PROMETHEUS.
WE'RE THE ONES STILL STANDING.
I...
I JUST...
THINK ABOUT IT IN BELLE REVE. AFTERTHOUGHT KNOWS THE PLACE, I'M SURE HE'LL SHOW YOU AROUND...
ONCE HE WAKES UP.
...HATE YOU...

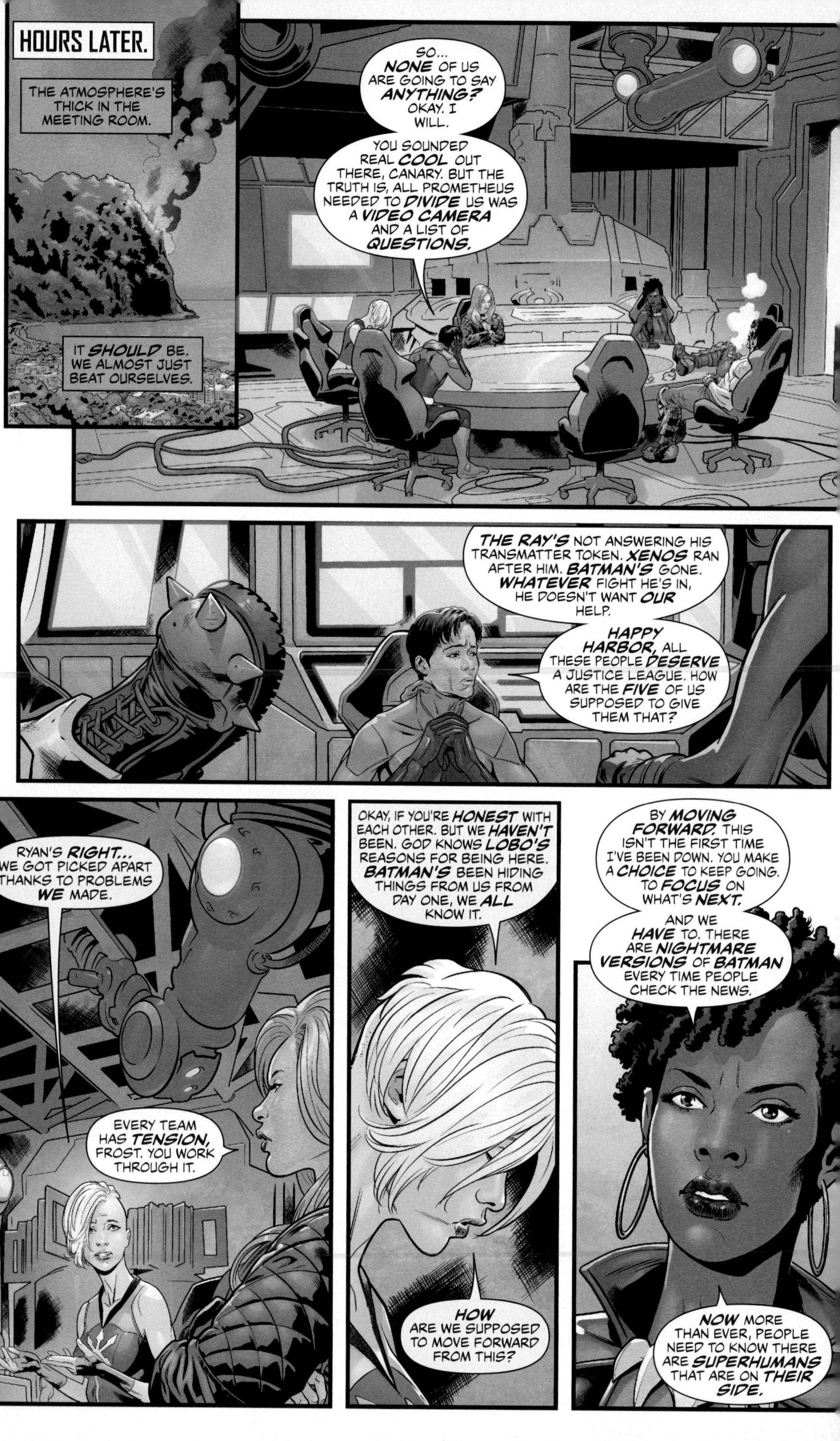
HOURS LATER.
THE ATMOSPHERE'S THICK IN THE MEETING ROOM.
IT SHOULD BE. WE ALMOST JUST BEAT OURSELVES.
SO... NONE OF US ARE GOING TO SAY ANYTHING? OKAY. I WILL.
YOU SOUNDED REAL COOL OUT THERE, CANARY. BUT THE TRUTH IS, ALL PROMETHEUS NEEDED TO DIVIDE US WAS A VIDEO CAMERA AND A LIST OF QUESTIONS.
THE RAY'S NOT ANSWERING HIS TRANSMATTER TOKEN. XENOS RAN AFTER HIM. BATMAN'S GONE. WHATEVER FIGHT HE'S IN, HE DOESN'T WANT OUR HELP.
HAPPY HARBOR, ALL THESE PEOPLE DESERVE A JUSTICE LEAGUE. HOW ARE THE FIVE OF US SUPPOSED TO GIVE THEM THAT?
RYAN'S RIGHT... WE GOT PICKED APART THANKS TO PROBLEMS WE MADE.
EVERY TEAM HAS TENSION, FROST. YOU WORK THROUGH IT.
OKAY, IF YOU'RE HONEST WITH EACH OTHER. BUT WE HAVEN'T BEEN. GOD KNOWS LOBO'S REASONS FOR BEING HERE. BATMAN'S BEEN HIDING THINGS FROM US FROM DAY ONE, WE ALL KNOW IT.
HOW ARE WE SUPPOSED TO MOVE FORWARD FROM THIS?
BY MOVING FORWARD. THIS ISN'T THE FIRST TIME I'VE BEEN DOWN. YOU MAKE A CHOICE TO KEEP GOING. TO FOCUS ON WHAT'S NEXT.
AND WE HAVE TO. THERE ARE NIGHTMARE VERSIONS OF BATMAN EVERY TIME PEOPLE CHECK THE NEWS.
NOW MORE THAN EVER, PEOPLE NEED TO KNOW THERE ARE SUPERHUMANS THAT ARE ON THEIR SIDE.

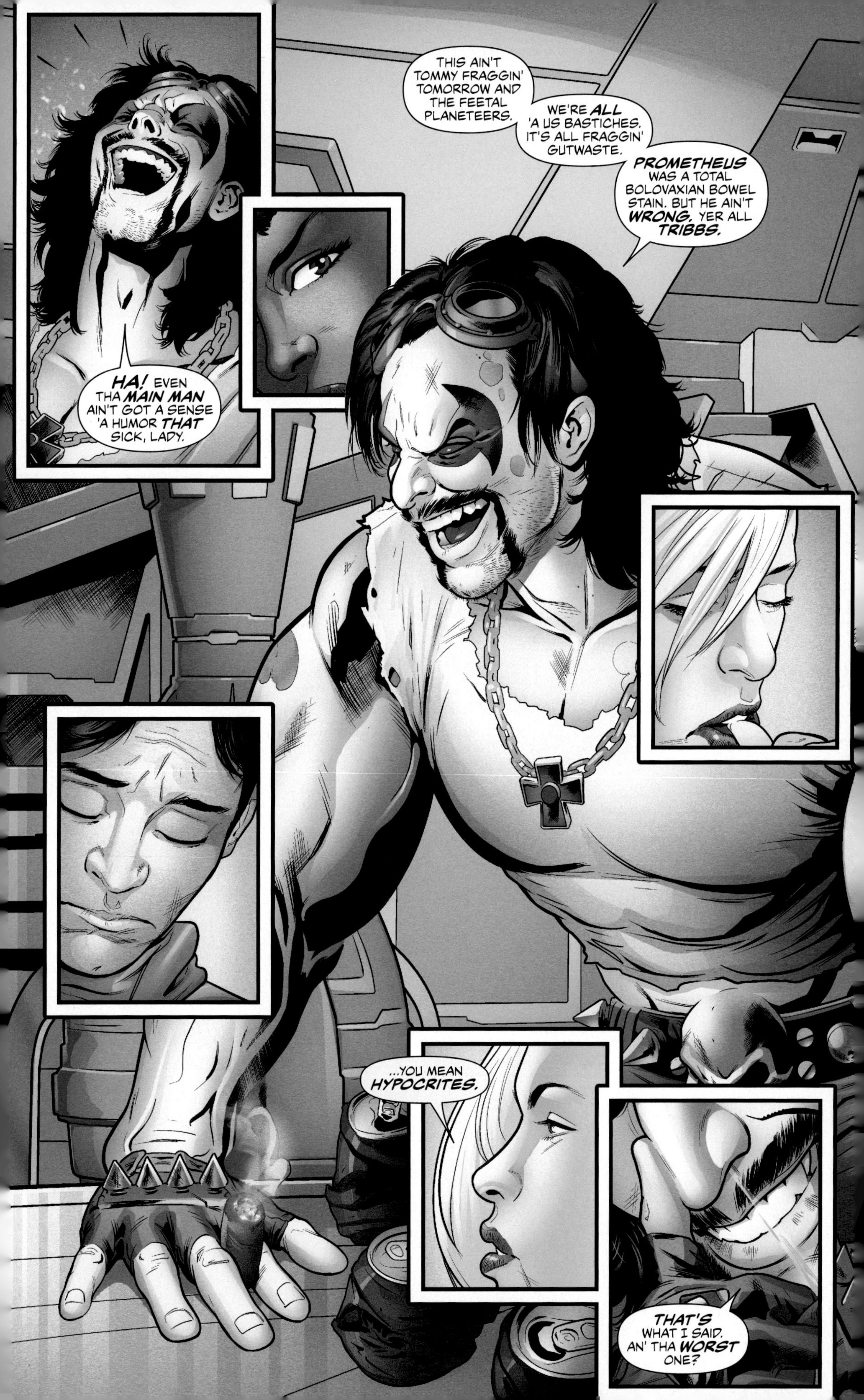
HA! EVEN THA MAIN MAN AIN'T GOT A SENSE 'A HUMOR THAT SICK, LADY.
THIS AIN'T TOMMY FRAGGIN' TOMORROW AND THE FEETAL PLANETEERS.
WE'RE ALL 'A US BASTICHES. IT'S ALL FRAGGIN' GUTWASTE.
PROMETHEUS WAS A TOTAL BOLOVAXIAN BOWEL STAIN. BUT HE AIN'T WRONG. YER ALL TRIBBS.
...YOU MEAN HYPOCRITES.
THAT'S WHAT I SAID. AN' THA WORST ONE?

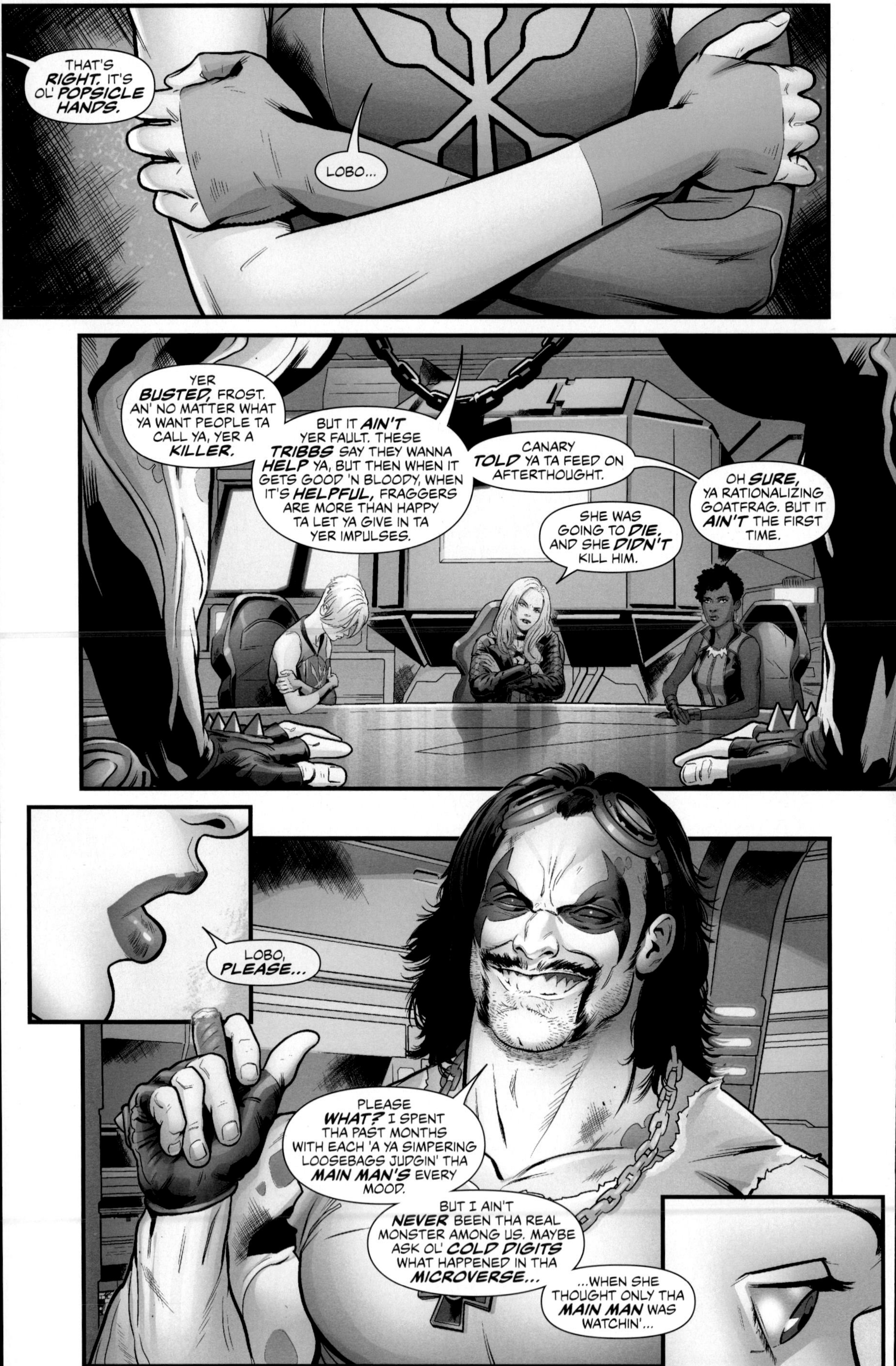
THAT'S RIGHT. IT'S OL' POPSICLE HANDS.
LOBO...
YER BUSTED, FROST. AN' NO MATTER WHAT YA WANT PEOPLE TA CALL YA, YER A KILLER.
BUT IT AIN'T YER FAULT. THESE TRIBBS SAY THEY WANNA HELP YA, BUT THEN WHEN IT GETS GOOD 'N BLOODY, WHEN IT'S HELPFUL, FRAGGERS ARE MORE THAN HAPPY TA LET YA GIVE IN TA YER IMPULSES.
CANARY TOLD YA TA FEED ON AFTERTHOUGHT.
SHE WAS GOING TO DIE, AND SHE DIDN'T KILL HIM.
OH SURE, YA RATIONALIZING GOATFRAG. BUT IT AIN'T THE FIRST TIME.
LOBO, PLEASE...
PLEASE WHAT? I SPENT THA PAST MONTHS WITH EACH 'A YA SIMPERING LOOSEBAGS JUDGIN' THA MAIN MAN'S EVERY MOOD.
BUT I AIN'T NEVER BEEN THA REAL MONSTER AMONG US. MAYBE ASK OL' COLD DIGITS WHAT HAPPENED IN THA MICROVERSE...
...WHEN SHE THOUGHT ONLY THA MAIN MAN WAS WATCHIN'...

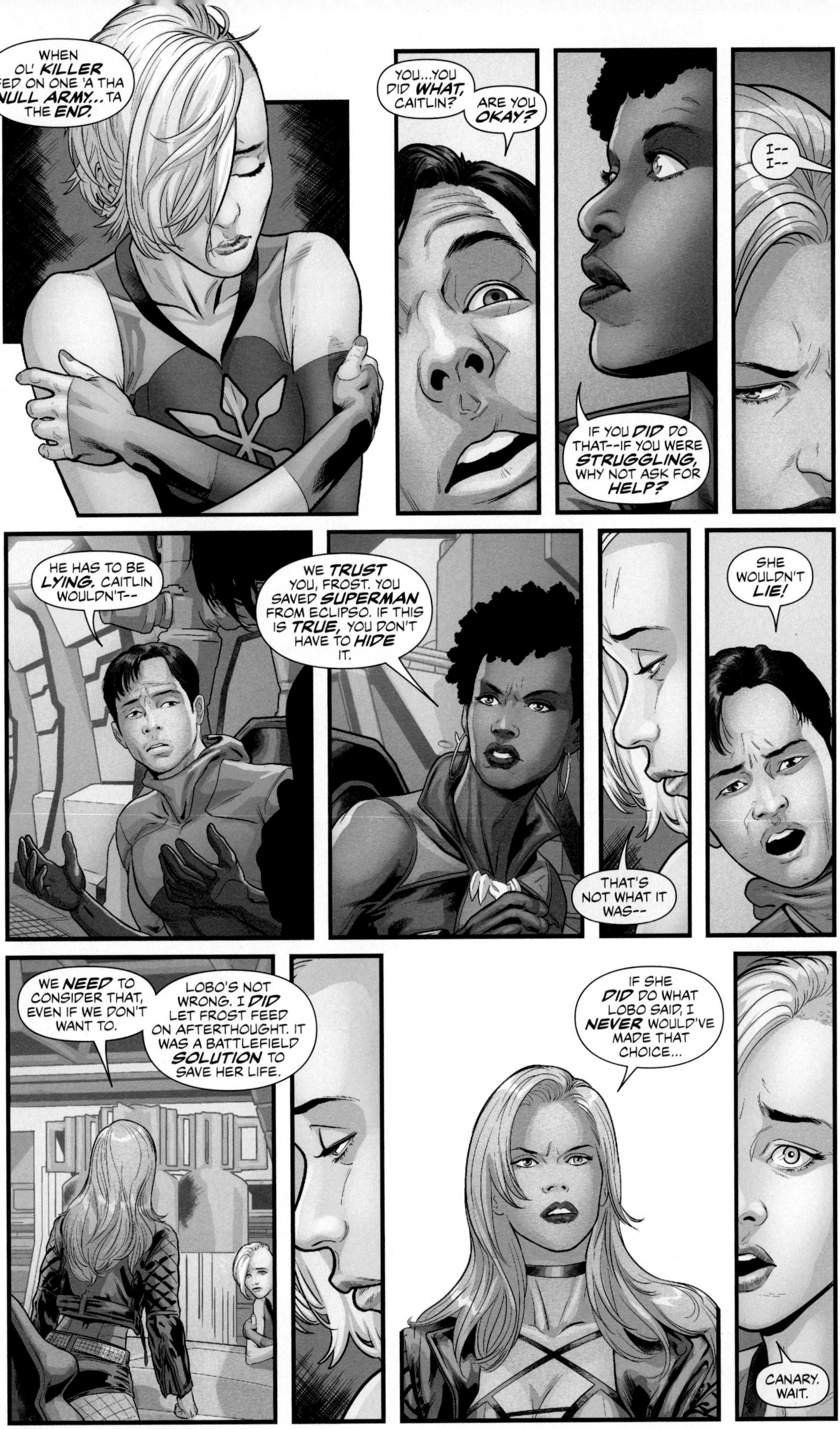
WHEN OL' KILLER FED ON ONE 'A THA NULL ARMY... TA THE END.
YOU...YOU DID WHAT, CAITLIN?
ARE YOU OKAY?
IF YOU DID DO THAT--IF YOU WERE STRUGGLING, WHY NOT ASK FOR HELP?
I-- I--
HE HAS TO BE LYING. CAITLIN WOULDN'T--
WE TRUST YOU, FROST. YOU SAVED SUPERMAN FROM ECLIPSO. IF THIS IS TRUE, YOU DON'T HAVE TO HIDE IT.
THAT'S NOT WHAT IT WAS--
SHE WOULDN'T LIE!
WE NEED TO CONSIDER THAT, EVEN IF WE DON'T WANT TO.
LOBO'S NOT WRONG. I DID LET FROST FEED ON AFTERTHOUGHT. IT WAS A BATTLEFIELD SOLUTION TO SAVE HER LIFE.
IF SHE DID DO WHAT LOBO SAID, I NEVER WOULD'VE MADE THAT CHOICE...
CANARY. WAIT.

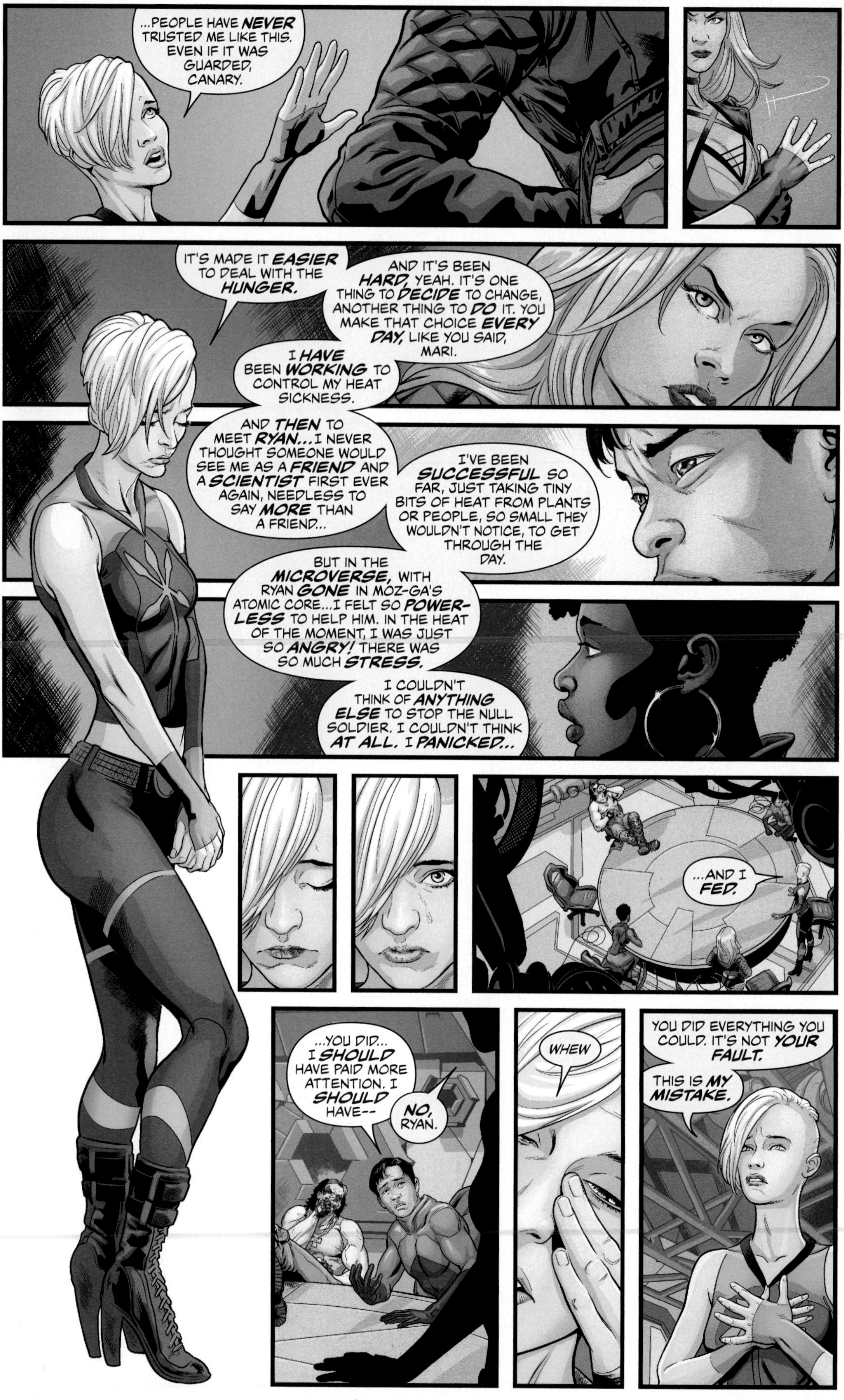
...PEOPLE HAVE NEVER TRUSTED ME LIKE THIS. EVEN IF IT WAS GUARDED, CANARY.
IT'S MADE IT EASIER TO DEAL WITH THE HUNGER.
AND IT'S BEEN HARD, YEAH. IT'S ONE THING TO DECIDE TO CHANGE, ANOTHER THING TO DO IT. YOU MAKE THAT CHOICE EVERY DAY, LIKE YOU SAID, MARI.
I HAVE BEEN WORKING TO CONTROL MY HEAT SICKNESS.
AND THEN TO MEET RYAN...I NEVER THOUGHT SOMEONE WOULD SEE ME AS A FRIEND AND A SCIENTIST FIRST EVER AGAIN, NEEDLESS TO SAY MORE THAN A FRIEND...
I'VE BEEN SUCCESSFUL SO FAR, JUST TAKING TINY BITS OF HEAT FROM PLANTS OR PEOPLE, SO SMALL THEY WOULDN'T NOTICE, TO GET THROUGH THE DAY.
BUT IN THE MICROVERSE, WITH RYAN GONE IN MÓZ-GA'S ATOMIC CORE...I FELT SO POWERLESS TO HELP HIM. IN THE HEAT OF THE MOMENT, I WAS JUST SO ANGRY! THERE WAS SO MUCH STRESS.
I COULDN'T THINK OF ANYTHING ELSE TO STOP THE NULL SOLDIER. I COULDN'T THINK AT ALL. I PANICKED...
...AND I FED.
...YOU DID... I SHOULD HAVE PAID MORE ATTENTION. I SHOULD HAVE--
NO, RYAN.
WHEW
YOU DID EVERYTHING YOU COULD. IT'S NOT YOUR FAULT.
THIS IS MY MISTAKE.

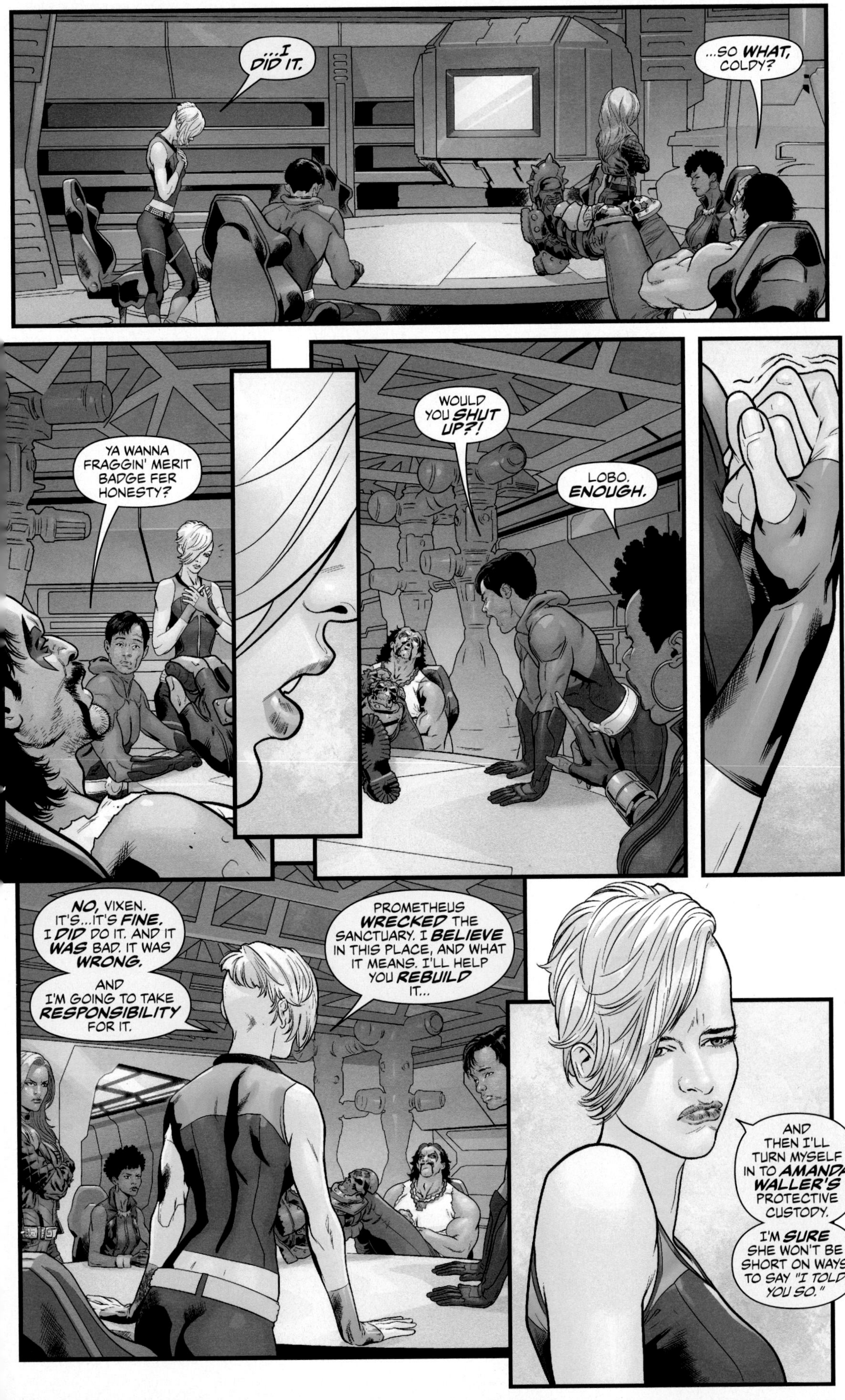
...I DID IT.
...SO WHAT, COLDY?
YA WANNA FRAGGIN' MERIT BADGE FER HONESTY?
WOULD YOU SHUT UP?!
LOBO. ENOUGH.
NO, VIXEN. IT'S...IT'S FINE. I DID DO IT. AND IT WAS BAD. IT WAS WRONG.
AND I'M GOING TO TAKE RESPONSIBILITY FOR IT.
PROMETHEUS WRECKED THE SANCTUARY. I BELIEVE IN THIS PLACE, AND WHAT IT MEANS. I'LL HELP YOU REBUILD IT...
AND THEN I'LL TURN MYSELF IN TO AMANDA WALLER'S PROTECTIVE CUSTODY.
I'M SURE SHE WON'T BE SHORT ON WAYS TO SAY "I TOLD YOU SO."

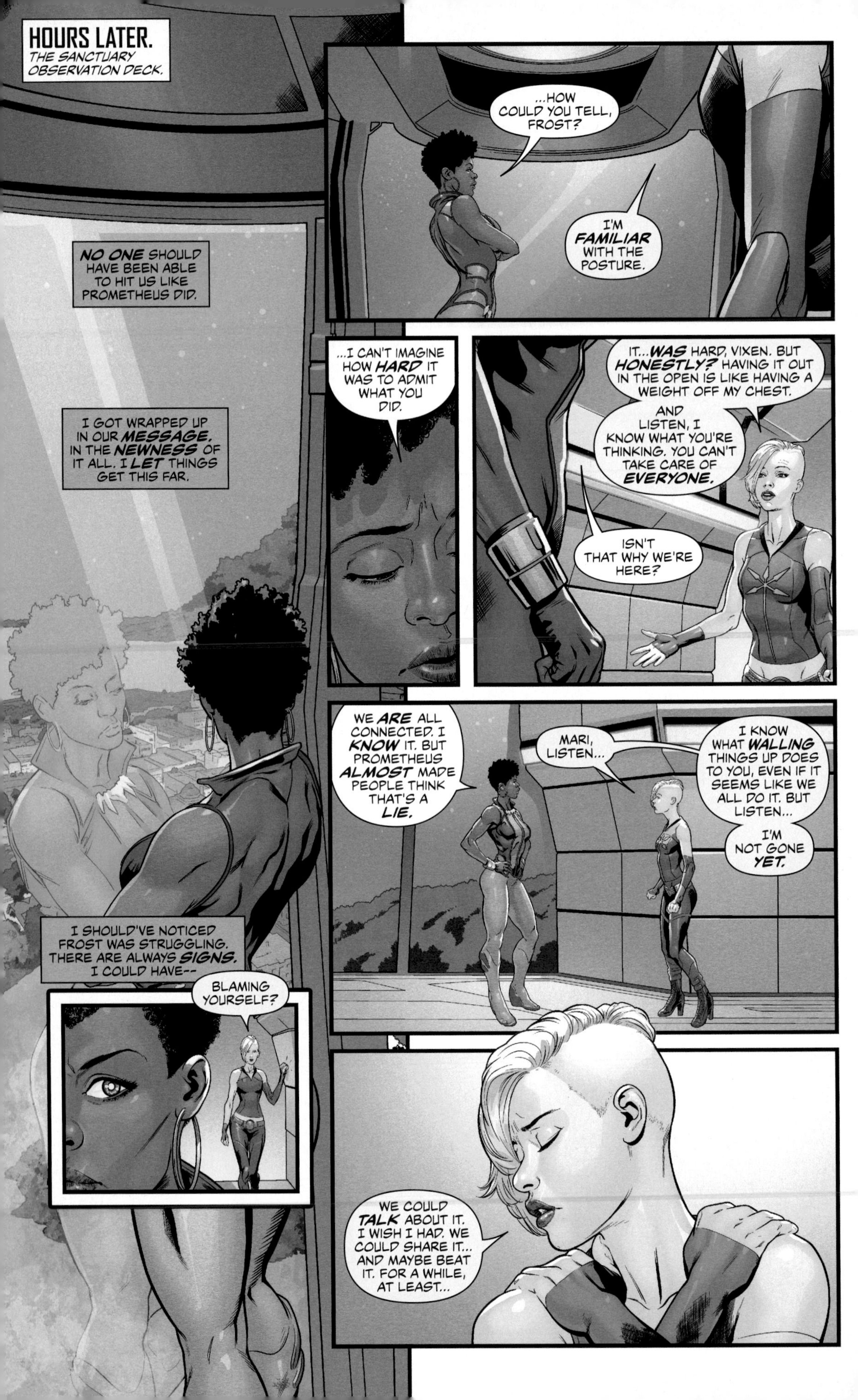
HOURS LATER. THE SANCTUARY OBSERVATION DECK.
...HOW COULD YOU TELL, FROST?
I'M FAMILIAR WITH THE POSTURE.
NO ONE SHOULD HAVE BEEN ABLE TO HIT US LIKE PROMETHEUS DID.
...I CAN'T IMAGINE HOW HARD IT WAS TO ADMIT WHAT YOU DID.
IT...WAS HARD, VIXEN. BUT HONESTLY? HAVING IT OUT IN THE OPEN IS LIKE HAVING A WEIGHT OFF MY CHEST.
AND LISTEN, I KNOW WHAT YOU'RE THINKING. YOU CAN'T TAKE CARE OF EVERYONE.
ISN'T THAT WHY WE'RE HERE?
I GOT WRAPPED UP IN OUR MESSAGE. IN THE NEWNESS OF IT ALL. I LET THINGS GET THIS FAR.
WE ARE ALL CONNECTED. I KNOW IT. BUT PROMETHEUS ALMOST MADE PEOPLE THINK THAT'S A LIE.
MARI, LISTEN...
I KNOW WHAT WALLING THINGS UP DOES TO YOU, EVEN IF IT SEEMS LIKE WE ALL DO IT. BUT LISTEN...
I'M NOT GONE YET.
I SHOULD'VE NOTICED FROST WAS STRUGGLING. THERE ARE ALWAYS SIGNS. I COULD HAVE--
BLAMING YOURSELF?
WE COULD TALK ABOUT IT. I WISH I HAD. WE COULD SHARE IT... AND MAYBE BEAT IT. FOR A WHILE, AT LEAST...

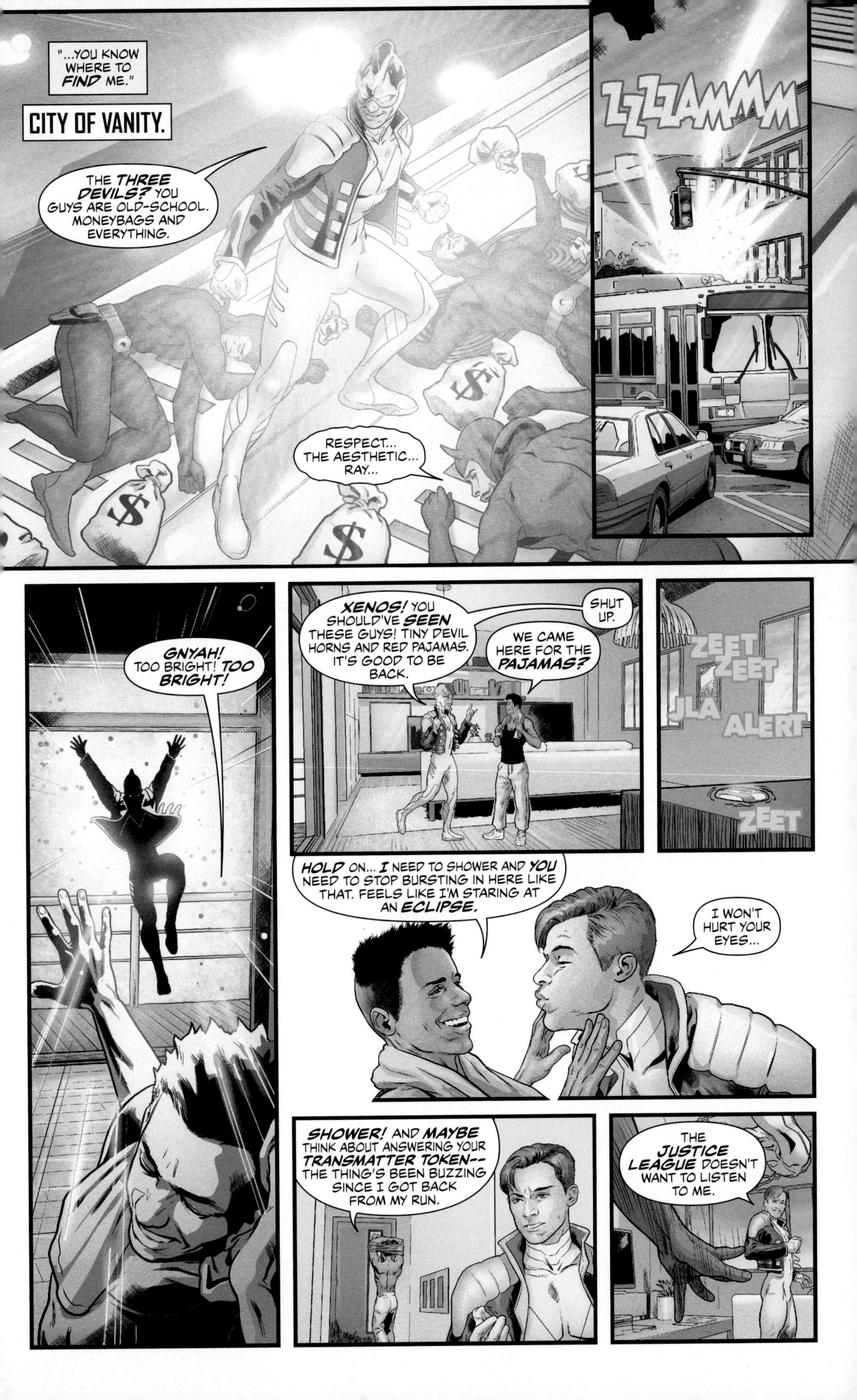
"...YOU KNOW WHERE TO FIND ME."
CITY OF VANITY.
THE THREE DEVILS? YOU GUYS ARE OLD-SCHOOL. MONEYBAGS AND EVERYTHING.
RESPECT... THE AESTHETIC... RAY...
ZZZZAMMM
GNYAH! TOO BRIGHT! TOO BRIGHT!
XENOS! YOU SHOULD'VE SEEN THESE GUYS! TINY DEVIL HORNS AND RED PAJAMAS. IT'S GOOD TO BE BACK.
WE CAME HERE FOR THE PAJAMAS?
SHUT UP.
ZEET ZEET
JLA ALERT
ZEET
HOLD ON... I NEED TO SHOWER AND YOU NEED TO STOP BURSTING IN HERE LIKE THAT. FEELS LIKE I'M STARING AT AN ECLIPSE.
I WON'T HURT YOUR EYES...
SHOWER! AND MAYBE THINK ABOUT ANSWERING YOUR TRANSMATTER TOKEN-- THE THING'S BEEN BUZZING SINCE I GOT BACK FROM MY RUN.
THE JUSTICE LEAGUE DOESN'T WANT TO LISTEN TO ME.

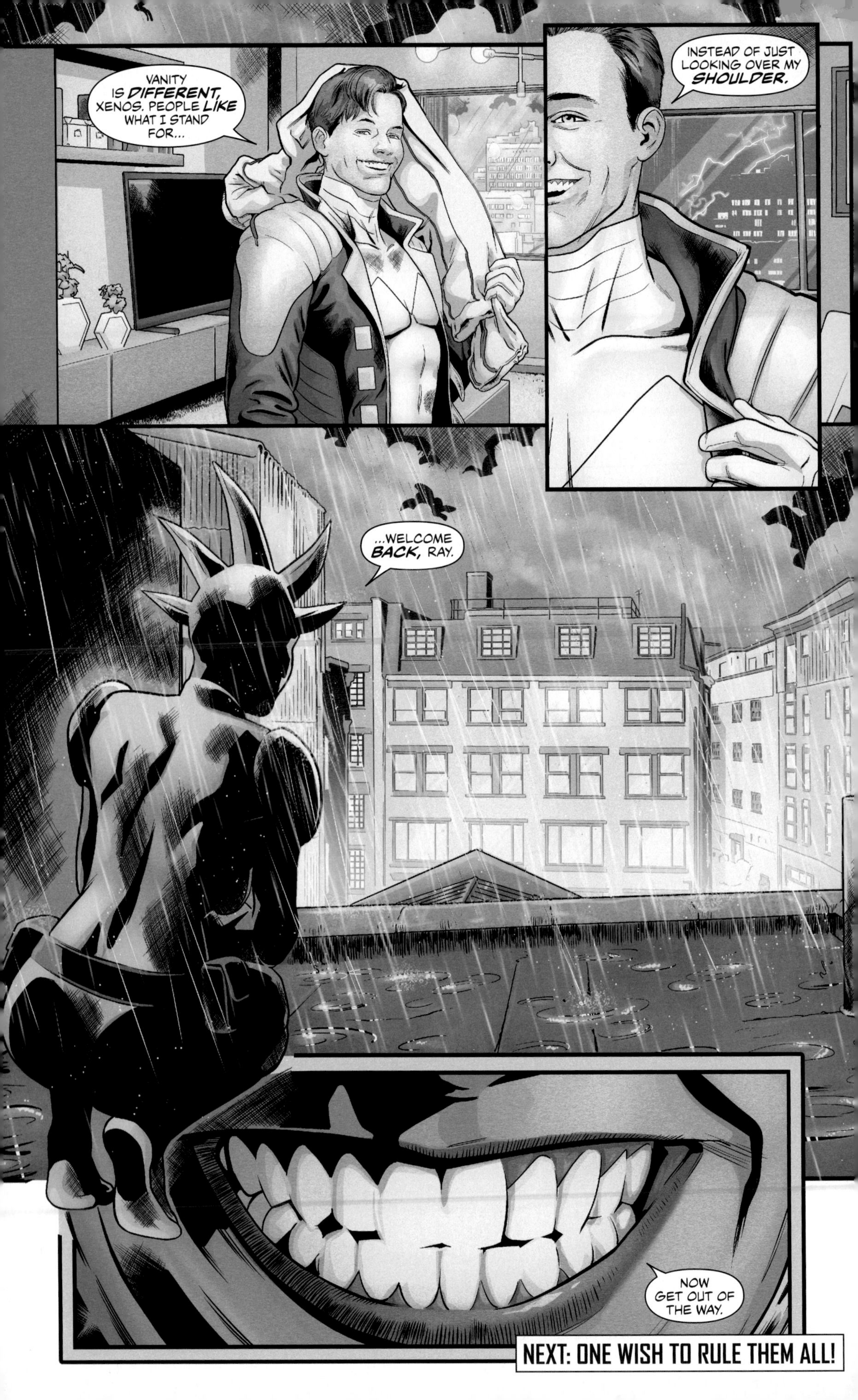
VANITY IS DIFFERENT, XENOS. PEOPLE LIKE WHAT I STAND FOR...
INSTEAD OF JUST LOOKING OVER MY SHOULDER.
...WELCOME BACK, RAY.
NOW GET OUT OF THE WAY.
NEXT: ONE WISH TO RULE THEM ALL!

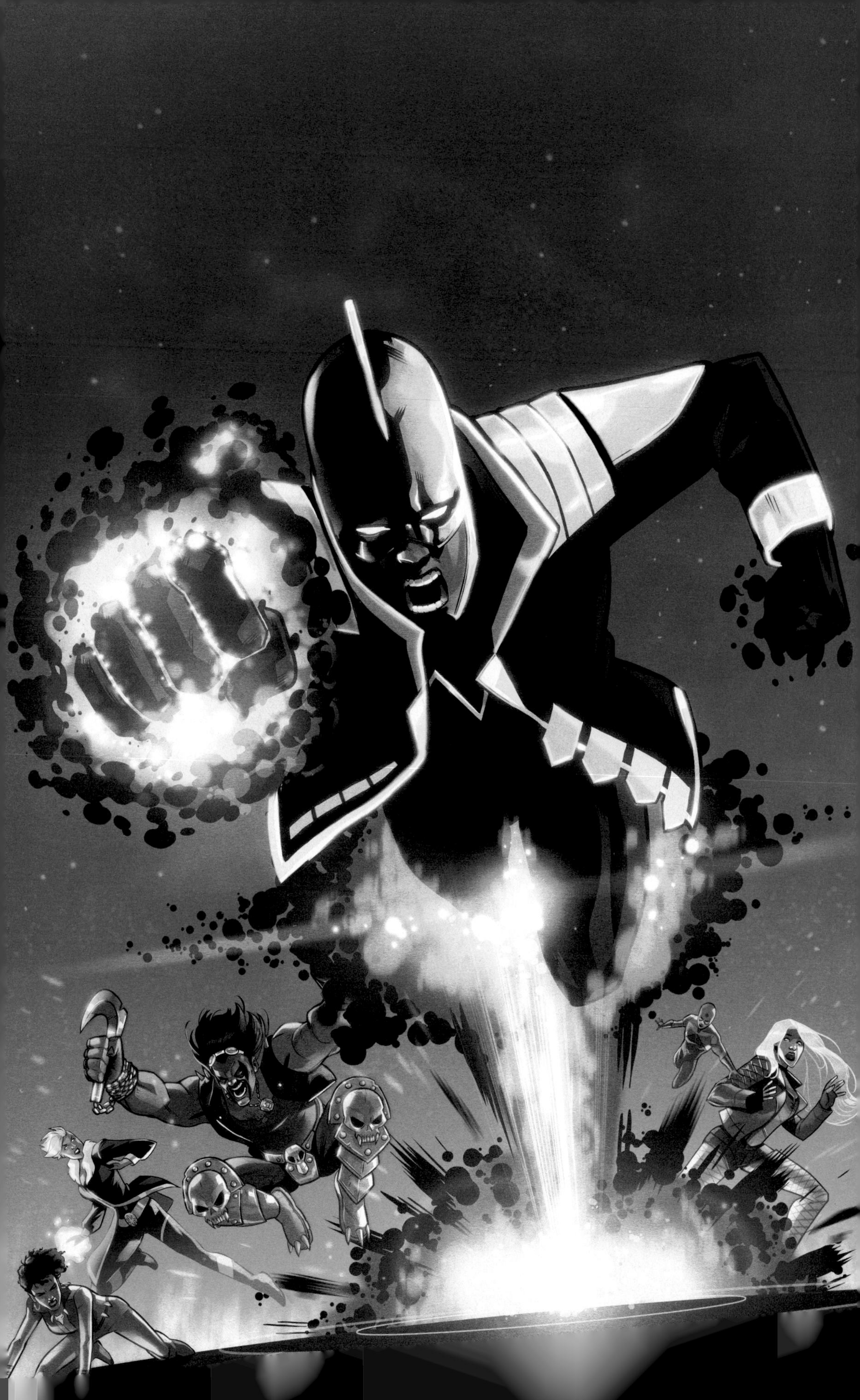

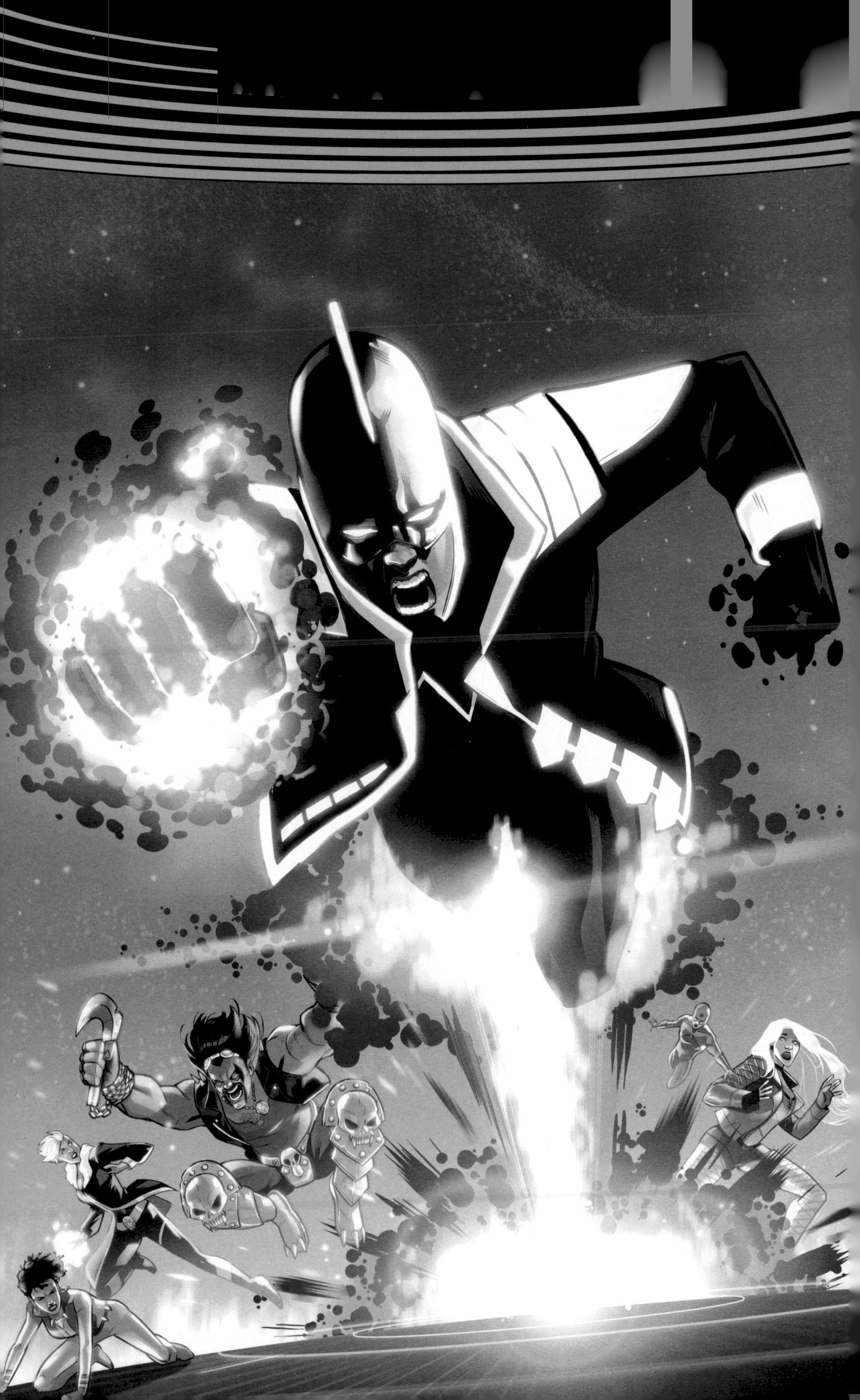

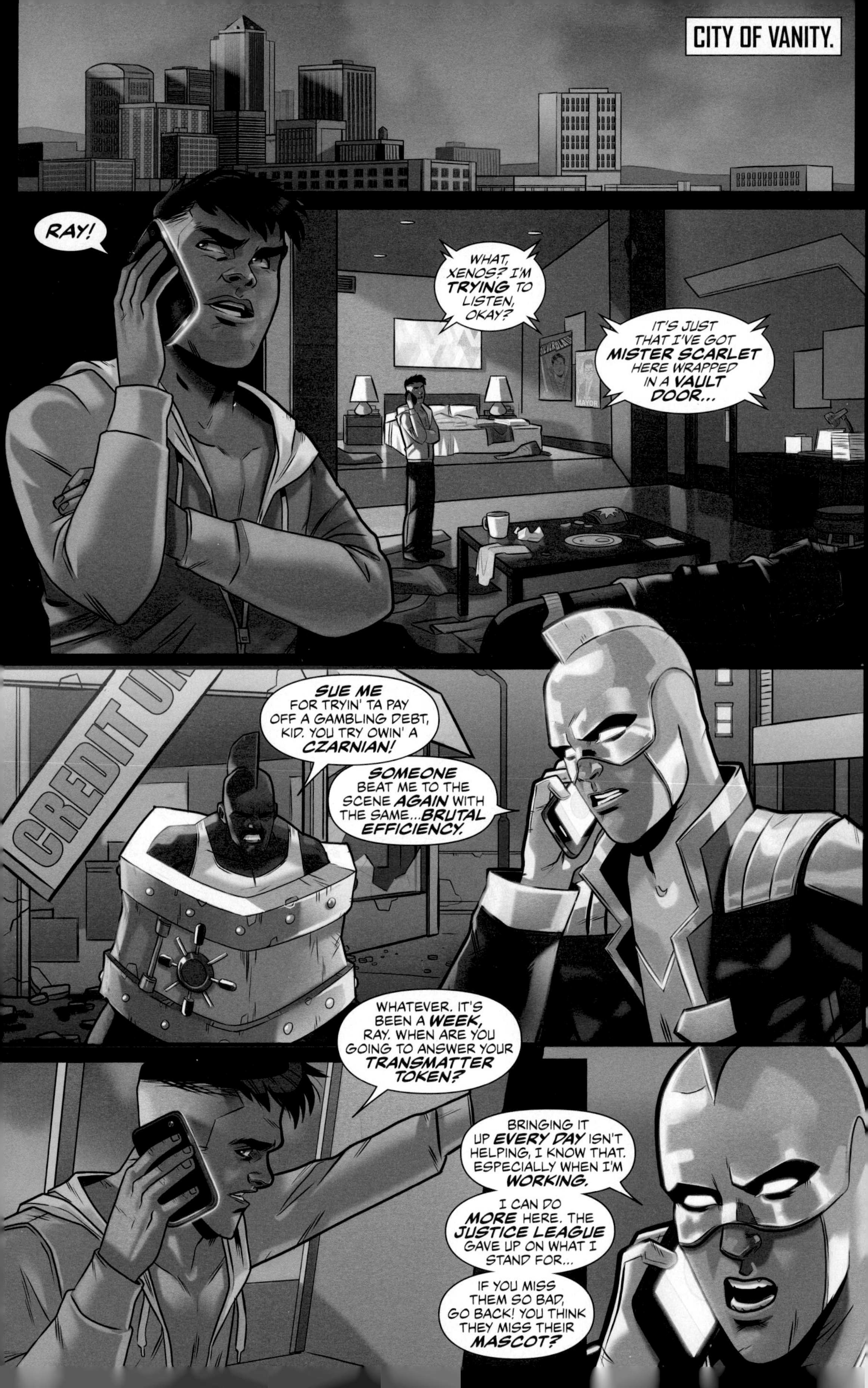
CITY OF VANITY.
RAY!
WHAT, XENOS? I'M TRYING TO LISTEN, OKAY?
IT'S JUST THAT I'VE GOT MISTER SCARLET HERE WRAPPED IN A VAULT DOOR...
CREDIT U
SUE ME FOR TRYIN' TA PAY OFF A GAMBLING DEBT, KID. YOU TRY OWIN' A CZARNIAN!
SOMEONE BEAT ME TO THE SCENE AGAIN WITH THE SAME...BRUTAL EFFICIENCY.
WHATEVER. IT'S BEEN A WEEK, RAY. WHEN ARE YOU GOING TO ANSWER YOUR TRANSMATTER TOKEN?
BRINGING IT UP EVERY DAY ISN'T HELPING, I KNOW THAT. ESPECIALLY WHEN I'M WORKING.
I CAN DO MORE HERE. THE JUSTICE LEAGUE GAVE UP ON WHAT I STAND FOR...
IF YOU MISS THEM SO BAD, GO BACK! YOU THINK THEY MISS THEIR MASCOT?

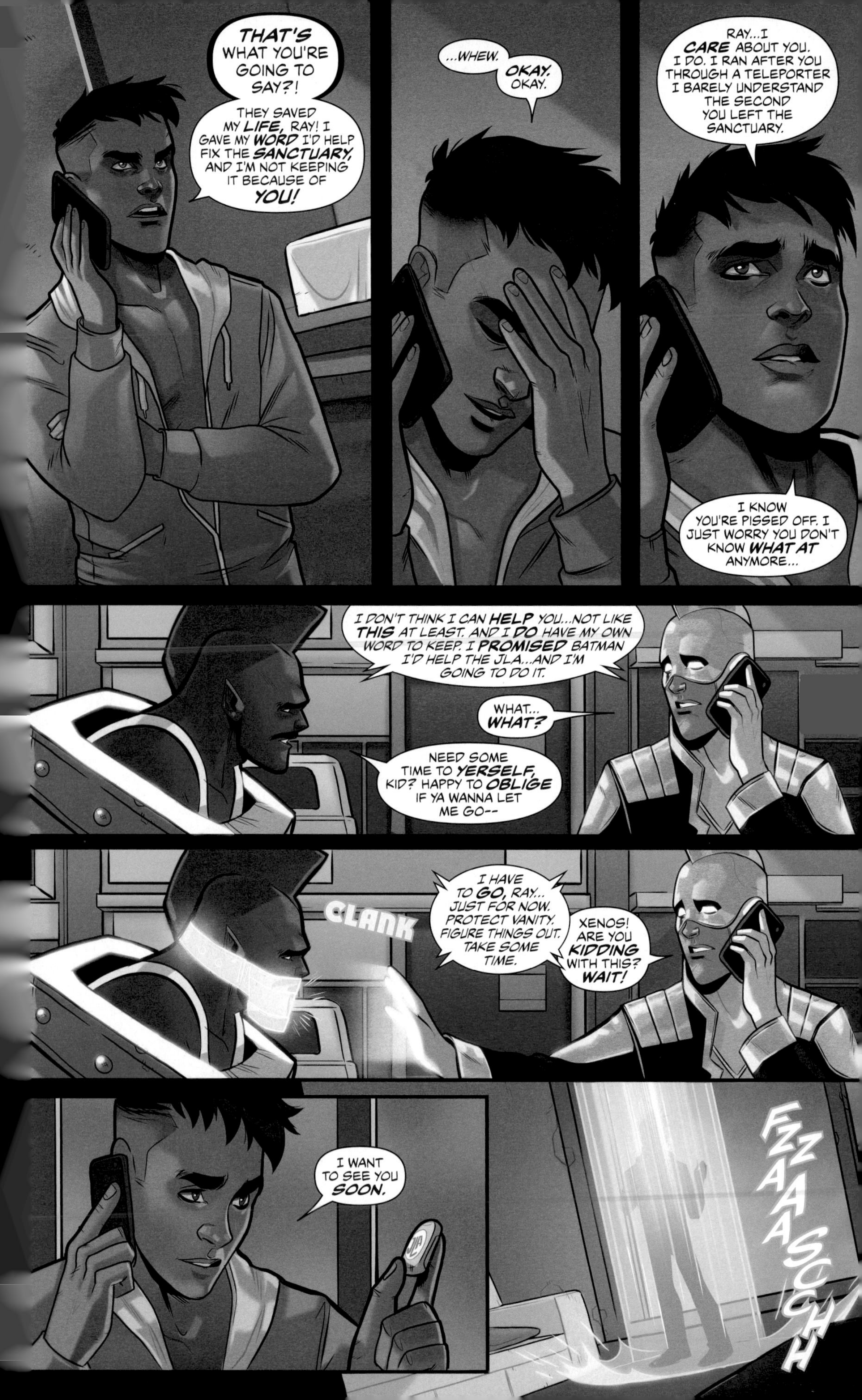
THAT'S WHAT YOU'RE GOING TO SAY?!
THEY SAVED MY LIFE, RAY! I GAVE MY WORD I'D HELP FIX THE SANCTUARY, AND I'M NOT KEEPING IT BECAUSE OF YOU!
...WHEW. OKAY. OKAY.
RAY...I CARE ABOUT YOU. I DO. I RAN AFTER YOU THROUGH A TELEPORTER I BARELY UNDERSTAND THE SECOND YOU LEFT THE SANCTUARY.
I KNOW YOU'RE PISSED OFF. I JUST WORRY YOU DON'T KNOW WHAT AT ANYMORE...
I DON'T THINK I CAN HELP YOU...NOT LIKE THIS AT LEAST. AND I DO HAVE MY OWN WORD TO KEEP. I PROMISED BATMAN I'D HELP THE JLA...AND I'M GOING TO DO IT.
WHAT... WHAT?
NEED SOME TIME TO YERSELF, KID? HAPPY TO OBLIGE IF YA WANNA LET ME GO--
CLANK
I HAVE TO GO, RAY... JUST FOR NOW. PROTECT VANITY. FIGURE THINGS OUT. TAKE SOME TIME.
XENOS! ARE YOU KIDDING WITH THIS? WAIT!
I WANT TO SEE YOU SOON.
FZZAAASCHH

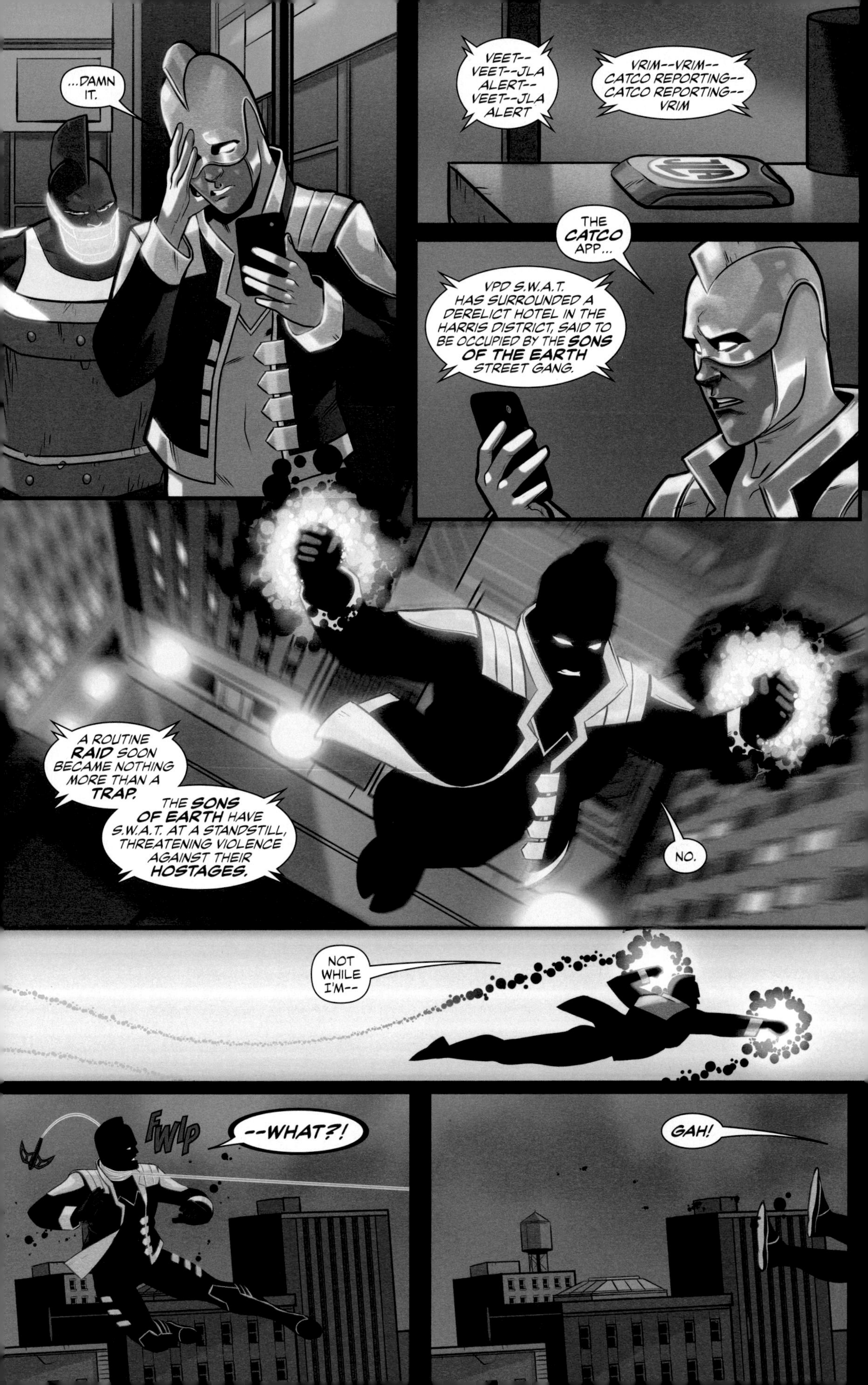

...DAMN IT.
VEET-- VEET--JLA ALERT-- VEET--JLA ALERT
VRIM--VRIM-- CATCO REPORTING-- CATCO REPORTING-- VRIM
THE CATCO APP...
VPD S.W.A.T. HAS SURROUNDED A DERELICT HOTEL IN THE HARRIS DISTRICT, SAID TO BE OCCUPIED BY THE SONS OF THE EARTH STREET GANG.
A ROUTINE RAID SOON BECAME NOTHING MORE THAN A TRAP.
THE SONS OF EARTH HAVE S.W.A.T. AT A STANDSTILL, THREATENING VIOLENCE AGAINST THEIR HOSTAGES.
NO.
NOT WHILE I'M--
FWIP
--WHAT?!
GAH!

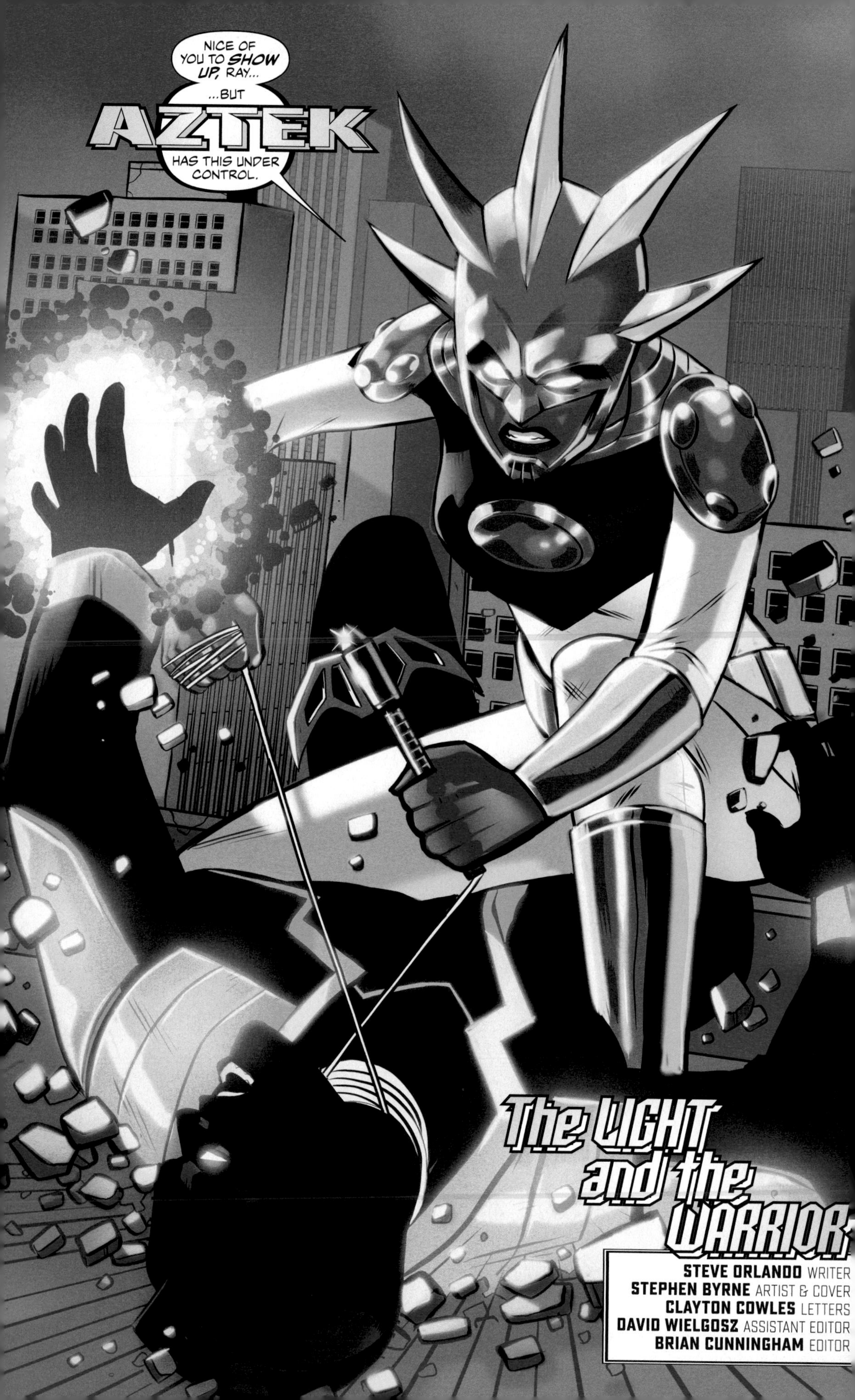

NICE OF YOU TO SHOW UP, RAY...
...BUT
AZTEK
HAS THIS UNDER CONTROL.
The LIGHT and the WARRIOR
STEVE ORLANDO WRITER
STEPHEN BYRNE ARTIST & COVER
CLAYTON COWLES LETTERS
DAVID WIELGOSZ ASSISTANT EDITOR
BRIAN CUNNINGHAM EDITOR

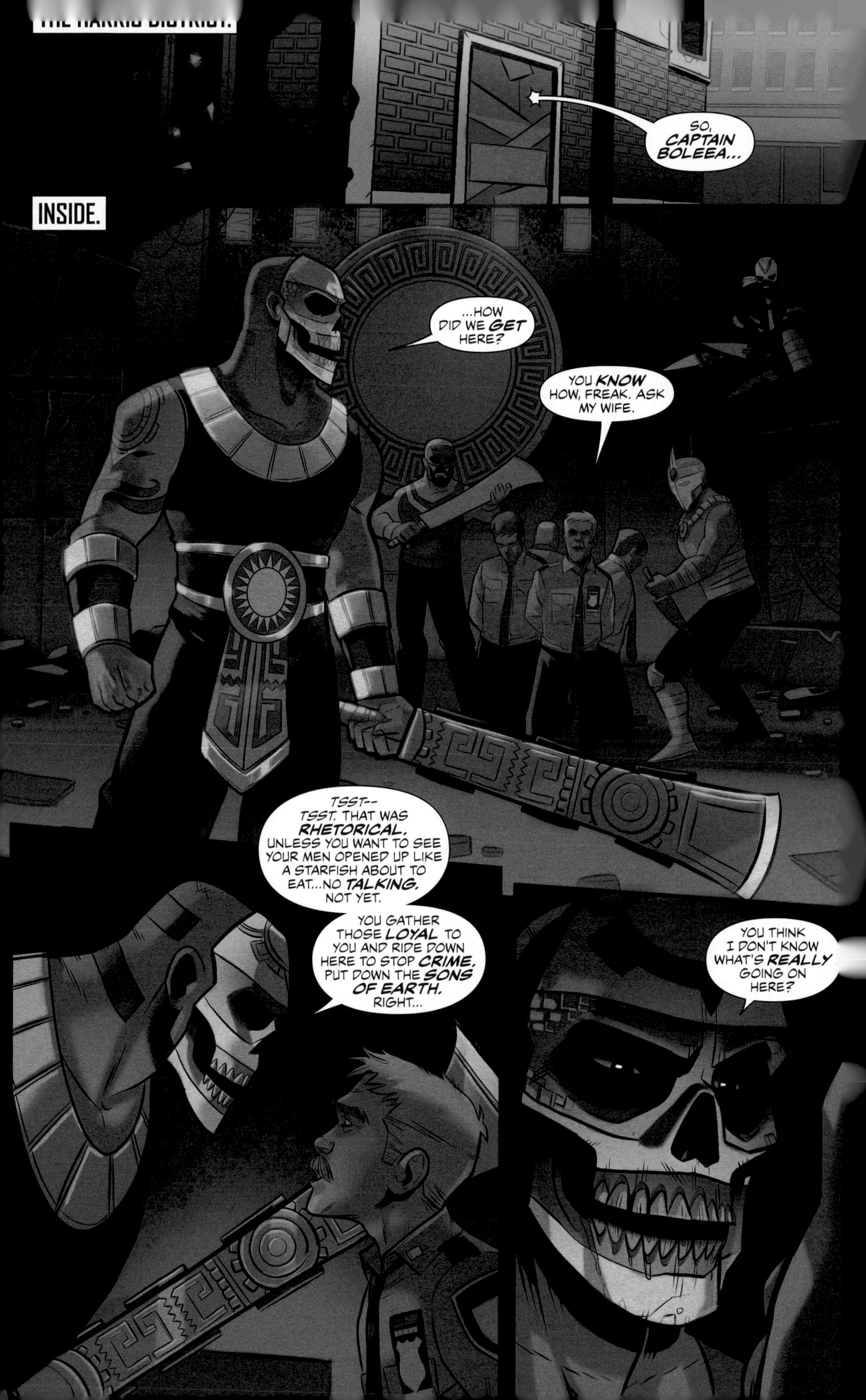
SO, CAPTAIN BOLEEA...
INSIDE.
...HOW DID WE GET HERE?
YOU KNOW HOW, FREAK. ASK MY WIFE.
TSST-- TSST. THAT WAS RHETORICAL. UNLESS YOU WANT TO SEE YOUR MEN OPENED UP LIKE A STARFISH ABOUT TO EAT...NO TALKING. NOT YET.
YOU GATHER THOSE LOYAL TO YOU AND RIDE DOWN HERE TO STOP CRIME. PUT DOWN THE SONS OF EARTH. RIGHT...
YOU THINK I DON'T KNOW WHAT'S REALLY GOING ON HERE?

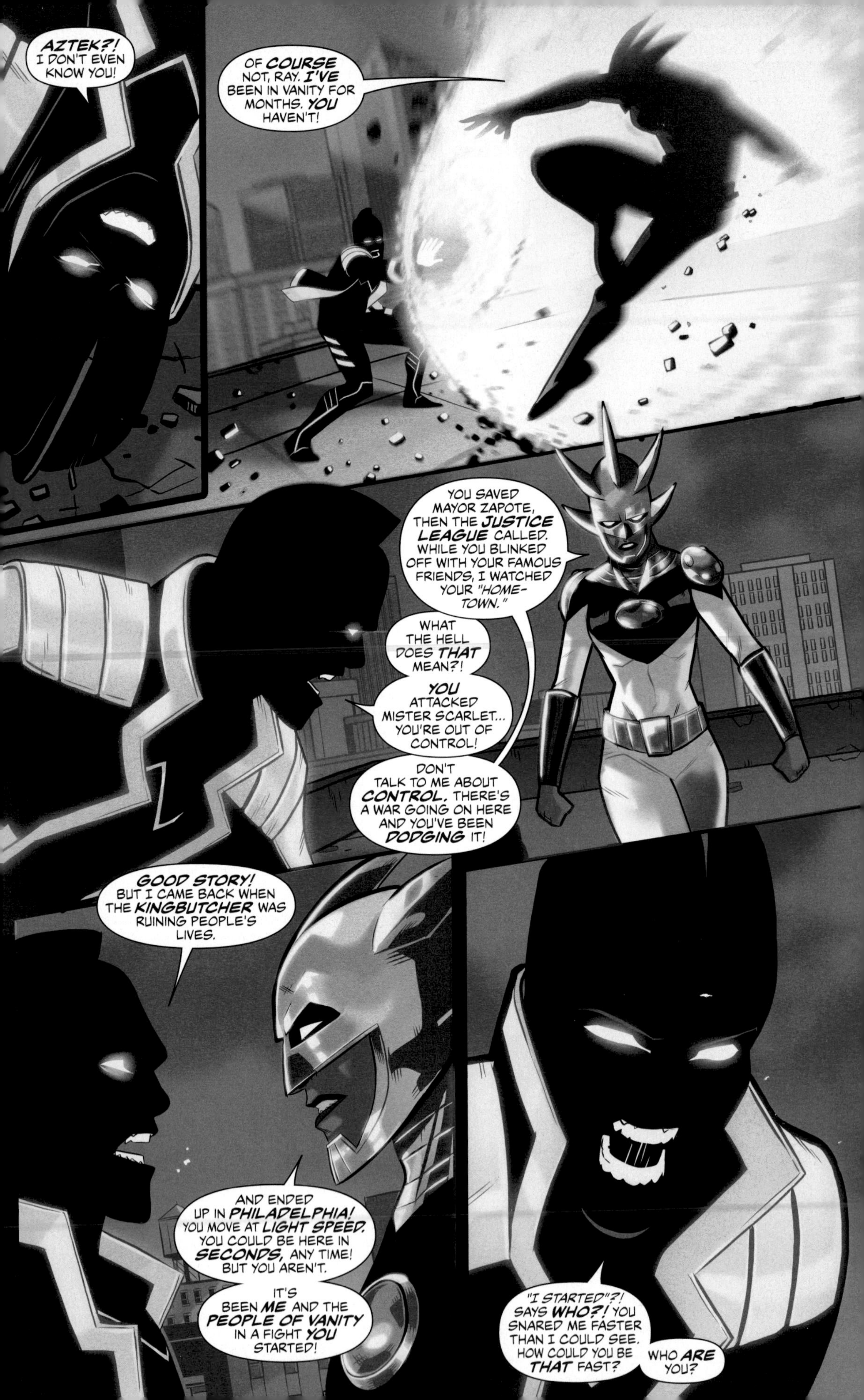
AZTEK?! I DON'T EVEN KNOW YOU!
OF COURSE NOT, RAY. I'VE BEEN IN VANITY FOR MONTHS. YOU HAVEN'T!
YOU SAVED MAYOR ZAPOTE, THEN THE JUSTICE LEAGUE CALLED. WHILE YOU BLINKED OFF WITH YOUR FAMOUS FRIENDS, I WATCHED YOUR "HOME-TOWN."
WHAT THE HELL DOES THAT MEAN?!
YOU ATTACKED MISTER SCARLET... YOU'RE OUT OF CONTROL!
DON'T TALK TO ME ABOUT CONTROL. THERE'S A WAR GOING ON HERE AND YOU'VE BEEN DODGING IT!
GOOD STORY! BUT I CAME BACK WHEN THE KINGBUTCHER WAS RUINING PEOPLE'S LIVES.
AND ENDED UP IN PHILADELPHIA! YOU MOVE AT LIGHT SPEED. YOU COULD BE HERE IN SECONDS, ANY TIME! BUT YOU AREN'T.
IT'S BEEN ME AND THE PEOPLE OF VANITY IN A FIGHT YOU STARTED!
"I STARTED"?! SAYS WHO?! YOU SNARED ME FASTER THAN I COULD SEE. HOW COULD YOU BE THAT FAST?
WHO ARE YOU?

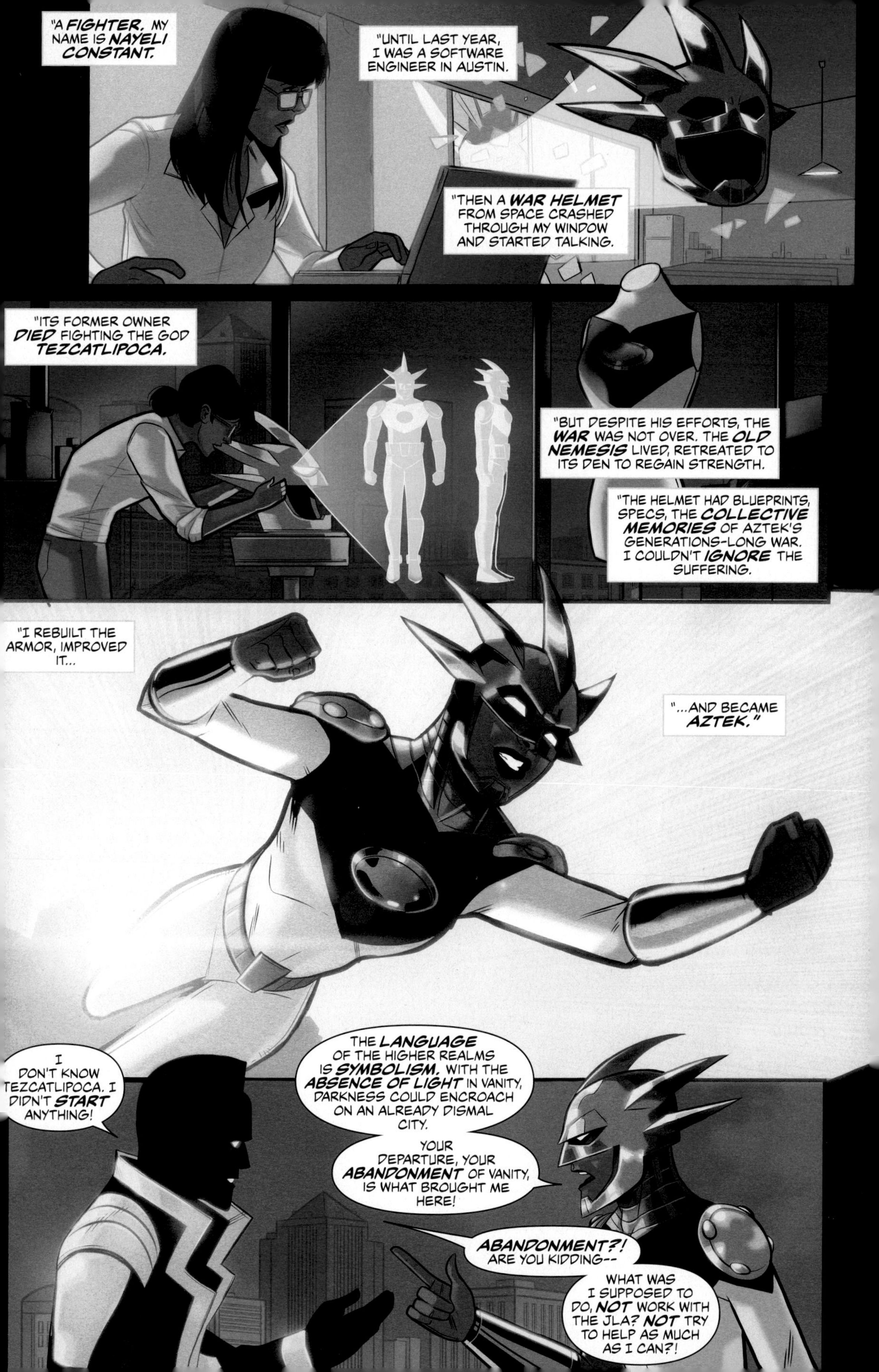
"A FIGHTER. MY NAME IS NAYELI CONSTANT.
"UNTIL LAST YEAR, I WAS A SOFTWARE ENGINEER IN AUSTIN.
"THEN A WAR HELMET FROM SPACE CRASHED THROUGH MY WINDOW AND STARTED TALKING.
"ITS FORMER OWNER DIED FIGHTING THE GOD TEZCATLIPOCA.
"BUT DESPITE HIS EFFORTS, THE WAR WAS NOT OVER. THE OLD NEMESIS LIVED, RETREATED TO ITS DEN TO REGAIN STRENGTH.
"THE HELMET HAD BLUEPRINTS, SPECS, THE COLLECTIVE MEMORIES OF AZTEK'S GENERATIONS-LONG WAR. I COULDN'T IGNORE THE SUFFERING.
"I REBUILT THE ARMOR, IMPROVED IT...
"...AND BECAME AZTEK."
I DON'T KNOW TEZCATLIPOCA. I DIDN'T START ANYTHING!
THE LANGUAGE OF THE HIGHER REALMS IS SYMBOLISM. WITH THE ABSENCE OF LIGHT IN VANITY, DARKNESS COULD ENCROACH ON AN ALREADY DISMAL CITY.
YOUR DEPARTURE, YOUR ABANDONMENT OF VANITY, IS WHAT BROUGHT ME HERE!
ABANDONMENT?! ARE YOU KIDDING--
WHAT WAS I SUPPOSED TO DO, NOT WORK WITH THE JLA? NOT TRY TO HELP AS MUCH AS I CAN?!

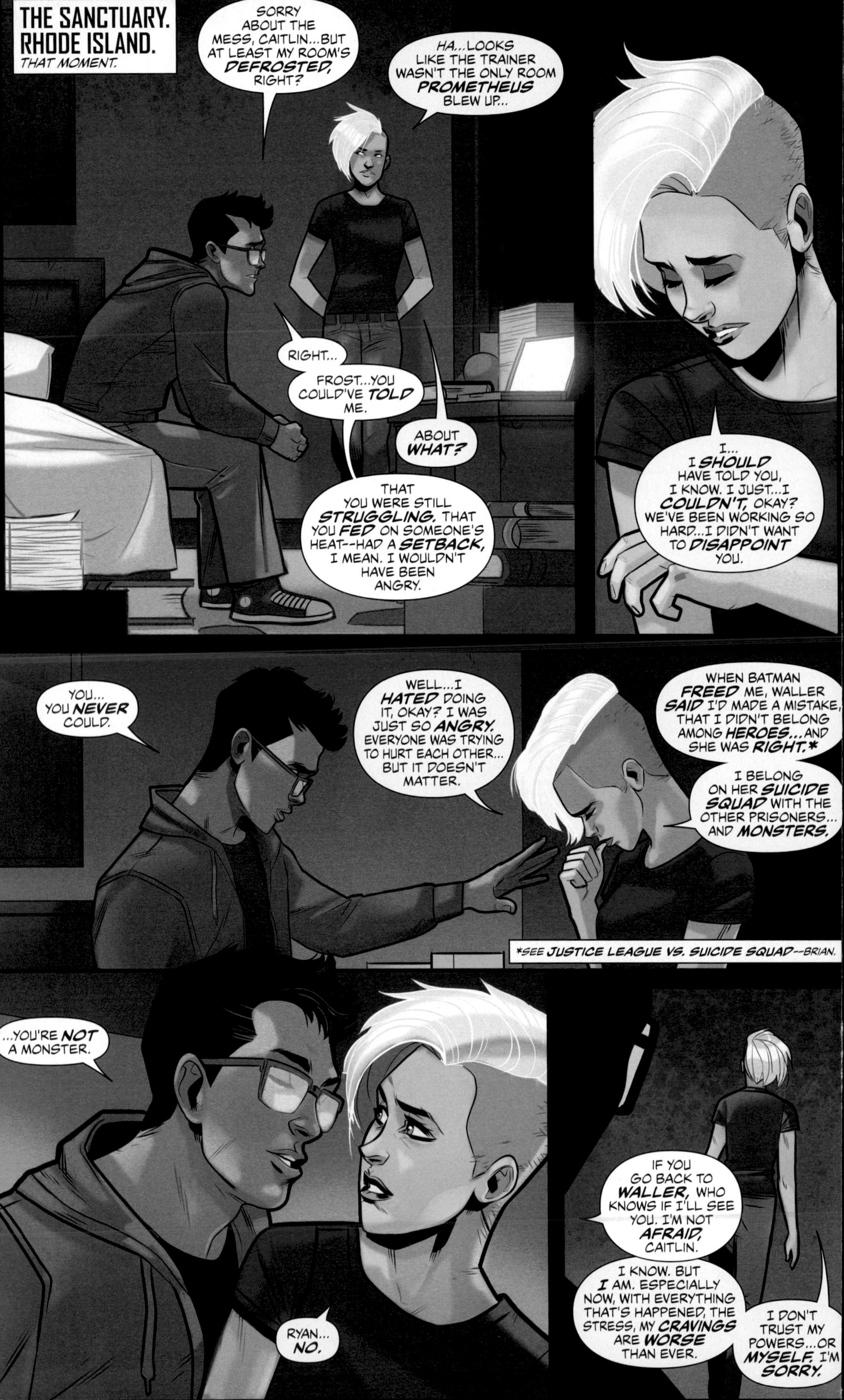
THE SANCTUARY. RHODE ISLAND. THAT MOMENT.
SORRY ABOUT THE MESS, CAITLIN...BUT AT LEAST MY ROOM'S DEFROSTED, RIGHT?
HA...LOOKS LIKE THE TRAINER WASN'T THE ONLY ROOM PROMETHEUS BLEW UP...
RIGHT...
FROST...YOU COULD'VE TOLD ME.
ABOUT WHAT?
THAT YOU WERE STILL STRUGGLING. THAT YOU FED ON SOMEONE'S HEAT--HAD A SETBACK, I MEAN. I WOULDN'T HAVE BEEN ANGRY.
I... I SHOULD HAVE TOLD YOU, I KNOW. I JUST...I COULDN'T, OKAY? WE'VE BEEN WORKING SO HARD...I DIDN'T WANT TO DISAPPOINT YOU.
YOU... YOU NEVER COULD.
WELL...I HATED DOING IT, OKAY? I WAS JUST SO ANGRY. EVERYONE WAS TRYING TO HURT EACH OTHER... BUT IT DOESN'T MATTER.
WHEN BATMAN FREED ME, WALLER SAID I'D MADE A MISTAKE, THAT I DIDN'T BELONG AMONG HEROES...AND SHE WAS RIGHT.*
I BELONG ON HER SUICIDE SQUAD WITH THE OTHER PRISONERS... AND MONSTERS.
*SEE JUSTICE LEAGUE VS. SUICIDE SQUAD--BRIAN.
...YOU'RE NOT A MONSTER.
RYAN... NO.
IF YOU GO BACK TO WALLER, WHO KNOWS IF I'LL SEE YOU. I'M NOT AFRAID, CAITLIN.
I KNOW. BUT I AM. ESPECIALLY NOW, WITH EVERYTHING THAT'S HAPPENED, THE STRESS, MY CRAVINGS ARE WORSE THAN EVER.
I DON'T TRUST MY POWERS...OR MYSELF. I'M SORRY.

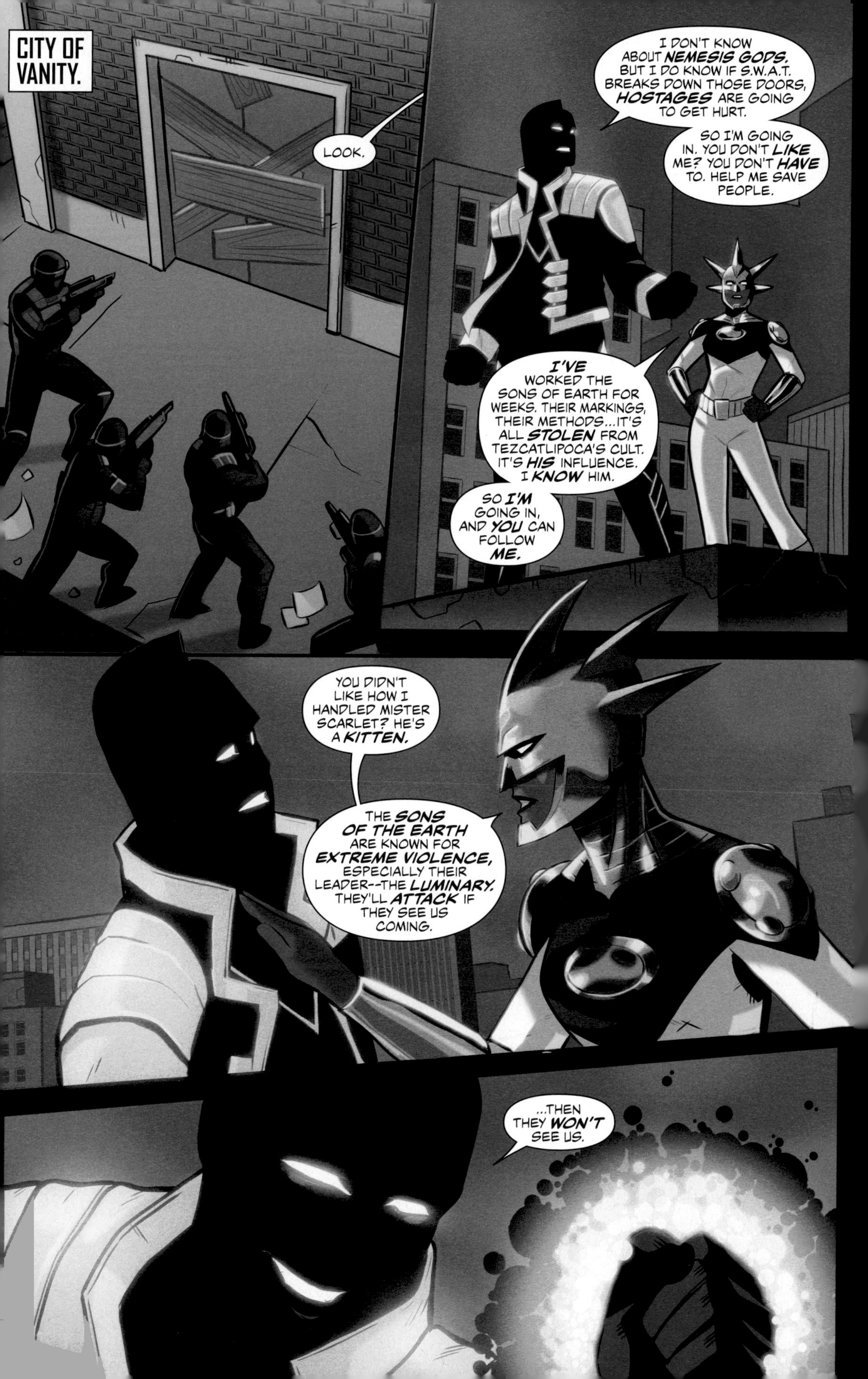
CITY OF VANITY.
LOOK.
I DON'T KNOW ABOUT NEMESIS GODS. BUT I DO KNOW IF S.W.A.T. BREAKS DOWN THOSE DOORS, HOSTAGES ARE GOING TO GET HURT.
SO I'M GOING IN. YOU DON'T LIKE ME? YOU DON'T HAVE TO. HELP ME SAVE PEOPLE.
I'VE WORKED THE SONS OF EARTH FOR WEEKS. THEIR MARKINGS, THEIR METHODS...IT'S ALL STOLEN FROM TEZCATLIPOCA'S CULT. IT'S HIS INFLUENCE. I KNOW HIM.
SO I'M GOING IN, AND YOU CAN FOLLOW ME.
YOU DIDN'T LIKE HOW I HANDLED MISTER SCARLET? HE'S A KITTEN.
THE SONS OF THE EARTH ARE KNOWN FOR EXTREME VIOLENCE, ESPECIALLY THEIR LEADER--THE LUMINARY. THEY'LL ATTACK IF THEY SEE US COMING.
...THEN THEY WON'T SEE US.

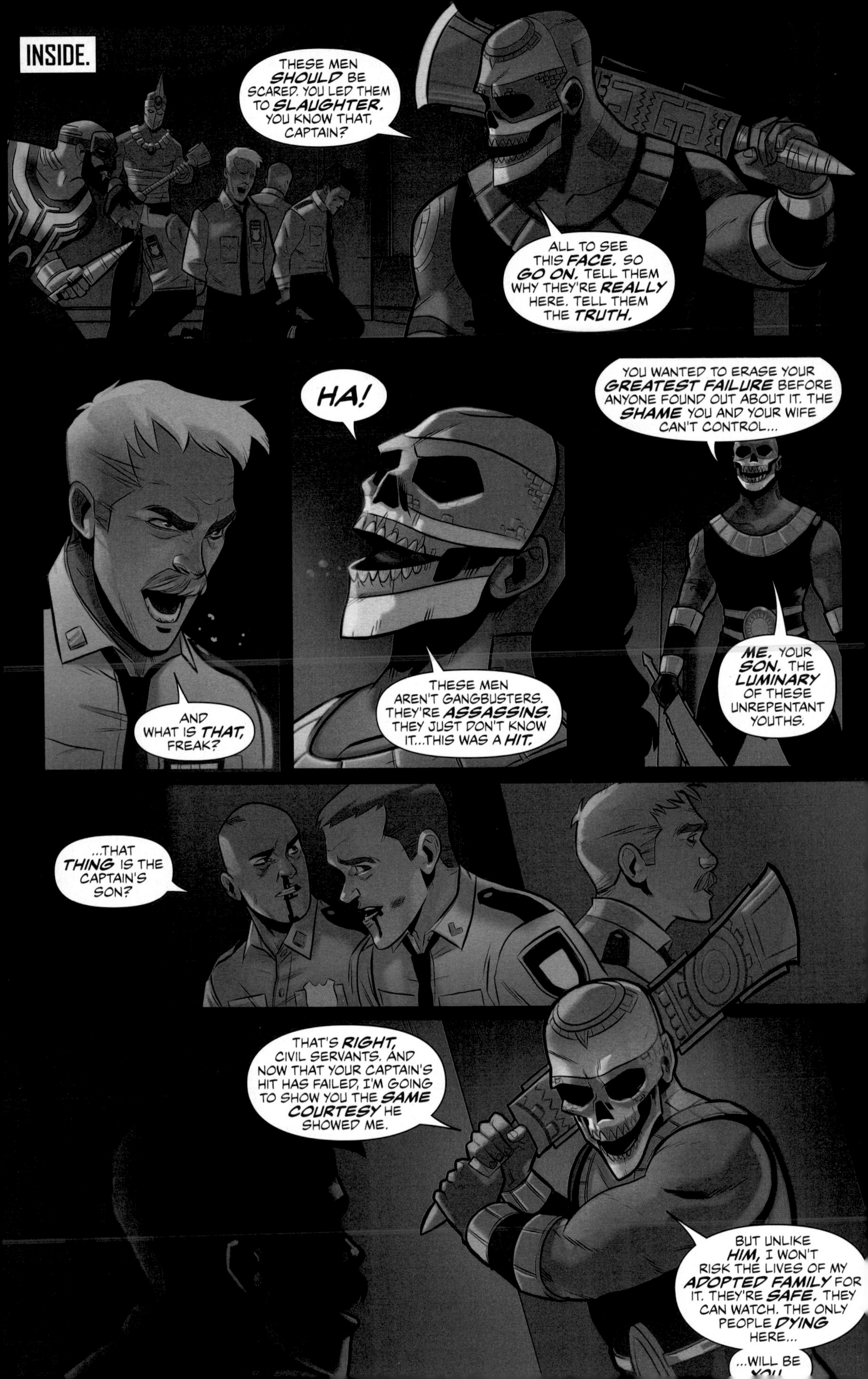
INSIDE.
THESE MEN SHOULD BE SCARED. YOU LED THEM TO SLAUGHTER. YOU KNOW THAT, CAPTAIN?
ALL TO SEE THIS FACE. SO GO ON. TELL THEM WHY THEY'RE REALLY HERE. TELL THEM THE TRUTH.
AND WHAT IS THAT, FREAK?
HA!
THESE MEN AREN'T GANGBUSTERS. THEY'RE ASSASSINS. THEY JUST DON'T KNOW IT...THIS WAS A HIT.
YOU WANTED TO ERASE YOUR GREATEST FAILURE BEFORE ANYONE FOUND OUT ABOUT IT. THE SHAME YOU AND YOUR WIFE CAN'T CONTROL...
ME. YOUR SON. THE LUMINARY OF THESE UNREPENTANT YOUTHS.
...THAT THING IS THE CAPTAIN'S SON?
THAT'S RIGHT, CIVIL SERVANTS. AND NOW THAT YOUR CAPTAIN'S HIT HAS FAILED, I'M GOING TO SHOW YOU THE SAME COURTESY HE SHOWED ME.
BUT UNLIKE HIM, I WON'T RISK THE LIVES OF MY ADOPTED FAMILY FOR IT. THEY'RE SAFE. THEY CAN WATCH. THE ONLY PEOPLE DYING HERE...
...WILL BE

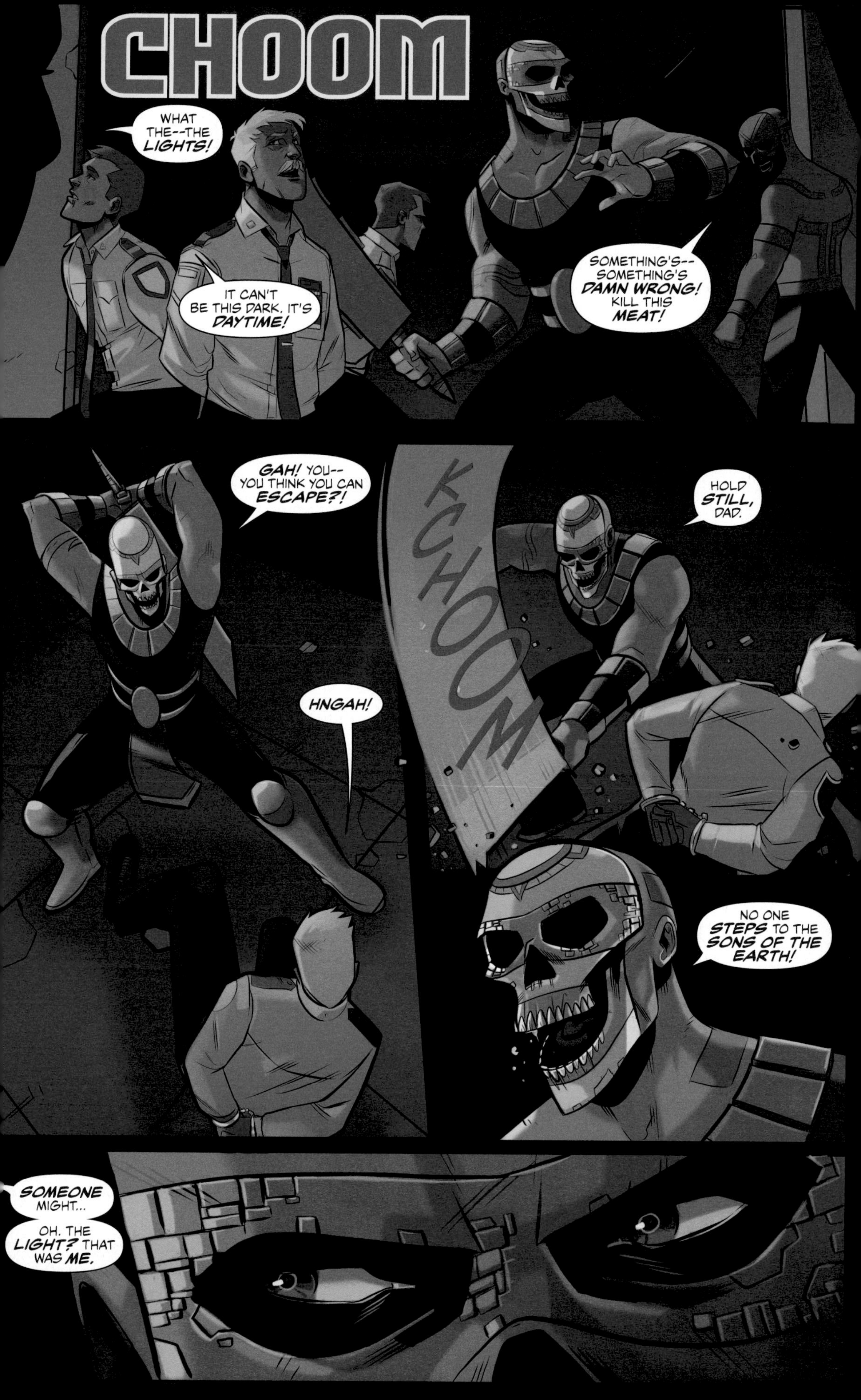
CHOOM
WHAT THE--THE LIGHTS!
IT CAN'T BE THIS DARK. IT'S DAYTIME!
SOMETHING'S-- SOMETHING'S DAMN WRONG! KILL THIS MEAT!
GAH! YOU-- YOU THINK YOU CAN ESCAPE?!
HNGAH!
KCHOOM
HOLD STILL, DAD.
NO ONE STEPS TO THE SONS OF THE EARTH!
SOMEONE MIGHT...
OH. THE LIGHT? THAT WAS ME.

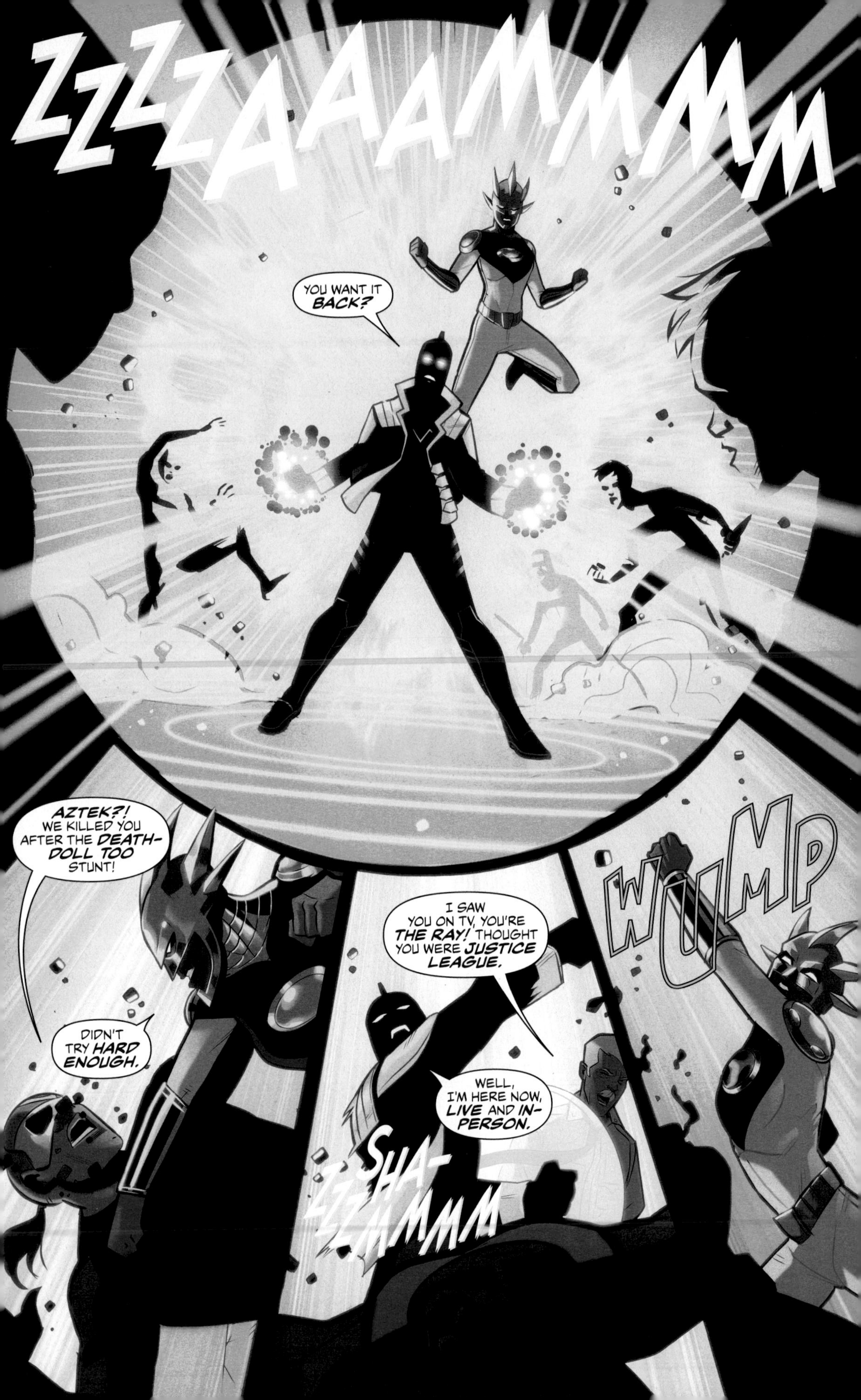
ZZZZAAAMMMMM
YOU WANT IT BACK?
AZTEK?! WE KILLED YOU AFTER THE DEATH-DOLL TOO STUNT!
DIDN'T TRY HARD ENOUGH.
I SAW YOU ON TV, YOU'RE THE RAY! THOUGHT YOU WERE JUSTICE LEAGUE.
WELL, I'M HERE NOW, LIVE AND IN-PERSON.
SHA-ZZZAMMMM
WUMP

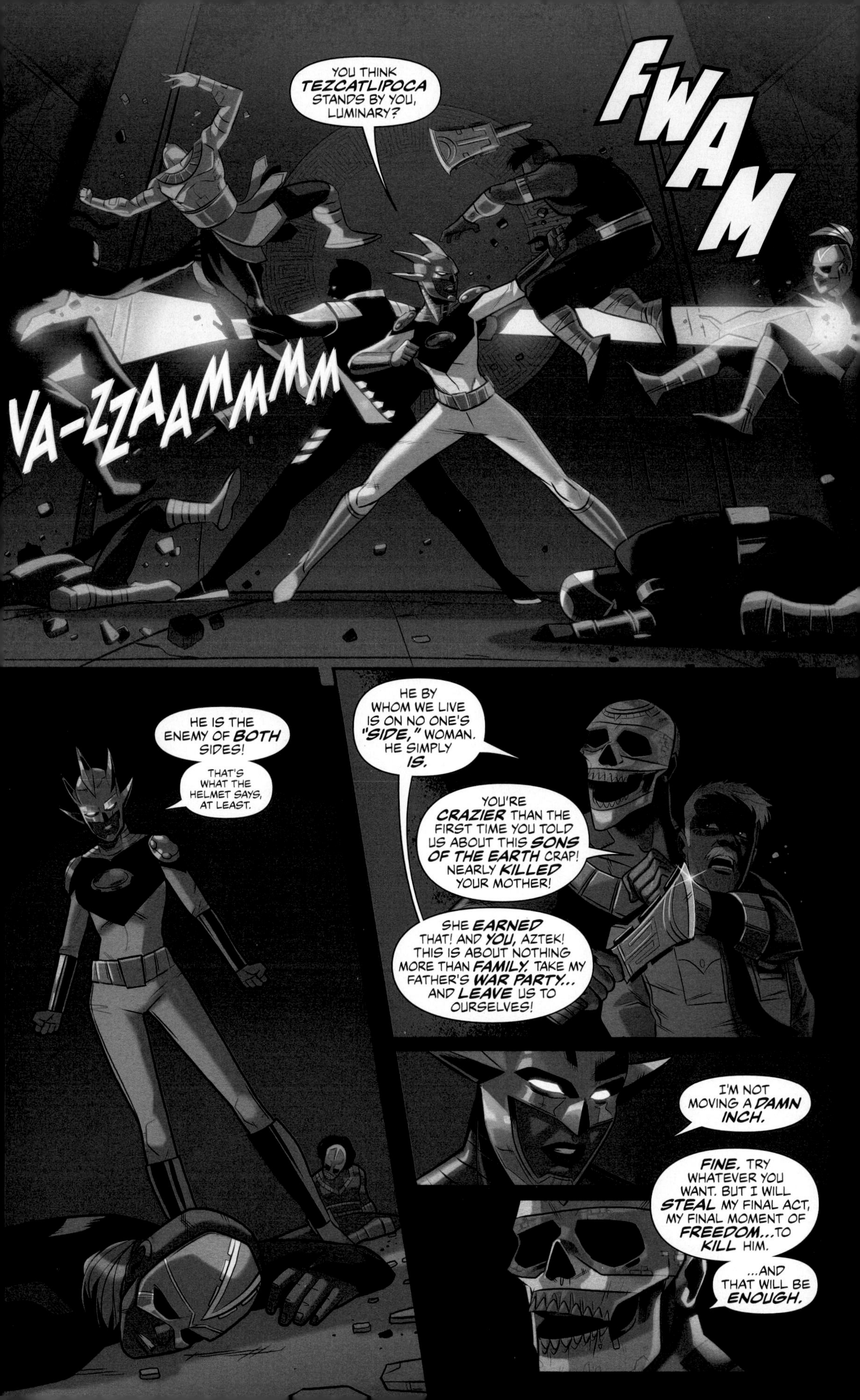

YOU THINK TEZCATLIPOCA STANDS BY YOU, LUMINARY?
FWAM
VA-ZZAAMMMM
HE IS THE ENEMY OF BOTH SIDES!
THAT'S WHAT THE HELMET SAYS, AT LEAST.
HE BY WHOM WE LIVE IS ON NO ONE'S "SIDE," WOMAN. HE SIMPLY IS.
YOU'RE CRAZIER THAN THE FIRST TIME YOU TOLD US ABOUT THIS SONS OF THE EARTH CRAP! NEARLY KILLED YOUR MOTHER!
SHE EARNED THAT! AND YOU, AZTEK! THIS IS ABOUT NOTHING MORE THAN FAMILY. TAKE MY FATHER'S WAR PARTY... AND LEAVE US TO OURSELVES!
I'M NOT MOVING A DAMN INCH.
FINE. TRY WHATEVER YOU WANT. BUT I WILL STEAL MY FINAL ACT, MY FINAL MOMENT OF FREEDOM...TO KILL HIM.
...AND THAT WILL BE ENOUGH.

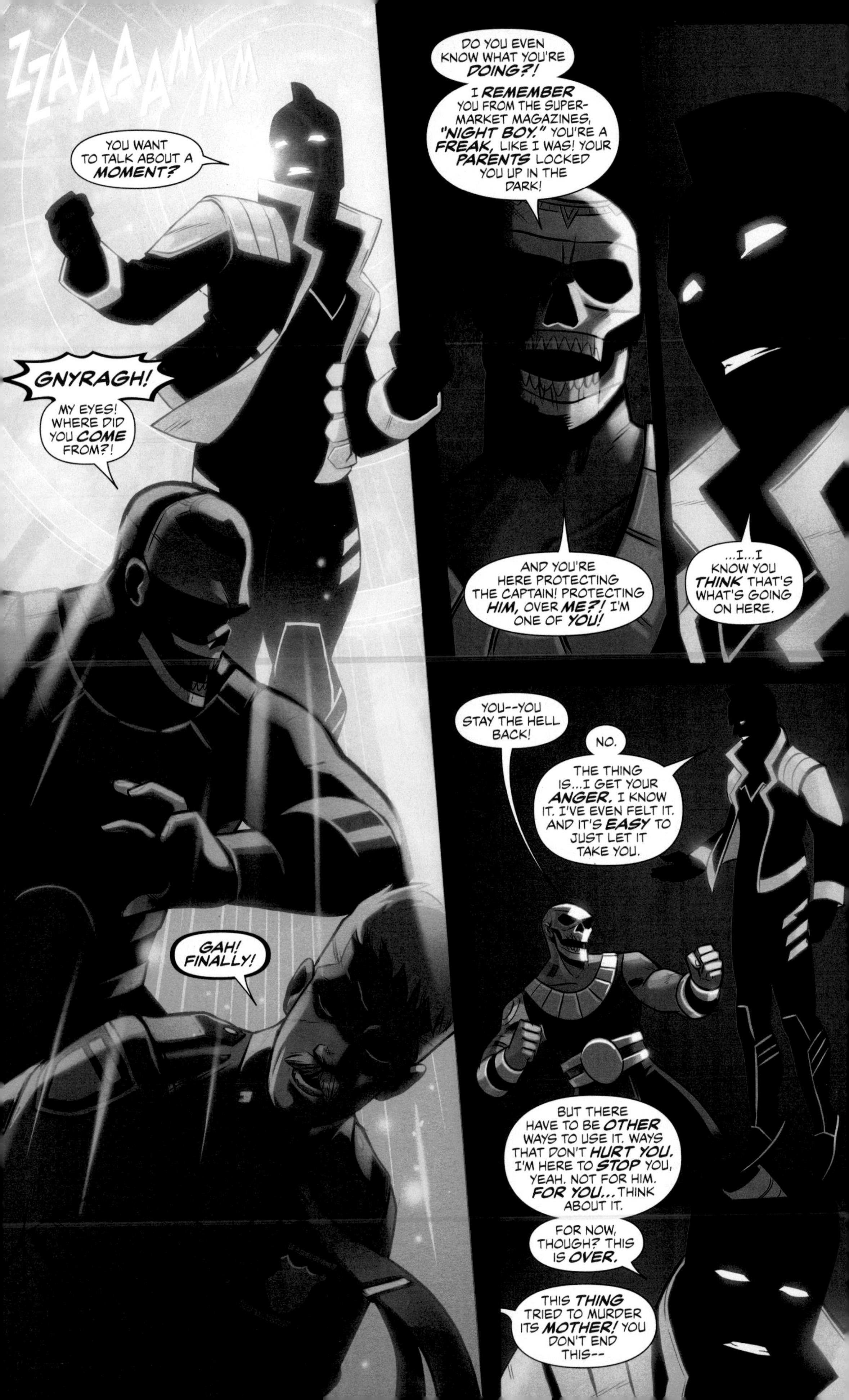
ZZAAAAMMM
YOU WANT TO TALK ABOUT A MOMENT?
GNYRAGH!
MY EYES! WHERE DID YOU COME FROM?!
GAH! FINALLY!
DO YOU EVEN KNOW WHAT YOU'RE DOING?!
I REMEMBER YOU FROM THE SUPER-MARKET MAGAZINES, "NIGHT BOY." YOU'RE A FREAK, LIKE I WAS! YOUR PARENTS LOCKED YOU UP IN THE DARK!
AND YOU'RE HERE PROTECTING THE CAPTAIN! PROTECTING HIM, OVER ME?! I'M ONE OF YOU!
...I...I KNOW YOU THINK THAT'S WHAT'S GOING ON HERE.
YOU--YOU STAY THE HELL BACK!
NO.
THE THING IS...I GET YOUR ANGER. I KNOW IT. I'VE EVEN FELT IT. AND IT'S EASY TO JUST LET IT TAKE YOU.
BUT THERE HAVE TO BE OTHER WAYS TO USE IT. WAYS THAT DON'T HURT YOU. I'M HERE TO STOP YOU, YEAH. NOT FOR HIM. FOR YOU... THINK ABOUT IT.
FOR NOW, THOUGH? THIS IS OVER.
THIS THING TRIED TO MURDER ITS MOTHER! YOU DON'T END THIS--

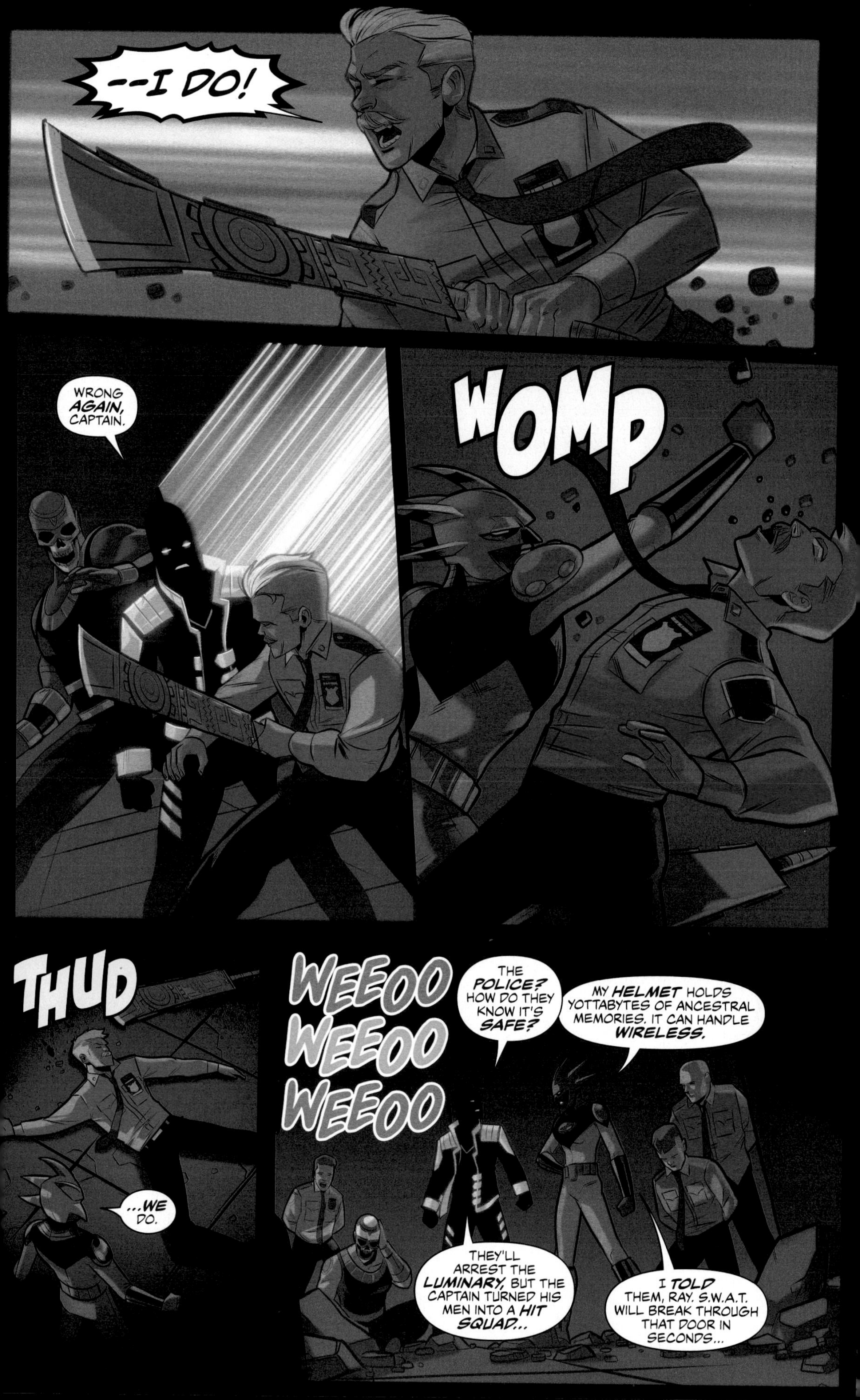
--I DO!
WRONG AGAIN, CAPTAIN.
WOMP
THUD
...WE DO.
WEEOO WEEOO WEEOO
THE POLICE? HOW DO THEY KNOW IT'S SAFE?
MY HELMET HOLDS YOTTABYTES OF ANCESTRAL MEMORIES. IT CAN HANDLE WIRELESS.
THEY'LL ARREST THE LUMINARY, BUT THE CAPTAIN TURNED HIS MEN INTO A HIT SQUAD...
I TOLD THEM, RAY. S.W.A.T. WILL BREAK THROUGH THAT DOOR IN SECONDS...

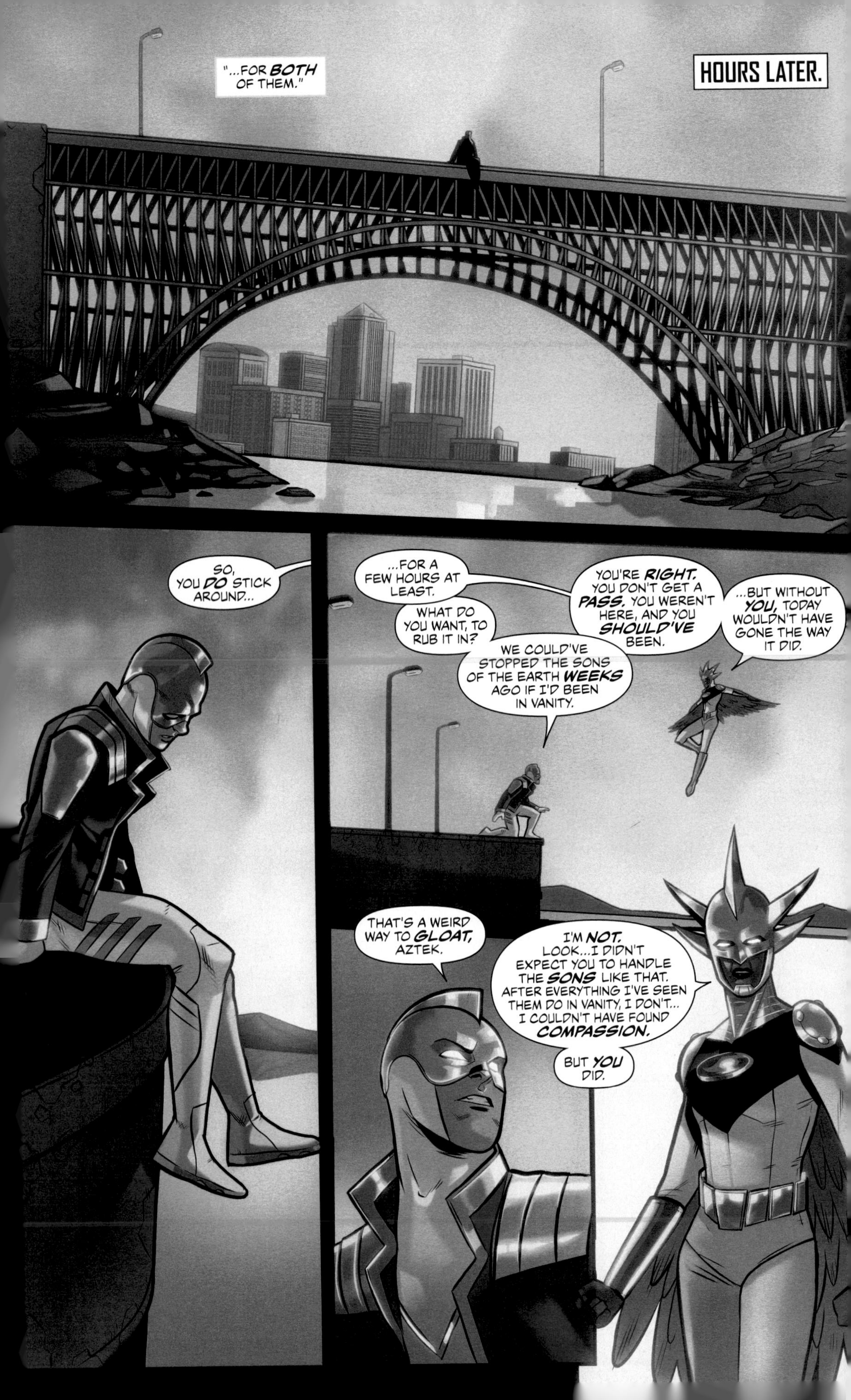
"...FOR BOTH OF THEM."
HOURS LATER.
SO, YOU DO STICK AROUND...
...FOR A FEW HOURS AT LEAST.
WHAT DO YOU WANT, TO RUB IT IN?
WE COULD'VE STOPPED THE SONS OF THE EARTH WEEKS AGO IF I'D BEEN IN VANITY.
YOU'RE RIGHT. YOU DON'T GET A PASS. YOU WEREN'T HERE, AND YOU SHOULD'VE BEEN.
...BUT WITHOUT YOU, TODAY WOULDN'T HAVE GONE THE WAY IT DID.
THAT'S A WEIRD WAY TO GLOAT, AZTEK.
I'M NOT. LOOK...I DIDN'T EXPECT YOU TO HANDLE THE SONS LIKE THAT. AFTER EVERYTHING I'VE SEEN THEM DO IN VANITY, I DON'T... I COULDN'T HAVE FOUND COMPASSION.
BUT YOU DID.

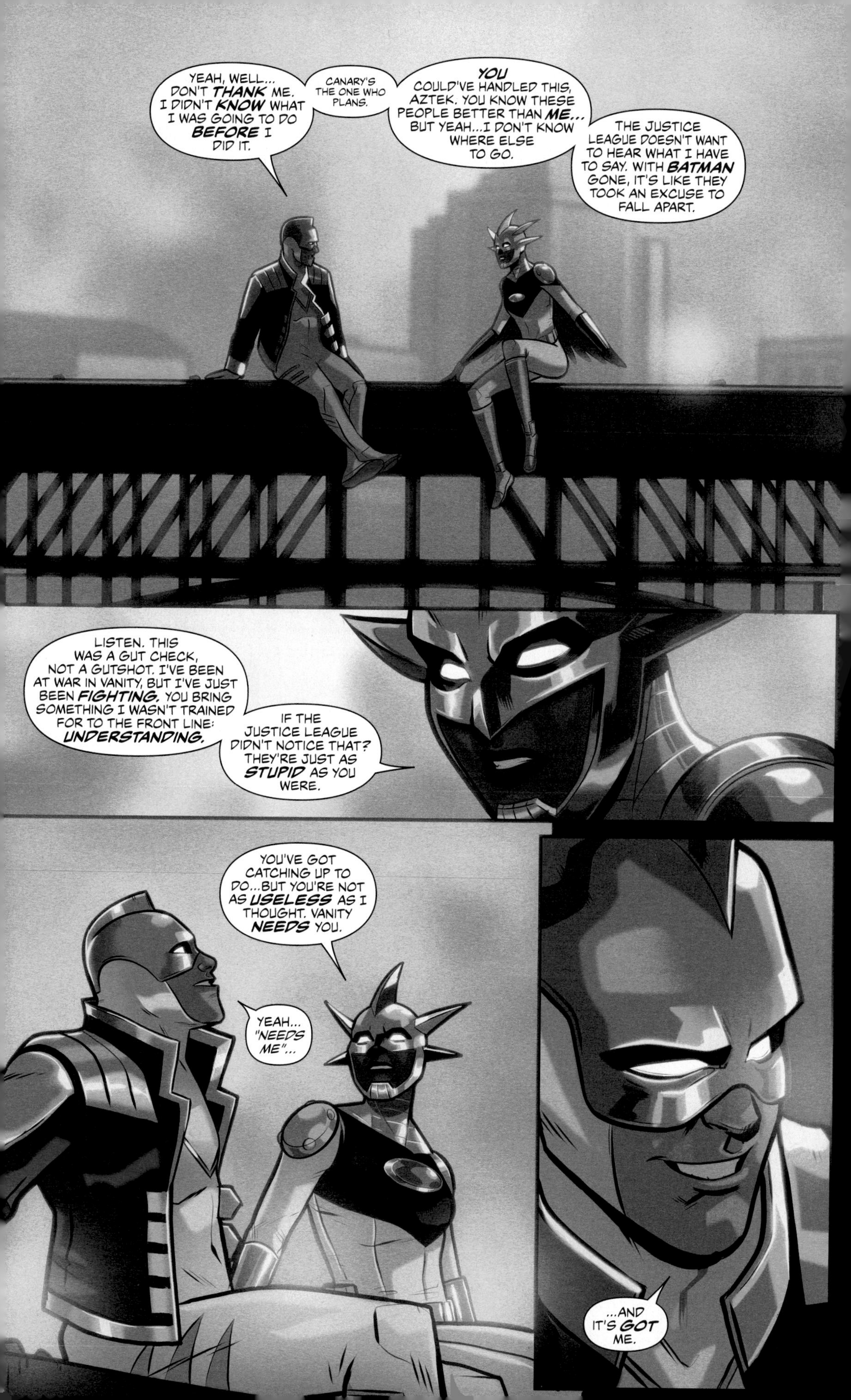
YEAH, WELL... DON'T THANK ME. I DIDN'T KNOW WHAT I WAS GOING TO DO BEFORE I DID IT.
CANARY'S THE ONE WHO PLANS.
YOU COULD'VE HANDLED THIS, AZTEK. YOU KNOW THESE PEOPLE BETTER THAN ME... BUT YEAH...I DON'T KNOW WHERE ELSE TO GO.
THE JUSTICE LEAGUE DOESN'T WANT TO HEAR WHAT I HAVE TO SAY. WITH BATMAN GONE, IT'S LIKE THEY TOOK AN EXCUSE TO FALL APART.
LISTEN. THIS WAS A GUT CHECK, NOT A GUTSHOT. I'VE BEEN AT WAR IN VANITY, BUT I'VE JUST BEEN FIGHTING. YOU BRING SOMETHING I WASN'T TRAINED FOR TO THE FRONT LINE: UNDERSTANDING.
IF THE JUSTICE LEAGUE DIDN'T NOTICE THAT? THEY'RE JUST AS STUPID AS YOU WERE.
YOU'VE GOT CATCHING UP TO DO...BUT YOU'RE NOT AS USELESS AS I THOUGHT. VANITY NEEDS YOU.
YEAH... "NEEDS ME"...
...AND IT'S GOT ME.

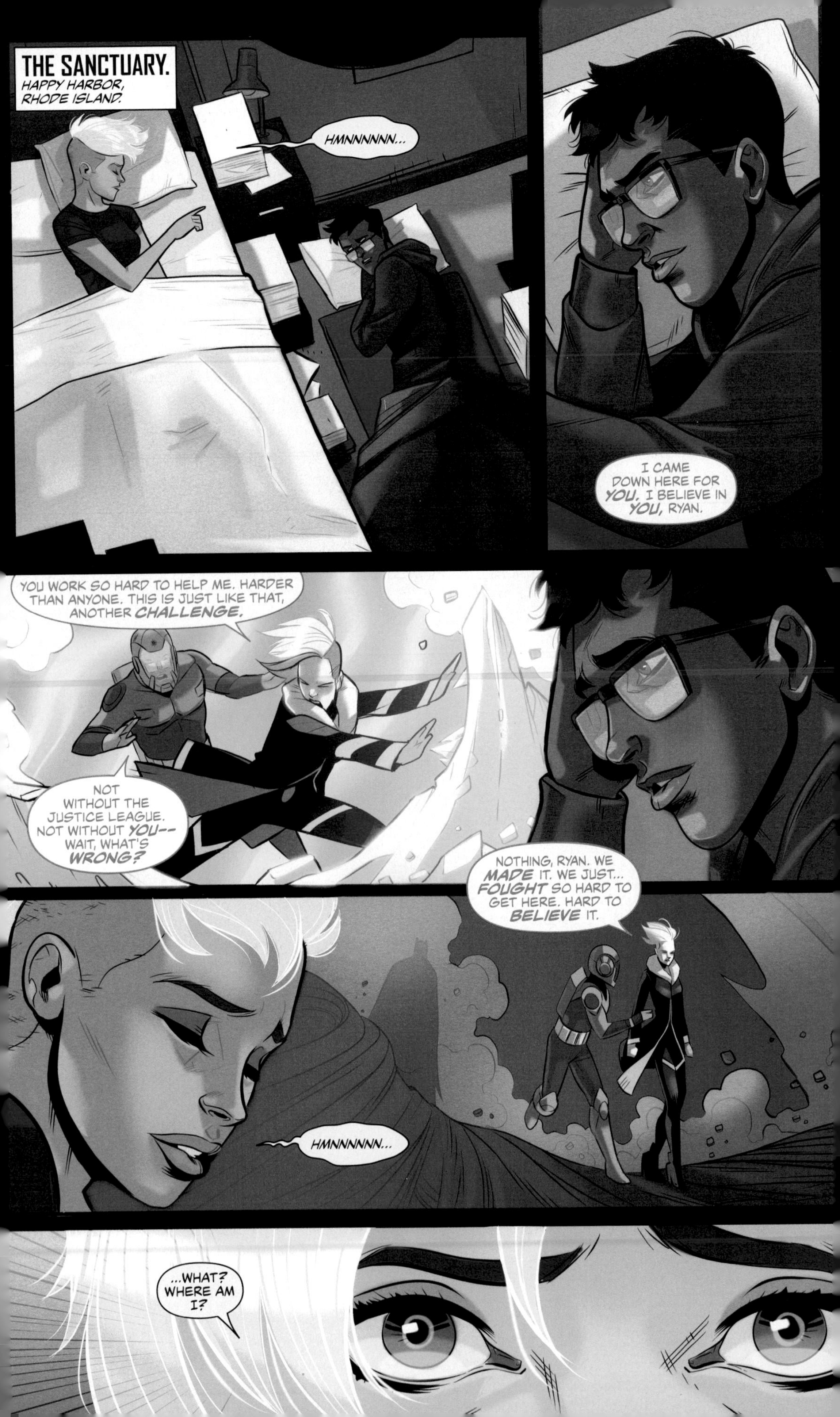
THE SANCTUARY.
HAPPY HARBOR, RHODE ISLAND.
HMNNNNNN...
I CAME DOWN HERE FOR YOU. I BELIEVE IN YOU, RYAN.
YOU WORK SO HARD TO HELP ME. HARDER THAN ANYONE. THIS IS JUST LIKE THAT, ANOTHER CHALLENGE.
NOT WITHOUT THE JUSTICE LEAGUE. NOT WITHOUT YOU-- WAIT, WHAT'S WRONG?
NOTHING, RYAN. WE MADE IT. WE JUST... FOUGHT SO HARD TO GET HERE. HARD TO BELIEVE IT.
HMNNNNNN...
...WHAT? WHERE AM I?

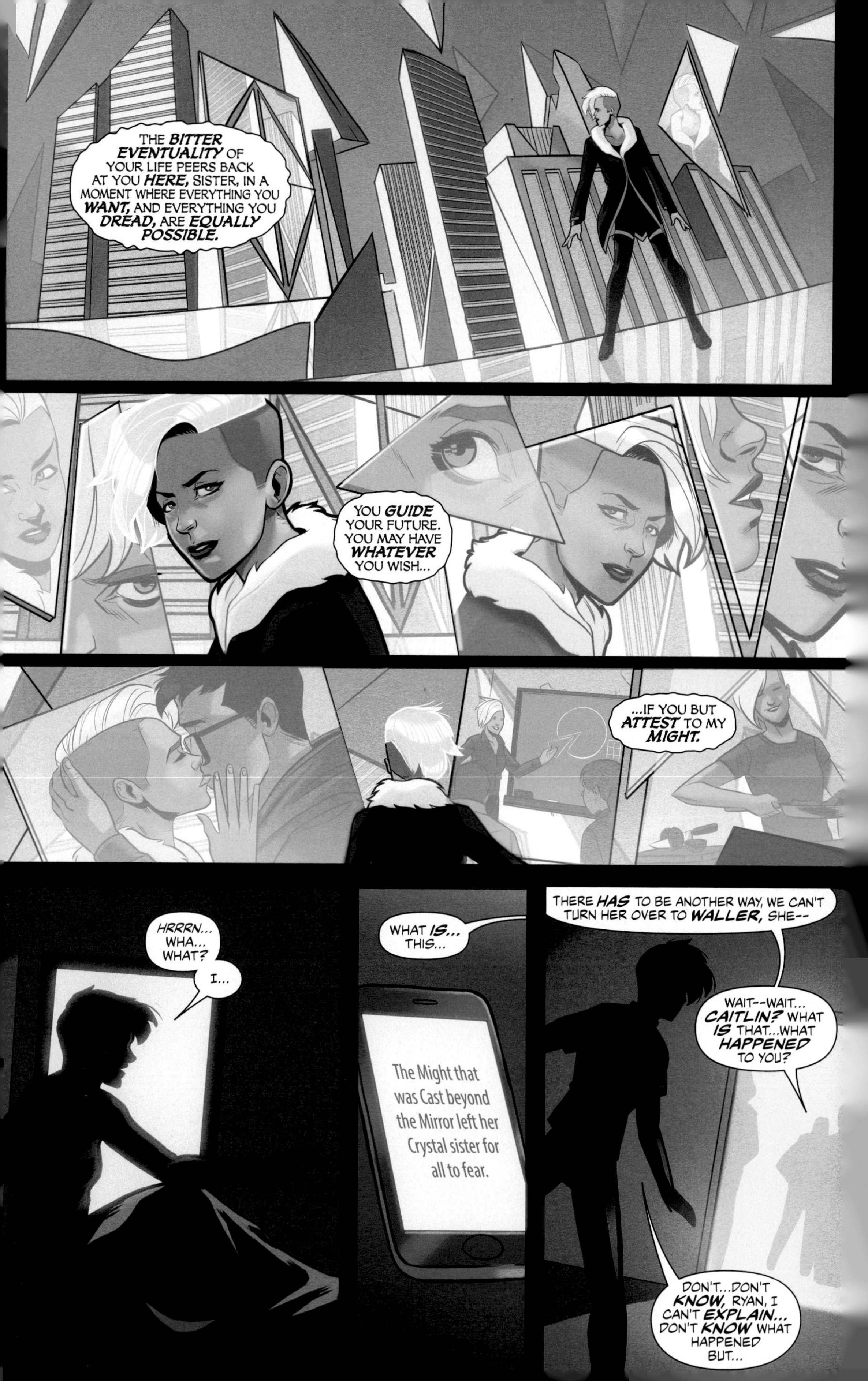
THE BITTER EVENTUALITY OF YOUR LIFE PEERS BACK AT YOU HERE, SISTER, IN A MOMENT WHERE EVERYTHING YOU WANT, AND EVERYTHING YOU DREAD, ARE EQUALLY POSSIBLE.
YOU GUIDE YOUR FUTURE. YOU MAY HAVE WHATEVER YOU WISH...
...IF YOU BUT ATTEST TO MY MIGHT.
HRRRN... WHA... WHAT?
I...
WHAT IS... THIS...
The Might that was Cast beyond the Mirror left her Crystal sister for all to fear.
THERE HAS TO BE ANOTHER WAY, WE CAN'T TURN HER OVER TO WALLER, SHE--
WAIT--WAIT... CAITLIN? WHAT IS THAT...WHAT HAPPENED TO YOU?
DON'T...DON'T KNOW, RYAN, I CAN'T EXPLAIN... DON'T KNOW WHAT HAPPENED BUT...

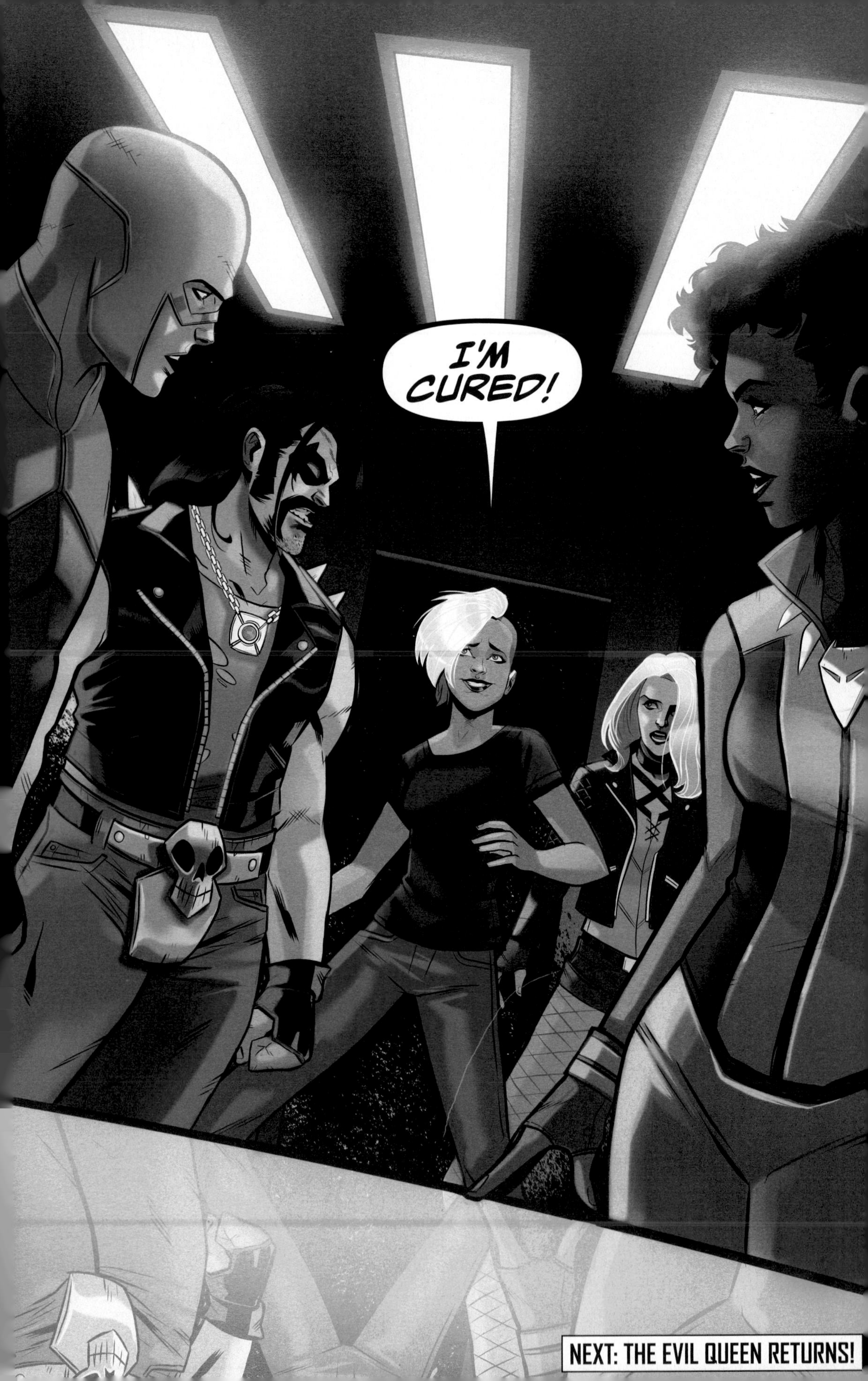
I'M CURED!
NEXT: THE EVIL QUEEN RETURNS!

JUSTICE LEAGUE OF AMERICA #18 variant cover
by DOUG MAHNKE & WIL QUINTANA

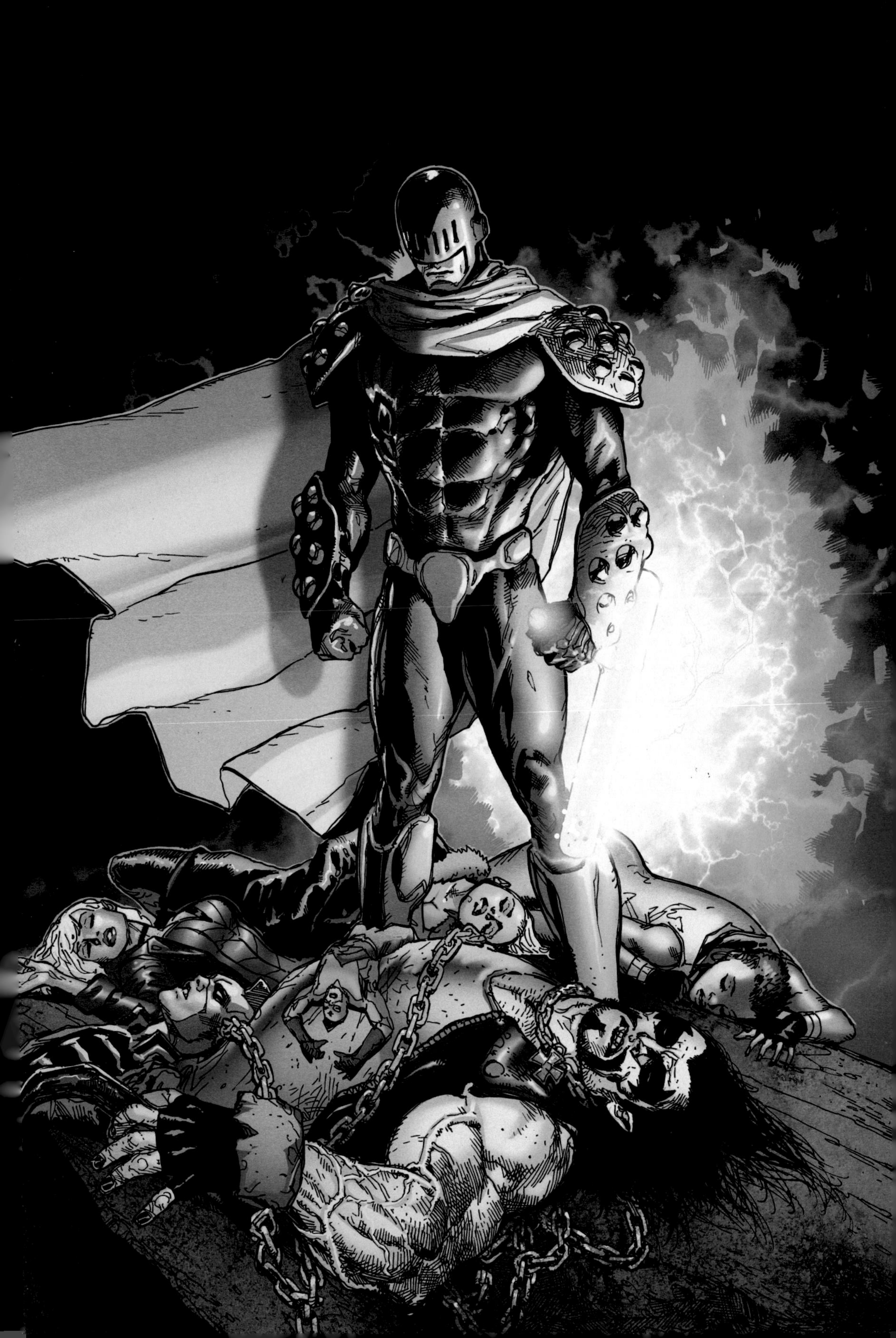

JUSTICE LEAGUE OF AMERICA #19 variant cover
by DOUG MAHNKE & WIL QUINTANA

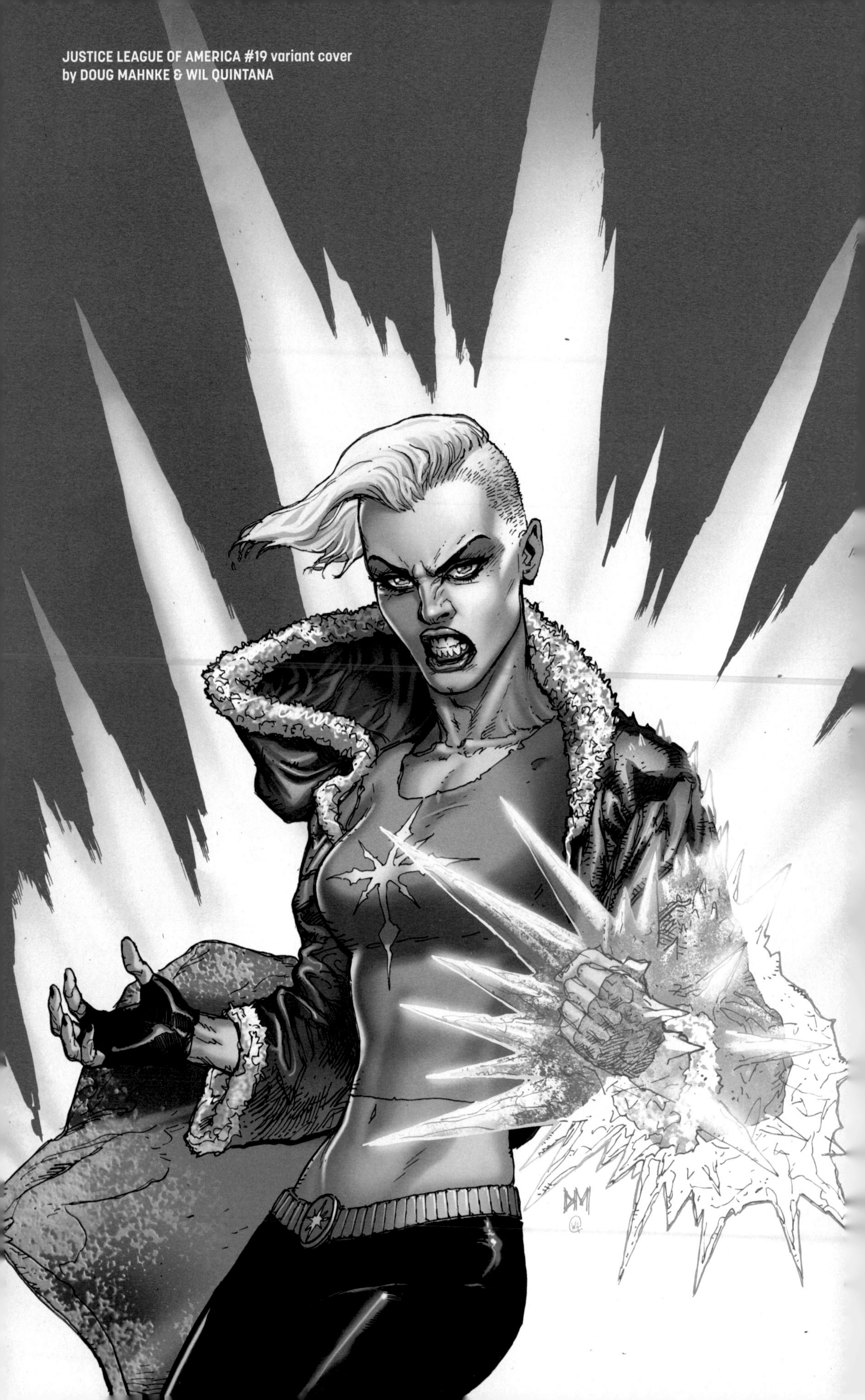

JUSTICE LEAGUE OF AMERICA #20 variant cover
by DOUG MAHNKE & WIL QUINTANA

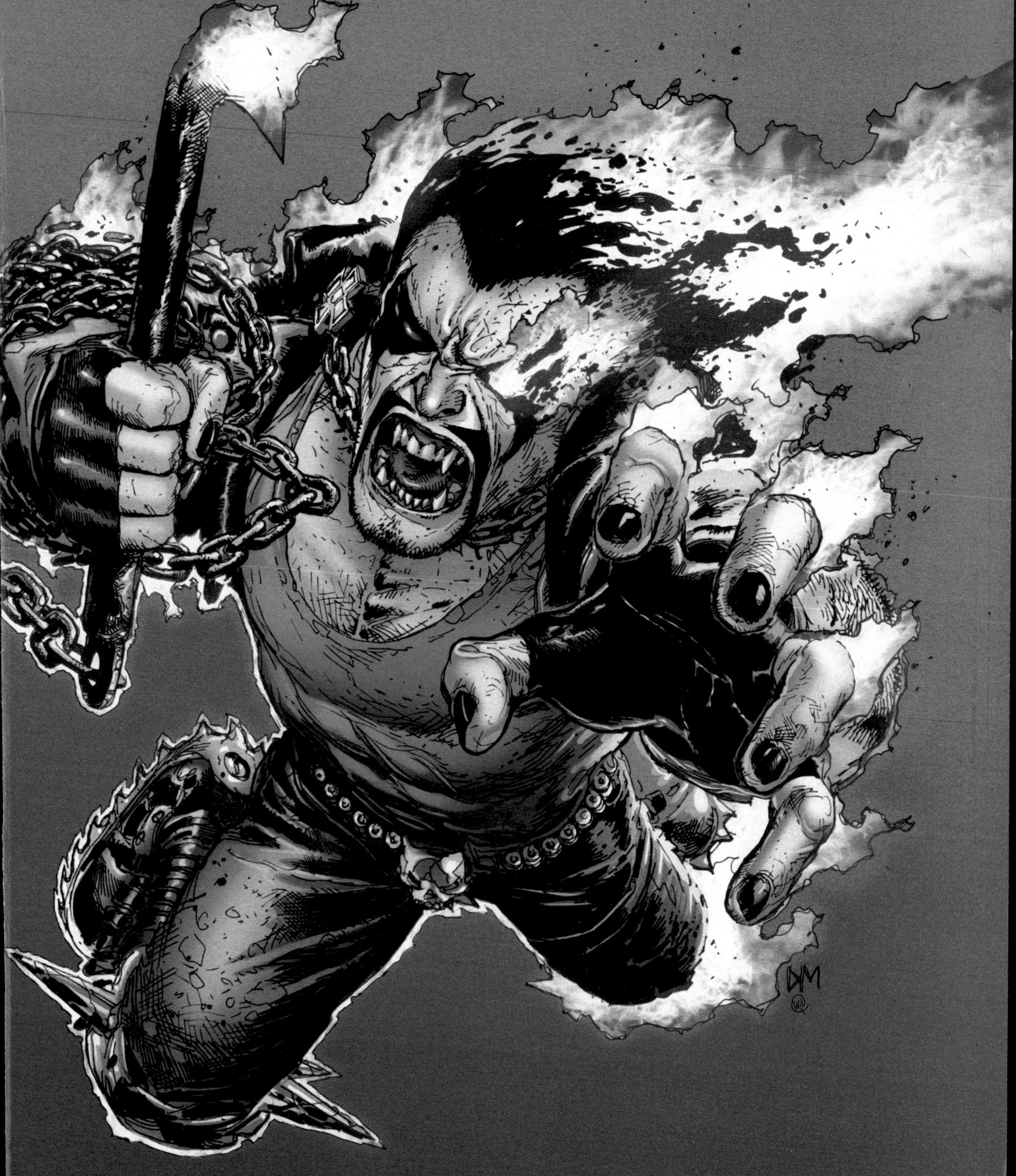

JUSTICE LEAGUE OF AMERICA #21 variant cover
by DOUG MAHNKE & WIL QUINTANA

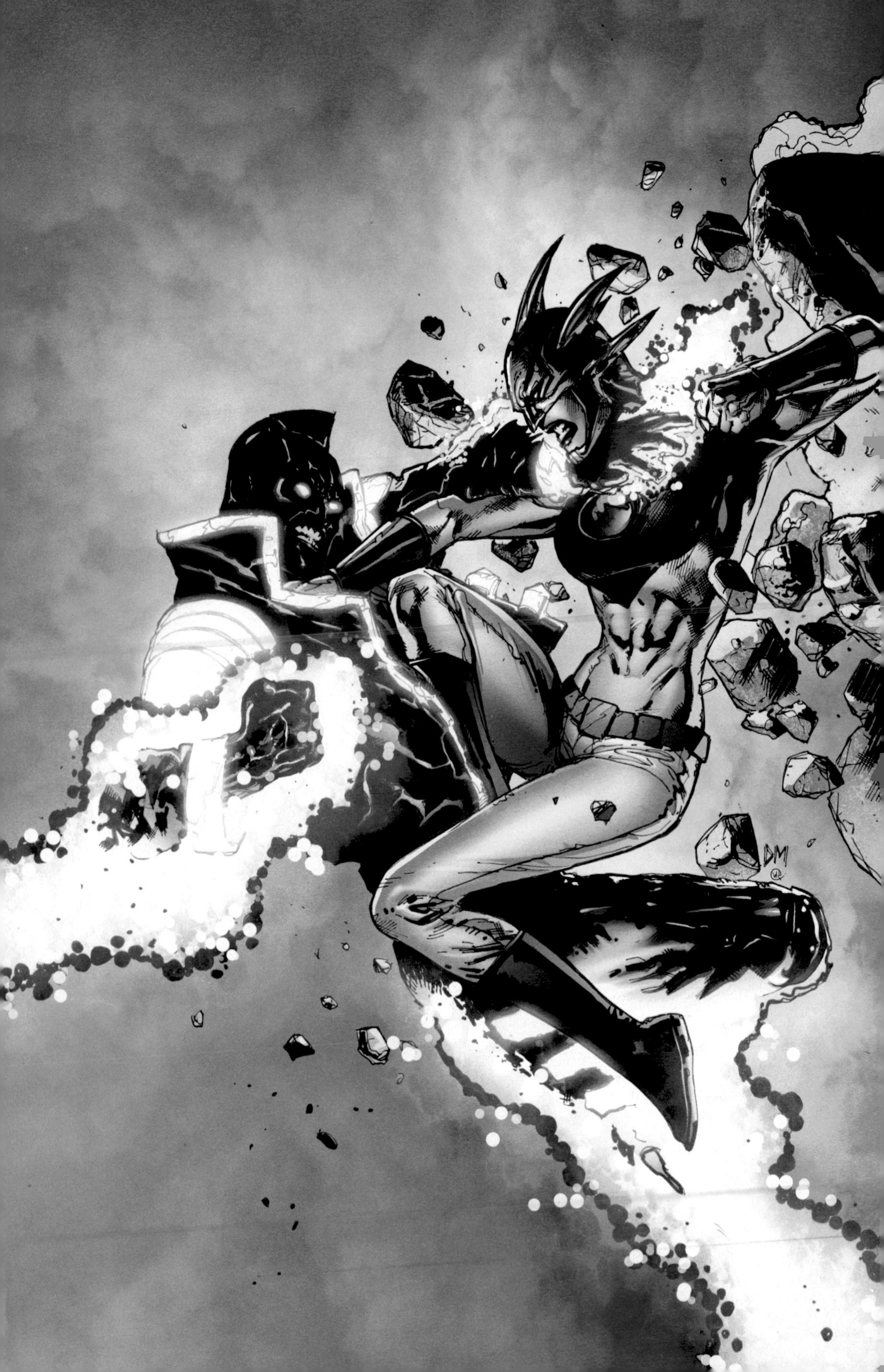